Editor
Erica N. Russikoff, M.A.

Editor in Chief
Karen J. Goldfluss, M.S. Ed.

Creative Director
Sarah M. Smith

Cover Artist
Barb Lorseyedi

Imaging
James Edward Grace
Amanda R. Harter

Publisher
Mary D. Smith, M.S. Ed.

TCR 3659

MW00444066

DAILY WA...

Reading

GRADE 8

- Over 150 nonfiction and fiction passages
- Follow-up questions for each passage target essential comprehension skills.
- Ideal for test preparation!

Reading

Teacher Created Resources

Author
Susan Mackey Collins, M. Ed.

Teacher Created Resources

12621 Western Avenue
Garden Grove, CA 92841
www.teachercreated.com

ISBN: 978-1-4206-3659-8

©2014 Teacher Created Resources
Reprinted, 2020
Made in U.S.A.

Teacher Created Resources

Table of Contents

The Great Quake—The Chicago Fire—The Dust Bowl—The Galveston Hurricane—The Black Death—Pompeii—The Sticky Explosion—The *Hindenburg*—The *Titanic*—The Twin Towers—The New Madrid Fault—Mount St. Helens: A Deadly Volcano—Chernobyl: A Nuclear Disaster—The Space Shuttle Catastrophe—Hurricane Katrina

William Driver—Thomas Jefferson—King Tut—Butch Cassidy—Milton Hershey—Helen Keller—Harry Houdini—Benjamin Franklin—Anne Frank—Amelia Earhart—Elvis Presley—Laura Ingalls Wilder—Rosa Parks—Princess Diana—Levi Strauss—Jesse James

History—Slavery—Independence—The Louisiana Purchase—The Wild West—Early Inventions—Women's Suffrage—The Roaring Twenties—The Great Depression—World War II—The Iron Curtain—Civil Rights—The Race into Space—The American-Indian Movement—Vietnam

Animal Rights—Bats—Monkeypox—Migration—Pythons—Bedbugs—Sleeping Sickness—Elephants—Sheep—Jellyfish—Ticks—Chinchillas—Animal Experiments—Service Animals

Table of Contents (cont.)

Introduction

The goal of this book is to improve students' reading and comprehension skills. The more experience a student has with reading and comprehending, the better reader and problem-solver he or she will be. *Daily Warm-Ups: Reading* contains a variety of passages to be read on a daily basis. Each passage is followed by comprehension questions. The questions that follow the passages are based on Bloom's Taxonomy and allow for higher-level thinking skills. Making this book a part of your daily classroom agenda can help your students' reading and comprehension abilities improve dramatically.

Nonfiction and Fiction

Daily Warm-Ups: Reading is divided into two sections: nonfiction and fiction. It is important for students to be exposed to a variety of reading genres and formats. The nonfiction section is divided into four categories. These categories are disasters, biographies, American history, and animals. By reading these nonfiction passages, your students will be exposed to a variety of nonfiction information, as well as questions to stimulate thinking on these subjects.

The fiction section of the book is divided into six categories. These categories are mythology, fairy tales/folklore, historical fiction, contemporary realism, mystery/suspense/adventure, and fantasy. Each story is followed by questions to stimulate thinking on the plot, characters, vocabulary, and sequence.

Comprehension Questions

Comprehension is the primary goal of any reading task. Students who comprehend what they read perform better on both tests and in life. The follow-up questions after each passage are written to encourage students to improve in recognizing text structure, visualizing, summarizing, and learning new vocabulary. Each of these skills can be found in scope-and-sequence charts as well as standards for reading comprehension. The different types of questions in *Daily Warm-Ups: Reading* are geared to help students with the following skills:

- Recognize the main idea
- Identify details
- Recall details
- Summarize
- Describe characters and character traits
- Classify and sort into categories
- Compare and contrast

- Make generalizations
- Draw conclusions
- Recognize fact
- Apply information to new situations
- Recognize sequence
- Understand vocabulary

Introduction *(cont.)*

Readability

Each of the reading passages in *Daily Warm-Ups: Reading* varies in difficulty to meet the various reading levels of your students. The passages have been categorized as follows: below grade level, at grade level, and above grade level. (See the Leveling Chart on page 6.)

Record Keeping

Use the Tracking Sheet on page 164 to record which warm-up exercises you have given to your students, or distribute copies of the sheet for students to keep their own records.

How to Make the Most of This Book

Here are some simple tips to supplement your educational strategies. They are only suggestions to help you make your students as successful in reading as possible.

- Read through the book ahead of time so you are familiar with each portion. The better you understand how the book works, the easier it will be to answer students' questions.

- Set aside a regular time each day to incorporate *Daily Warm-Ups* into your routine. Once the routine is established, students will look forward to and expect to work on reading strategies at that particular time.

- Make sure that any amount of time spent on *Daily Warm-Ups* is positive and constructive. This should be a time of practicing for success and recognizing it as it is achieved.

- Allot only about 10 minutes a day to *Daily Warm-Ups*. Too much time will not be useful; too little time will create additional stress.

- Be sure to model the reading and question-answering process at the beginning of the year. Model pre-reading questions, reading the passage, highlighting information that refers to the questions, and eliminating answers that are obviously wrong. Finally, refer back to the text once again to make sure the answers chosen are the best ones.

- Create and store overheads or interactive-whiteboard slides of each lesson so that you can review student work, concepts, and strategies as quickly as possible.

- Utilize peer tutors to assist struggling students.

- Offer small group time to students who need extra enrichment or opportunities for questions regarding the text. Small groups will allow many of these students, once they are comfortable with the format, to achieve success independently.

- Adjust the procedures, as you see fit, to meet the needs of all your students.

Leveling Chart

NONFICTION   ▲ = below grade level   ● = at grade level   ■ = above grade level

Disasters		Biographies		American History		Animals	
Page 9	■	Page 24	■	Page 40	▲	Page 55	■
Page 10	●	Page 25	■	Page 41	▲	Page 56	▲
Page 11	■	Page 26	●	Page 42	■	Page 57	●
Page 12	■	Page 27	●	Page 43	■	Page 58	●
Page 13	▲	Page 28	●	Page 44	■	Page 59	▲
Page 14	■	Page 29	●	Page 45	■	Page 60	●
Page 15	●	Page 30	■	Page 46	■	Page 61	●
Page 16	■	Page 31	■	Page 47	■	Page 62	▲
Page 17	■	Page 32	▲	Page 48	■	Page 63	▲
Page 18	▲	Page 33	●	Page 49	■	Page 64	▲
Page 19	■	Page 34	▲	Page 50	■	Page 65	▲
Page 20	■	Page 35	▲	Page 51	■	Page 66	●
Page 21	■	Page 36	●	Page 52	■	Page 67	■
Page 22	▲	Page 37	●	Page 53	■	Page 68	●
Page 23	●	Page 38	▲	Page 54	■		
		Page 39	▲				

FICTION   ▲ = below grade level   ● = at grade level   ■ = above grade level

Mythology		Fairy Tales/ Folklore		Historical		Contemporary Realism		Mystery/ Suspense/ Adventure		Fantasy	
Page 71	●	Page 87	▲	Page 103	▲	Page 117	▲	Page 133	▲	Page 148	▲
Page 72	▲	Page 88	▲	Page 104	▲	Page 118	▲	Page 134	▲	Page 149	▲
Page 73	▲	Page 89	▲	Page 105	▲	Page 119	▲	Page 135	▲	Page 150	▲
Page 74	●	Page 90	▲	Page 106	●	Page 120	▲	Page 136	▲	Page 151	▲
Page 75	■	Page 91		Page 107	▲	Page 121	▲	Page 137	▲	Page 152	▲
Page 76	●	Page 92	▲	Page 108	▲	Page 122	▲	Page 138	▲	Page 153	▲
Page 77	▲	Page 93	▲	Page 109	▲	Page 123	▲	Page 139	▲	Page 154	▲
Page 78	●	Page 94	▲	Page 110	▲	Page 124	▲	Page 140	▲	Page 155	▲
Page 79	▲	Page 95	▲	Page 111	▲	Page 125	▲	Page 141	▲	Page 156	▲
Page 80	●	Page 96	▲	Page 112	▲	Page 126	▲	Page 142	▲	Page 157	▲
Page 81	●	Page 97	▲	Page 113	▲	Page 127	▲	Page 143	▲	Page 158	▲
Page 82	▲	Page 98	●	Page 114	▲	Page 128	▲	Page 144	▲	Page 159	▲
Page 83	▲	Page 99	●	Page 115	▲	Page 129	▲	Page 145	■	Page 160	▲
Page 84	▲	Page 100	▲	Page 116	▲	Page 130	▲	Page 146	▲	Page 161	▲
Page 85	●	Page 101	▲			Page 131	▲	Page 147	▲	Page 162	▲
Page 86	▲	Page 102	▲			Page 132	▲			Page 163	▲

Nonfiction

Name_____

The Great Quake

Today, in most industrialized countries in the world, buildings are designed to withstand various, unexpected natural disasters. Safety measures are installed in modern-day designs to help contain the spread of fire, and design engineers make sure newer structures are deliberately planned to hold against the violent shifting of the earth during an unexpected earthquake. However, such deliberate design and planning was not the case during the early 1900s.

On April 18, 1906, in the morning hours of the day, the citizens of San Francisco, California, were witnesses to an earthquake so monumental the tremors were felt as far north as Oregon. Neither the city nor its people were prepared for what would happen next: the devastation of their city.

The actual earthquake only lasted two minutes. Of course, the violent tremors must have seemed much longer to the actual eyewitnesses, but the fires that came after the earthquake lasted for nearly three days. The enormous loss from the disaster included the lives of at least five hundred people, and an estimated three thousand acres of the city were destroyed. This disaster is often called simply the "Great Quake" because of the vast destruction that occurred.

Text Questions

1. After reading this passage, what can you predict will most likely happen to San Francisco in the future if another earthquake hits the city?
   a. The city will be less prepared than in 1906.
   b. Fires will ravage the city after an earthquake.
   c. The citizens will refuse to rebuild the city.
   d. The city will be better prepared due to modern-day designs and safety measures.

2. What is the meaning of the word *vast* as used in the last paragraph?
   a. extensive
   b. miniature
   c. simultaneous
   d. perpetual

3. Which would be the best source to learn more about the San Francisco Earthquake of 1906?
   a. a personal website by someone who currently resides in San Francisco
   b. a journal written by someone who survived the 1906 earthquake
   c. an atlas showing the epicenter of the 1906 quake
   d. an online encyclopedia entry about earthquakes

4. Using information from the text, what can you say is true about the 1906 earthquake?
   a. Flooding was a huge problem after the earthquake.
   b. The earthquake left everyone in the city without shelter.
   c. People were ill-prepared for any type of disaster in the 1900s.
   d. The destruction by fires after the earthquake caused major damage to San Francisco.

5. Using information from the passage, explain why the 1906 earthquake became known as the "Great Quake." Write at least two complete sentences.

   On April 18, 1906, in the morning hours of the day, the citizens of San Francisco, California were witnesses to an earthquake

Name_____

The Chicago Fire

In the state of Illinois on October 8, 1871, one of the most infamous events in the city of Chicago's history began: the Chicago Fire. The Chicago Fire of 1871 had such an enormous impact on the city that one of the four stars on the city's official flag stands for this event.

No one is certain what caused the fire, which burned for several days. Most historians believe the fire started in a barn owned by a Mrs. O'Leary. It is thought that perhaps a cow may have started the spark that led to the burning of Chicago by kicking over a lantern located in the barn. Regardless of the source, the damage from the fire was widespread. Fire destroyed four square miles of the city and cost more than 300 people their lives. Another 100,000 people lost their homes.

The determination of the citizens of Chicago to rebuild eventually saved their beloved city. Within four years, the people had rebuilt much of what was destroyed by the fire. Today, the city has overcome its bleak past, but no one will ever forget the disaster of 1871.

Text Questions

1. What personal quality did the citizens who survived the fire of 1871 need to be successful in rebuilding their city?
   a. weakness
   b. determination
   c. creativity
   d. imagination

2. Why does the author mention the star on Chicago's flag?
   a. To show the historical significance of the event to the citizens of Chicago.
   b. To explain that Chicago's flag has four stars.
   c. To show the city's flag has stars just as the flag of the United States of America has stars.
   d. To infer that one star has more significance than the other three stars.

3. Based on the information given, what can one conclude about the source of the fire?
   a. The source of the fire is not as significant as the actual event and the results of the fire.
   b. Historians feel compelled to find out the exact source of the fire.
   c. The citizens needed to know the source of the fire to stop such an event from ever occurring again.
   d. Electricity would be added to all new outdoor structures being built after the fire to prevent the use of lanterns or other sources of possible fire.

4. Which title would be a good alternative for this text?
   a. "Stop the Destruction"
   b. "Mrs. O'Leary's Cow"
   c. "The Citizens Rebuild"
   d. "The 1871 Chicago Inferno"

5. What was the author's purpose in writing this text?
   a. to entertain
   b. to persuade
   c. to inform
   d. to explain

Name_____

The Dust Bowl

Imagine day turned into night. The world is so covered in a thick, blinding dust that all sunlight is blocked out from view. Everyone around you is running from the cloud of dust that will suffocate its victims with a blanket of dust. Think it couldn't happen? Think again.

In the United States during the 1930s, an area in the middle of the country became known as the Dust Bowl. Huge dust storms ravaged areas in the states of Kansas, Oklahoma, Texas, Colorado, and New Mexico. The dust storms were mainly caused by a lack of planning on the part of those who continuously farmed the areas of land and a series of droughts that swept through the ravaged farmlands. The loose soil easily succumbed to the strong winds ready to sweep the land in huge clouds across the already suffering Midwestern states.

The environmental disaster caused over three million people to leave their homes in the Great Plains area. Those leaving hoped to find food, shelter, and a new way of life for their families by moving out West. Although some did find new homes, sadly, many of those people hoping for a better life were often forced to take whatever jobs they could find just to survive. People in other areas did not often treat the immigrants with kindness, believing the flux of people in their own lands would cause overcrowding and hardships for their own families. However, the Dust Bowl did have at least one positive effect on agriculture: people learned to implement farming practices that would save the soil and save the settlers of the Great Plains from facing such an economic disaster of such magnitude ever again.

Text Questions

1. Why do you think the author included the first paragraph in this reading passage?
   a. to provide a visual image for the reader
   b. to give factual information about the Dust Bowl
   c. to describe what it would be like to be blind
   d. to give a strong conclusion to the text

2. Compare the word *flux* as it is used in the third paragraph to the examples below. Choose the sentence that uses the word *flux* in a similar way.
   a. All of the computers were not working because the entire system was in a flux.
   b. The flux of tourists to the area caused overcrowding at every train station.
   c. Because of the flux in her temperature, the doctor worried about her recovery.
   d. She felt a flux of emotions when she was around her former boyfriend.

3. What is one inference the reader can make about the Dust Bowl of the 1930s?
   a. With better soil management, much of the Dust Bowl could have been prevented.
   b. Lack of rain was the only cause of the Dust Bowl.
   c. The Great Plains should be prepared to face another disaster similar to what occurred in the 1930s.
   d. The Great Depression was the key cause of the dust storms that ravaged the Great Plains.

4. Which sentence would be a good concluding sentence for the first paragraph?
   a. Don't ever stop thinking about it.
   b. The Dust Bowl of the 1930s was an environmental and natural disaster that caused unimaginable tragedy.
   c. Earthquakes, tornadoes, and hurricanes are all natural disasters that can occur in the United States.
   d. Having a farm on the Great Plains was the dream of many immigrants.

5. Which statement is <u>not</u> a fact about the Dust Bowl?
   a. The Dust Bowl was the worst natural disaster of all time.
   b. The Dust Bowl occurred in the Great Plains.
   c. Many farmers of the Great Plains moved West.
   d. Lack of rain was one cause of the Dust Bowl.

Name_____

The Galveston Hurricane

Coastal towns are changed forever when hurricane winds strike. On September 8, 1900, the citizens of Galveston, Texas, found out how true this would be for them. The city was ravaged by winds that reached nearly 130 miles per hour. Unlike today's world, where weather stations are often able to give warnings about impending hurricanes, leaving people time to prepare for upcoming storms, those living in the 1900s had no way of knowing the magnitude of what was about to happen.

When the storm was over, one-sixth of Galveston's population—approximately 10,000 people—was gone.

The death toll was staggering, but especially sad were the deaths of many children. At St. Mary's orphanage in Galveston, all but three of the children living there were reported to have perished that day.

Thousands were left homeless after the hurricane. Volunteer agencies such as the Red Cross rushed to help those in need. Through the caring of others and the help of its citizens, Galveston managed to rebuild; however, those who survived the hurricane would be forever changed by what had occurred.

Text Questions

1. What does the text imply about the hurricane of 1900 and the events surrounding the storm?

    a. Galveston was prepared for a storm of this magnitude.
    b. The citizens were taken by surprise at the force of the storm.
    c. People who live in coastal towns are always ready to leave when bad weather erupts.
    d. Many people in Galveston were homeless before the storm ever hit.

2. Choose the best definition for the word *coastal* as it is used in the first paragraph.

    a. a slope or area that is downhill
    b. a rural area
    c. a town built near the ocean
    d. a city that is a tourist attraction

3. Which statement is not a fact about the story?

    a. The Galveston hurricane occurred on September 8, 1900.
    b. Winds from the hurricane reached nearly 130 mph.
    c. Citizens of Galveston knew the risk they were taking by living in a coastal city.
    d. Many children died as a result of the Galveston hurricane.

4. Where in the text can you find information about the number of deaths as a result of the hurricane?

    a. the title of the text
    b. the first paragraph
    c. the second paragraph
    d. the third paragraph

5. Which would be the best source to learn about other hurricanes that have happened in Texas?

    a. a newspaper article about the hurricane that hit Galveston on September 8th
    b. an encyclopedia entry about hurricanes
    c. a research paper comparing the world's worst hurricanes and tsunamis
    d. a book about natural disasters in the state of Texas

Name_____

The Black Death

Plagues of all types have haunted humans since the dawn of civilization. One of the worst plagues to strike was during the mid 1300s. This plague was so deadly it became known as the Black Death.

The Black Death began to be seen in Europe in 1347 and lasted for nearly four years. During this time in history, Europeans were doing much trade with those living in Asia. Unfortunately, trading did not just bring new goods to the Europeans; it also brought new diseases. The unsuspecting adventurers never realized they were importing rats, who came as stowaways, into the previously uninfected areas. These rats carried with them the deadly plague, which quickly spread to the human inhabitants of the area.

Various diseases were a part of the Black Death. The bubonic plague was one type of disease that spread quickly throughout Europe during the middle 1300s. Some of the diseases could even spread through the air, and those infected would be dead in less than twenty-four hours. Literally, millions of people died as a result of the deadly sickness. No wonder history has given this plague the name the Black Death.

Text Questions

1. What can you infer about the plague from the first paragraph?
   a. Plagues such as this one happened often in Europe and Asia.
   b. The Black Death was devastating during the mid 1300s.
   c. Vaccinations for diseases were developed as a result of the Black Death.
   d. People should have stopped all trade with other countries during the plague.

2. What is the main idea of this text?
   a. The Black Death was one of the deadliest plagues known to Europe.
   b. Trading goods with people from different countries is not always a good idea.
   c. Most plagues could be controlled if people were more aware of what caused various diseases.
   d. People from earlier civilizations lived dangerous lives.

3. Which is a synonym for the word *various* as it is used in the third paragraph?
   a. some
   b. different
   c. remarkable
   d. similar

4. Which statement best explains how the plague was brought from Asia to Europe?
   a. The plague was carried through the air.
   b. Deadly diseases were already in Europe and did not come from trading with Asia.
   c. People were infected with the plague from ingesting fish and seafood from other regions.
   d. Rats, traveling with goods from Asia, brought the deadly disease with them.

5. What happened to Europe's population as a result of the Black Death?
   a. The population remained the same.
   b. The population decreased.
   c. The population slightly increased.
   d. The population doubled in size.

Name_____

Pompeii

In 79 A.D., the ancient Roman city of Pompeii was destroyed by the eruption of a nearby volcano, Mt. Vesuvius. Although many other cities in history have been victims to eruptions of volcanoes and their deadly gas, lava, and ash, what makes Pompeii especially interesting is what happened years later.

In 1748, explorers in the Italian region where Pompeii once stood made an incredible discovery. Buried underneath layers of dirt, the city of Pompeii remained preserved. The original volcanic explosion had happened so quickly that most of the citizens were unable to escape. Their remains and the buildings of the city were still there, preserved, as if the year was still 79 A.D. instead of 1748. Some were frozen as if running from the fiery inferno while others were engaged in normal daily activities. The layers of dust had frozen the day in history.

Archeologists would later begin the careful process of excavating the now famous city from the layers of ash. The tragedy of Pompeii is the loss of the city and the approximately two thousand people who died during the eruption. Ironically, the deadly eruption helped preserve Pompeii so that no one will ever forget the name of this ancient Roman civilization.

Text Questions

1. What was the author's purpose in writing this text?
   a. to inform
   b. to entertain
   c. to persuade
   d. to explain

2. Citing information from the text, compare the discovery of Pompeii to another famous, historical discovery such as explorer Robert Ballard's discovery of the sunken *Titanic* or any other well-known discovery.

   _____

   _____

   _____

3. What conclusion can be drawn about the people of Pompeii in the year 79 A.D.?
   a. Most of the citizens were farmers.
   b. Women and men were treated equally.
   c. The citizens of Pompeii were not prepared for the eruption of Mt. Vesuvius.
   d. The people of Pompeii were unconcerned about living near an active volcano.

4. Using the information from the text, what can you infer an archeologist might do as part of his or her job?
   a. Study modern events to better understand connections to the past.
   b. Teach history at the university level.
   c. Create buildings that have similar qualities of architectural designs of the past.
   d. Excavate and study past civilizations and their artifacts.

5. Which of the following statements can be proven true from the information given in the text?
   a. Archaeologists believe Pompeii is the greatest historical discovery of its kind.
   b. Mt. Vesuvius will erupt again within the next ten years.
   c. All of the citizens of Pompeii could have survived the eruption if they had been given adequate warning that they were in danger.
   d. The 1748 discovery of Pompeii is considered a significant historical discovery.

Name_____

The Sticky Explosion

Molasses is a dark, sweet, sticky substance that most people only think about using for baking. However, enjoying molasses as a treat is not all this food is known for, especially to anyone who lived in Boston, Massachusetts, during the early 1900s. In fact, these people learned that molasses can be dangerous.

On January 15, 1919, disaster struck at the United States Industrial Alcohol Company. A tank holding 2.5 million gallons of molasses exploded. A wave of hot molasses poured from the tank burning and destroying whatever or whomever was unlucky enough to be in its path.

The spread of the molasses was not contained to the Industrial Alcohol Company building. The substance spread throughout the street, taking down structures, animals, and people. Twenty-one people died as a result of the explosion. Cleanup of the sticky substance took weeks. The source of the explosion was eventually blamed on the tank, which was described as simply not being large enough to hold the amount of molasses that it had contained.

Text Questions

1. Which would be a good source to learn more about the production of molasses?
   a. a website of a company currently producing molasses
   b. a flyer advertising where to purchase organic products, including molasses
   c. an article comparing honey and molasses
   d. a newspaper from 1919 with articles about the molasses explosion

2. Which statement is a fact about the story?
   a. Twenty-one people died as a result of the molasses explosion.
   b. The Industrial Alcohol Company knew there were problems with the molasses tank but did nothing to stop the explosion.
   c. The people of Boston, Massachusetts, fought for the closing of the industrial plant after the explosion occurred.
   d. The source of the explosion was never discovered.

3. What does the word *source* mean as it is used in the third paragraph?
   a. resource
   b. cause
   c. ending
   d. supply

4. What conclusion can be drawn about the molasses explosion in Boston?
   a. In any industrialized plant, proper equipment and safety measures must be ensured at all times for the safety of everyone.
   b. Infectious disease can be a result of any natural disaster.
   c. Molasses will always be made in the United States regardless of past dangers in the process.
   d. People who do not consume molasses would not be interested in the 1919 explosion.

5. Using information from the text, explain what could have been done to prevent the explosion at the factory.

   _____

   _____

   _____

Name_____

The *Hindenburg*

In the 1930s, the nation of Germany was well known for its amazing flying machines known as dirigibles. These airships were enormous structures that were somewhat similar in shape to the blimps of today but much larger in size and more opulent in design. Another difference between the flying structures is the German dirigibles were filled with hydrogen, an extremely explosive substance.

The *Hindenburg* was one of the Zepplin Company's best airships. The airship began making flights to the United States in 1936. On May 3, 1937, passengers and crew would board the airship for what would become its final flight.

The flight to New Jersey was in itself unremarkable. Neither the crew nor its passengers reported any major problems during the three-day flight. But on the afternoon of May 6, thunderstorms were near the area where the airship was to land. Since hydrogen is flammable, lightning was always a concern for those flying on the *Hindenburg*. That day the crew managed to get the ship to its landing spot and dropped the ropes to secure the great airship just as tragedy struck.

A giant explosion rocked the airship, and within thirty-two seconds, the airship was lost in flames. Remarkably, sixty-seven of the ninety-seven people who were on board the *Hindenburg* managed to survive by reaching safety on the ground below.

The actual cause of the explosion remains a mystery, but one thing is certain: the explosion of the *Hindenburg* ended the era of the great airships.

Text Questions

1. What did the German dirigibles use as their main source of power?
   a. gasoline
   b. diesel
   c. hydrogen
   d. oxygen

2. Why was lightning a concern for anyone flying on the *Hindenburg*?
   a. The flight of the airship would not be as smooth.
   b. The pilot could not see well during storms with lightning.
   c. Stormy weather often caused motion sickness for many of the passengers on board.
   d. Lightning could cause an electric spark near the highly flammable airship.

3. From reading the text, what can one infer about traveling on the *Hindenburg*?
   a. The passage was very similar to modern-day airplanes.
   b. Passengers stayed on board the airships for several days.
   c. Most people would rather ride a ship from Europe to the Americas.
   d. The crew of the *Hindenburg* were only kind to German passengers.

4. Which country was known for creating and maintaining the flying dirigibles?
   a. Europe
   b. America
   c. Italy
   d. Germany

5. Using information from the text, explain how passengers might have survived the explosion of the *Hindenburg*.

_____

_____

_____

16

Name_____

The *Titanic*

In 1912, one of the most majestic ships of all times—the *Titanic*—set sail for America from England. The ship held not only some of the world's wealthiest people but also hundreds of immigrants hoping to find a new life in America. Sadly, many of those on board never reached American shores.

On the fifth night of the ship's first voyage, disaster struck when the ship came into deadly contact with an iceberg in the Atlantic Ocean. The force of the contact caused the ship, which had once been called "unsinkable," to be doomed.

By the end of the night, 1,500 of the 2,200 people on board would be dead. Too few lifeboats and inadequate safety procedures caused the demise of those who might have survived the terrible tragedy. For many, what happened to the *Titanic* is considered one of the greatest shipwrecks of all time.

Text Questions

1. What does the word *majestic* mean as it is used in the first paragraph?
   a. grand
   b. colossal
   c. enlightened
   d. imposing

2. What is the meaning of the last sentence—"what happened to the Titanic is considered one of the greatest shipwrecks of all time"?
   a. The ship was the largest to ever sink.
   b. There was a plethora of people who died when the ship sank.
   c. The shipwreck is a tragedy no one will ever forget.
   d. The story of the shipwreck is known by people in both England and America.

3. Based on the text, which of the following statements can be proven true?
   a. The *Titanic* was the grandest ship of its time.
   b. The immigrants on board the *Titanic* felt lucky to be going to America.
   c. There were not enough lifeboats for the number of passengers on board the *Titanic*.
   d. The ship's voyage was taking longer than expected.

4. What was the author's purpose in writing this text?
   a. to entertain
   b. to persuade
   c. to encourage
   d. to inform

5. Which would be the best source to learn more about icebergs?
   a. an encyclopedia
   b. an atlas
   c. an almanac
   d. a dictionary

Name_____

The Twin Towers

The side-by-side towers in New York City, which were home to Manhattan's World Trade Center, were more commonly known as the Twin Towers. Each skyscraper was an incredible one hundred and ten stories high. Then, on September 11, 2001, the World Trade Center was attacked by terrorists. What happened on that date in history should never be forgotten.

The attack on September 11th was not the first time the area had been targeted. In 1993, a bomb had been detonated in the North Tower. This explosion killed six people and injured thousands of others. The tower, however, was able to withstand the explosive power of the blast.

In 2001, both towers were attacked. Two planes were flown directly into the buildings. The effect of these attacks was immediately catastrophic. Neither building was built to withstand such structural damage, and the collapse of each building was imminent. The south tower fell in less than one hour after being attacked, and the north tower collapsed soon afterwards. Both towers were completely gone. The land where the World Trade Center once stood is now known as Ground Zero. The day when the towers were attacked is remembered as one of the most infamous days in America's history.

Text Questions

1. What is most likely the reason the World Trade Center buildings were also called the Twin Towers?
   a. The two buildings had similar working hours.
   b. The two buildings were built on the same acre of land.
   c. The two buildings were identical in design.
   d. The two buildings were nothing alike.

2. Which statement is a fact about the story?
   a. The World Trade Center was attacked more than once.
   b. The buildings would have survived the attack if they had not been identical in design.
   c. September 11, 2001, is the most infamous date in America's history.
   d. No one should ever construct another building at Ground Zero.

3. Which is a synonym for the word *infamous* as it is used in the last paragraph?
   a. notorious
   b. fabulous
   c. famous
   d. cordial

4. Which title would be a good alternative for this text?
   a. "September: A Bad Month"
   b. "The End of Time"
   c. "The World Trade Center Attack"
   d. "A Day When All Hope Died"

5. Using information from the third paragraph, list three things in sequential order that happened that day.

   a. _____

   b. _____

   c. _____

Name_____

The New Madrid Fault

In 1812, an earthquake caused by the New Madrid fault caused such seismic activity that the Mississippi River actually flowed backwards. The first tremors began in 1811, giving warning that the New Madrid Fault was about to get interesting. This fault line, which is named after the city New Madrid and is located along the Mississippi River in the state of Arkansas, would soon produce an earthquake that would have likely measured well above an eight on the Richter scale.

Unlike the San Francisco earthquake of 1906, this area near the New Madrid fault was sparsely populated. However, some towns were totally wiped out when the tremors caused landslides that covered the areas below them. Then, in February of 1812, the largest of the earthquakes would strike the area.

The quake that hit the region in February of 1812 is estimated to have measured at a strength of 8.8 and is undoubtedly one of the strongest earthquakes to ever hit this region. The tremors were so strong that church bells rang in Boston, Massachusetts, from the shaking of the earth. Waterfalls were created in the mighty Mississippi as the riverbed shifted and people unlucky enough to be on the water were killed instantly in the tumultuous waters. Reelfoot Lake in Tennessee was created as the earth shifted and water from the Mississippi poured into the new depressions of the ground.

The activity finally began to wane in March of the same year, but the landscape of the area had been permanently changed. Towns had been destroyed, fields were flooded, and new lakes were created. Historians estimate that the series of events eventually caused the deaths of over one thousand people.

Text Questions

1. Based on the text, which statement is <u>not</u> true?
   a. The New Madrid fault is located near the Mississippi River.
   b. Tremors from the New Madrid fault were so strong that the effects were felt as far away as Boston, Massachusetts.
   c. There were no serious injuries as a result of the earthquakes because there were no large towns.
   d. At one point, the Mississippi River flowed backwards as a result of the earthquakes.

2. Which would be the best source to learn more about the New Madrid Fault?
   a. a book about major fault lines in the United States
   b. a book about major earthquakes that have happened throughout the world
   c. an online encyclopedia entry about major earthquakes in the United States
   d. an online site about the history of the Mississippi River

3. Which is an antonym for the word *sparsely* as it is used in the second paragraph?
   a. barely
   b. lightly
   c. thinly
   d. densely

4. What is the main idea of this text?
   a. In the past, the New Madrid fault caused major damage near the Mississippi River.
   b. The earthquakes caused by the New Madrid fault were worse than the 1906 San Francisco earthquake.
   c. People all over the world should know about the life-changing effects of earthquakes.
   d. The New Madrid fault is still a serious threat in today's world.

5. Using the information in the text, list two things that happened as a result of the earthquakes.

   a. _____

   b. _____

Name_____

Mount St. Helens: A Deadly Volcano

Modern history has had its share of deadly volcanic eruptions. Mount St. Helens, located in the state of Washington, was once called "the Smoking Mountain" by Native Americans. The once smoking mountain was becoming extremely active, and by March of 1980, the activity within the volcano had begun to increase significantly.

Because of the increased activity, those living near the mountain were encouraged to evacuate. Unfortunately, not everyone listened to the warnings and left the area. One can only assume that those who chose to stay did not realize just how dangerous the situation was about to become.

Then, on May 18, 1980, the area around the volcano was hit with an earthquake. Parts of the mountain began to shift and one of the largest landslides ever recorded followed as a result of the earthquake. But the mountain wasn't finished. The volcano erupted with a blast that took out trees and leveled the area as far as twelve miles from the point of the blast. The explosion caused the debris from the landslide to become liquefied, and everything was propelled by the force of the explosion down the mountain at speeds surpassing one hundred miles an hour. The rush of debris, in turn, flooded the surrounding riverbanks, causing them to overflow and destroy everything in their path.

Despite the warnings, everyone did not reach safety. Fifty-seven people died as a result of this natural disaster. Scientists continue to monitor the still active volcano and hope such a catastrophe as what occurred in 1980 will not repeat itself in the near future.

Text Questions

1. Using information from the text, explain why people may not have evacuated the area around Mount St. Helens.

   _____

   _____

   _____

2. What was the author's purpose in writing this text?

   a. to explain
   b. to entertain
   c. to persuade
   d. to inform

3. Which statement is an opinion?

   a. Mount St. Helens led to the deaths of fifty-seven people.
   b. The eruption in 1980 of Mount St. Helens is, without a doubt, the worst natural disaster to ever occur in North America.
   c. The state of Washington experienced an earthquake and a volcanic explosion on the same day.
   d. Mount St. Helens was called "the Smoking Mountain" by Native Americans.

4. Why were the residents of the mountain encouraged to evacuate?

   a. The volcano was showing signs of increased activity.
   b. The property around the volcano was being used by the government for an interstate highway.
   c. Animals trying to escape volcanic activity were causing a stampede.
   d. Secret government experiments were taking place near the mountain.

5. Which would be a good primary source about the 1980 volcanic eruption?

   a. a website about volcanic eruptions in South America
   b. an atlas with maps showing the Pacific Northwest
   c. a letter written about the volcanic explosion by a survivor from the area
   d. an encyclopedia entry about volcanoes

20

Name_____

Chernobyl: A Nuclear Disaster

In the 1970s, the Chernobyl nuclear plant, located in the Ukraine, was one of the largest nuclear power plants on the planet. In 1986, the facility would experience an explosion that would forever change how much of the world viewed nuclear power. The effects of one fateful day would change the surrounding area forever.

Not until years after the incident would those investigating the cause finally be able to understand the origins of the disaster. An explosion in the reactors created a power surge that eventually led to an explosion that blew the lid off the nuclear reactor. This explosion caused radioactive material to spread to surrounding areas. Many of those areas were inhabited by civilians who were now exposed to dangerous levels of radiation.

Thirty-two people died as an immediate result of the explosion. The radiation that spread out from the facility would contaminate millions of acres. Eventually thousands of people died and thousands of others suffered from radiation poisoning and cancers caused from the nuclear explosion. Those people who lived near Chernobyl but did not die all lost their homes because of the contamination. Chernobyl was officially shut down in 2000, but the disastrous results of the nuclear meltdown remain even today.

Text Questions

1. Which statement is true about the text?
   a. Because of the Chernobyl disaster, nuclear power is no longer used today.
   b. After the meltdown, scientists managed to contain radiation within the area of the nuclear facility.
   c. Inhabitants of the area surrounding Chernobyl were not affected by the nuclear explosion.
   d. Thirty-two people died as an immediate result of the explosion, but many more would die as a result of the nuclear meltdown.

2. Which sentence in the first paragraph best foreshadows the fact that the nuclear meltdown would have long-term effects?
   a. In the 1970s, the Chernobyl nuclear plant, located in the Ukraine, was one of the largest nuclear power plants on the planet.
   b. In 1986, the facility would experience an explosion that would forever change how much of the world viewed nuclear power.
   c. The effects of one fateful day would change the surrounding area forever.
   d. Those people who lived near Chernobyl but did not die all lost their homes because of the contamination.

3. According to the text, which event most likely caused the nuclear meltdown?
   a. a loss of electricity in the facility
   b. a bird flying into some electrical wires outside the plant
   c. an unexpected freeze that caused a sudden drop in temperatures
   d. an explosion in the reactors that caused a power surge

4. After reading this text, what can one conclude about the nuclear plant at Chernobyl?
   a. The plant will reopen within the next decade.
   b. It will continue to provide power from the portions of the plant that were not affected by the explosion.
   c. The people living in the area hope to see the facility providing nuclear power within the near future.
   d. The plant is no longer in operation.

5. Why were people outside of the plant affected by the explosion?
   a. Nuclear radiation spread through the air.
   b. People came to the site to see what had happened.
   c. Vehicles leaving the plant unknowingly carried radiation outside of the facility.
   d. Birds flying in the vicinity of the facility carried radiation to other areas.

Name_____

The Space Shuttle Catastrophe

On February 1, 2003, the space shuttle *Columbia* exploded. The mission was the twenty-eighth trip made by the space shuttle. The crew of seven would die in a fiery explosion as the ship attempted to reenter Earth's atmosphere.

The start of the demise of the shuttle and its crew actually began with the shuttle's liftoff. Within the beginning of the launch, a piece of insulation broke off from the propellant tank. The piece of foam hit the edge of the left wing of the shuttle. This damage to the wing would later prove disastrous.

The wings of the shuttle were protected by heat-resistant tiles. When the foam hit the wing, some of the tiles were dislodged. Without the protection of this equipment, heat and wind would enter the wing during its ascent into the atmosphere. The result would cause the wing to blow apart from the struggling shuttle.

At 8:58, witnesses began seeing the first debris from the shuttle hit the ground. By 9:00 a.m., the shuttle and its crew were gone. The space shuttle program remained grounded until a complete investigation could be done, and the program did not resume until July 2005.

Text Questions

1. Which is most likely the reason the space shuttle exploded?
   a. Bad weather caused lightning strikes that caused a fire on board the *Columbia*.
   b. The space shuttle was blown off course from its original landing site.
   c. The space shuttle missed its original take-off date.
   d. Insulation broke off during liftoff and damaged the left wing.

2. Why was the space shuttle program grounded until 2005?
   a. to determine the cause of the accident
   b. to allow time for the completion of a new space shuttle
   c. to allow time to train new astronauts
   d. to determine which space shuttle and crew would be used for the next mission

3. What is this passage mostly about?
   a. the importance of the space program
   b. the explosion of the space shuttle *Columbia*
   c. the end of the space shuttle program
   d. the history of the United States' space program

4. What was the author's purpose in writing this text?
   a. to persuade
   b. to entertain
   c. to inform
   d. to explain

5. Which would be a good secondary source if someone wanted to know more about one of the astronauts on *Columbia's* last mission?
   a. an autobiography by one of the seven astronauts on the mission
   b. a fiction book about space travel in the future
   c. a biography about one of the seven astronauts on the mission
   d. an almanac about space travel in the United States

Name_____

Hurricane Katrina

On August 29, 2005, Hurricane Katrina hit the United States' Gulf Coastal area. Winds from the hurricane struck land at 100 to 140 miles per hour. Katrina is estimated to have caused over one hundred billion dollars in damages to areas in the United States.

Why was this hurricane so catastrophic? One reason is the amount of area affected by the storm. The damaging winds reached over four hundred miles across the continent. People in Louisiana, Mississippi, and Alabama all felt the effects of Katrina's raging wind and rain. The storm also caused levees to fail, which led to massive flooding. After the storm, many were left without food, water, or shelter.

As the storm was predicted to approach New Orleans, the mayor issued a mandatory evacuation. For those unable to leave, the city stadium—the Superdome—would be used as a temporary shelter. Despite the evacuation order, many people without funds or transportation were unable to leave. Eventually, some ten thousand people would seek shelter in the Superdome and still others chose to wait out the storm in their own homes despite the order to leave.

Although the aftermath of Hurricane Katrina was horrific, many heroes came out of such a terrible tragedy. People risked their lives to save others. People offered what they had to help those in need. Sadly, nearly two thousand people died. The effects of Hurricane Katrina can still be seen today despite the efforts of those hoping to rebuild what was lost.

Text Questions

1. Using information from the text, list two reasons people may have been unable to leave New Orleans once the mandatory evacuation order was given.

   a. _____

   b. _____

2. Using clues from the text, what is the purpose of a levee?
   a. to direct traffic
   b. to control floodwaters
   c. to control levels of radiation
   d. to mandate evacuations

3. Why did the mayor order a mandatory evacuation?
   a. He felt that everyone needed to go on vacation.
   b. He believed the city would be destroyed.
   c. He wanted the city all to himself.
   d. He felt conditions would become unsafe for the people there.

4. After reading this passage, what is one thing that could be done to protect the people of New Orleans in the event of future hurricanes?
   a. Everyone could be given a car so they could more easily evacuate.
   b. The levees could be strengthened to hold back floodwaters.
   c. All people living in New Orleans should move to other cities.
   d. There are no safety measures that could be done to protect from future hurricanes.

5. Which is a synonym for the word *catastrophic* as it is used in the second paragraph?
   a. wonderful
   b. satisfying
   c. majestic
   d. terrible

Name_____

William Driver

At the start of the Civil War, the people in the state of Tennessee struggled with the decision of whether to stay with the Union or to join the Confederacy. Eventually, the state would be the last to secede. However, there were people living in the state who would remain loyal to the Union. One such person was Captain William Driver. Driver is best known for a special flag he owned and hid during the Civil War, affectionately called "Old Glory."

William Driver was born in 1803 and was apprenticed to a blacksmith. Hating his situation, Driver ran away and became a cabin boy on a ship. His father told him not to come home until he had his own ship and was captain. Eventually, Driver did become a captain of his own ship. The people of his hometown in Salem, Massachusetts, were all very proud of Driver and made

him a huge flag that was twelve feet by twenty-four feet, which he nicknamed "Old Glory." Driver eventually sailed around the world and even rescued the descendants of the crew that had mutinied against their captain on the British ship the *HMS Bounty*.

Later, Driver would retire to Nashville, Tennessee, leaving the sea behind and becoming a clerk at his brother's store. During the Civil War, he hid "Old Glory" by sewing the flag into a quilt. When Tennessee was taken over by Union soldiers, the soldiers asked Driver to raise his flag over the state's capitol. As people heard about Driver and his flag, others began calling the American flag "Old Glory," a nickname that is still used today for the flag of the United States of America.

Text Questions

1. Summarize the text in two complete sentences.

   _____

   _____

   _____

2. Using information from the text, which statement best explains why William Driver hid the American flag during the Civil War?

   a. He knew he would be without an easy source for heat, and the large flag would make his quilt thicker and warmer.
   b. He liked the feeling of safety he had being covered with the American flag.
   c. He wanted to hide the flag from his neighbors.
   d. He was worried the Confederates would take or harm the Union flag.

3. Which statement best explains Driver's feelings about the flag?

   a. The flag represented his loyalty to the Union.
   b. The flag was a memento from his younger days.
   c. The flag reminded him how proud his father was when he became captain of his own ship.
   d. The flag was not special to Driver.

4. What is the meaning of the word *secede* as it is used in the first paragraph?

   a. to win   c. to remain
   b. to lose   d. to leave

5. After reading the text, what inference can you make about William Driver?

   a. He rarely finished anything he started.
   b. He was a person with an extremely strong will.
   c. He had become sick of the ocean as he aged.
   d. He missed his days as captain of his own ship.

Name_____

Thomas Jefferson

Thomas Jefferson, the third president of the United States and author of the Declaration of Independence, was born in 1743. Jefferson was born in the South into one of Virginia's most prominent families. Always an avid learner, Jefferson was determined to receive a top-notch education. He attended William and Mary, a college in Williamsburg, Virginia, and went on to study law.

Jefferson would later become involved in politics. He felt strongly that the American colonies should seek independence from Great Britain. His beliefs and eloquence with words would help lead him to his most significant written work: the Declaration of Independence. Jefferson was actually part of a five-person committee, but the other men chose Jefferson

to actually write the first draft. Jefferson's work was a document that would eloquently explain the importance of freedom and equality. The Declaration of Independence also listed the reasons the colonies wanted to be free.

In 1803, while president, Jefferson purchased land that tremendously increased the size of the United States. This purchase, known as the Louisiana Purchase, vastly increased the new country's size.

Jefferson's death was a sad time for the nation. He died in his home, Monticello, on July 4, 1826. Ironically, this date was also the fiftieth anniversary of the Declaration of Independence.

Text Questions

1. Which statement is a fact about the story?

    a. Without Thomas Jefferson's ideals, the Declaration of Independence could have never been written.
    b. Thomas Jefferson was the author of the Declaration of Independence.
    c. The Declaration of Independence is the most eloquently written document in all of American history.
    d. Thomas Jefferson is one of the greatest presidents in American history.

2. What was one purpose of the Declaration of Independence?

    a. to help boost Thomas Jefferson's political career
    b. to free all slaves living in the American colonies
    c. to explain the reasons Americans felt they were being taxed unfairly by Great Britain
    d. to list reasons and explain why the American colonies felt they should be free from Great Britain's rule

3. What is Monticello?

    a. the first draft of the Declaration of Independence
    b. the home of Thomas Jefferson
    c. the name of Thomas Jefferson's first son
    d. a type of violin

4. What is the main idea of this text?

    a. to explain the importance of the Declaration of Independence
    b. to explain the importance of the Louisiana Purchase
    c. to give information about Thomas Jefferson's education
    d. to give information about the importance of Thomas Jefferson to America's history

5. Based on the text, which statement would most likely be true about Jefferson?

    a. A good education was most important to Jefferson.
    b. Jefferson believed all men should reside in Virginia.
    c. One of Jefferson's finest achievements is the Declaration of Independence.
    d. Jefferson assumed he would die on Independence Day.

Name_____

King Tut

Tutankhamun, best known as King Tut, was born around 1341 B.C. The ruler of Egypt did not live a long life. In fact, he died near the age of eighteen or nineteen. Why then do so many people know about the boy who ruled Egypt?

Tutankhamun was buried in the area known as the Valley of the Kings. Because of his early death, many historians believe he was buried in a tomb that was most likely built for someone else since his own tomb would not have been completed at the time. Tut's body went through the ceremonial preservation system known as mummification. This process took many days, and certain organs were removed from the body and preserved in Canopic jars. Ironically, the brain was not considered an important organ and was removed from the body but not preserved. Seventy days after his death, King Tut's body was sealed in the Egyptian tomb.

In 1922, a remarkable discovery was made. An archeologist named Howard Carter found the tomb that had been sealed so long ago. As he and his team entered the tomb, they found the inside had been preserved and an interior chamber was painted with the story of the Egyptian leader's funeral and journey to his life after death. The tomb was filled with treasures from Tut's life. The crew would also find the final resting place of the boy ruler. His body had been preserved for more than three thousand years along with the magnificent artifacts and treasures no grave robbers had ever disturbed. Carter's find has helped make King Tut one of the most recognized and well-known ancient leaders of all time.

Text Questions ....

1. Using information from the text, summarize why King Tut is well-known many years after his death.

   _____

   _____

2. Why do historians believe Tutankhamun was most likely buried in someone else's tomb?
   a. The tomb was more elaborate than where he should have been buried.
   b. Because of his young age, he had to be buried in the Valley of the Kings.
   c. His own tomb would not have been completed at his death since he died at such a young age.
   d. The painted wall murals the archaeologists found explained he was buried in the wrong tomb.

3. After reading the text, what can one conclude about Tutankhamun?
   a. He was a well-loved ruler during his lifetime.
   b. He made many important political decisions during his lifetime.
   c. His young age was a benefit to his ability to rule ancient Egypt.
   d. He is known by generations today because of the discovery of his tomb.

4. List three things in sequential order that happen in the passage.

   a. _____

   b. _____

   c. _____

5. If someone wanted to know more about Tutankhamun, which source would be the least helpful in gathering information?
   a. an encyclopedia entry about Tutankhamun
   b. a brochure about a museum tour of artifacts from King Tut's tomb
   c. a website with original newspaper articles about Howard Carter's discovery of Tutankhamun's tomb.
   d. an atlas showing the location of the Valley of the Kings

Name_____

Butch Cassidy

Robert Leroy Parker is probably not a name most people know. However, Parker's pseudonym, Butch Cassidy, is synonymous as one of the most notorious bank robbers in America's history. Born in 1866, Parker would later team up with Harry Longabaugh, the Sundance Kid, and proceed to rob banks and trains with a group of outlaws known throughout the West as the Wild Bunch.

Butch Cassidy was the oldest of thirteen children. He was raised in Utah, and his family struggled financially. He left home as a teenager, hoping to find a way out of the poverty he had known as a child. He eventually found work on a ranch. He then met Mike Cassidy, a horse and cattle thief. For whatever reason, Robert Leroy Parker admired the older Cassidy and changed his name to Butch Cassidy.

Cassidy's first major robbery occurred in 1889, when he and his gang stole over twenty thousand dollars from a bank in Colorado. Eventually he was caught and spent two years in jail. Sadly, after his release, he was not reformed, and he continued his life as a criminal. With his gang known as the Wild Bunch, he would embark on a successful string of train and bank robberies.

The Union Pacific Railroad, a frequent target of the gang, was desperate to have the band of outlaws stopped. They hired the Pinkerton Detective Agency to track down and stop Butch Cassidy and his group of thieves. They eventually drove the robbers out of the United States and into South America. What happened to Butch Cassidy from there, no one actually knows. Some argue he changed his name yet again and went on to live a long life in South America. Others claim he died in a shootout, and still others say he came back to the United States to live. Although no one knows for sure what became of Butch Cassidy, he is remembered as one of the legendary outlaws of the West.

Text Questions

1. Which is a synonym for the word *pseudonym* as it is used in the first paragraph?
   a. first name
   b. false name
   c. legal name
   d. last name

2. From the information in the text, which statement best explains why Parker changed his name?
   a. He did not like his own name.
   b. He did not like his old name because he had been named after his father.
   c. Since he had run away, he did not want his parents to be able to find him.
   d. He wanted to start a new life with the name of someone he admired.

3. If you had to write a report about the life of Butch Cassidy, which source would be a primary source?
   a. an entry on a website about the Wild West and the outlaws who lived during the late 1800s
   b. a biography about Butch Cassidy
   c. letters written by Butch Cassidy while he was in jail
   d. a newspaper article about the Union Pacific Railroad Company

4. Summarize the text in two complete sentences.

   _____

   _____

5. According to the text, which of the following might have happened to Butch Cassidy?
   a. He died trying to cross the border into South America.
   b. He was buried in an unmarked grave in South America.
   c. He married and moved to Australia.
   d. He changed his name and lived out the rest of his life in South America.

Name_____

Milton Hershey

Most people have heard of Hershey chocolates. But did you know the candy was named after Milton Hershey? Milton Hershey was born in 1857 in Pennsylvania. He began learning to make candy at the age of fourteen. Success would not come easily. His hard work and determination as he learned how to make candy would help him become one of the world's most famous makers of chocolate.

Milton Hershey's first real success came when he started a company called Lancaster Caramel Company. At this point, he mainly made caramels. Then, in 1893, he attended the World's Columbian Exposition where he was able to see how chocolate was made. It was during this time that he started the Hershey Chocolate Company. His passion was to create world-class milk chocolate. Within three years, he had sold his caramel

company and was building a factory in Pennsylvania to make his new chocolates. The doors to the factory opened in 1905. By 1907, the Hershey's Kiss was created. The town in Pennsylvania where Milton Hershey built his factory is now called Hershey.

Hershey did more than start a candy company. He wanted to help the entire community with his success. The philanthropist gave money to support schools, churches, parks, and other endeavors—all to help those who lived in the area. One of his largest projects was opening the Hershey Industrial School for orphaned boys to have a home and an outstanding education. Today, both boys and girls can attend what is now known as the Milton Hershey School. Although Hershey died in 1945, his legacy continues.

Text Questions

1. Which adjective best describes Milton Hershey?

   a. stubborn
   b. determined

   c. selfish
   d. cowardly

2. Using information from the text, explain why you chose the answer for question one.

   _____

   _____

   _____

3. What does the word *philanthropist* mean as it is used in the third paragraph?

   a. someone who saves most of the money he or she makes
   b. someone who gives money to be used to help others
   c. someone who has very little money
   d. someone who is extremely wealthy

4. What is the main idea of the third paragraph?

   a. Milton Hershey was selfish and thought only of himself.
   b. Milton Hershey was driven to make the best chocolate in the world.
   c. Milton Hershey regretted his decision to sell his caramel company.
   d. Milton Hershey used his success to help others.

5. Which title would be a good alternative for this text?

   a. "Milton Hershey's Legacy"
   b. "Hershey Chocolate Tastes Great"
   c. "A New Kind of Chocolate"
   d. "A Boy from Pennsylvania"

28

Name_____

Helen Keller

Helen Keller's life is one of the most inspirational stories ever told. Born in 1880 in Tuscumbia, Alabama, Keller became sick when she was near the age of two. Her illness left her blind, deaf, and mute. Her vocal chords were not impaired from the illness, but because she could not hear how words were pronounced, she could not learn to say them. With no way to communicate, there seemed to be little hope of her being able to learn, even though she had already begun to say words at just six months old.

Experts are unsure exactly what illness Helen Keller had. Regardless, the high fever produced from the illness caused the loss of her sight and hearing. As a child, she found ways to communicate with her family. Just as one might hug someone to show affection or place a finger over a person's mouth to advise them to be quiet, she developed methods to let others know what she wanted or needed; however, her behavior was unpredictable, and she would often have uncontrollable tantrums.

Searching for help, the Keller family was introduced to Anne Sullivan from the Perkins Institute for the Blind. Sullivan moved to Alabama to work with her new student. Miraculously, Sullivan made a breakthrough with her pupil. One day, as she spelled the word *water* into Helen's hand and ran water from a pump onto Helen's hand, everything seemed to come together for Helen. She understood that the symbols stood for the words.

Helen Keller went on to graduate from Radcliffe College at the age of twenty-four. She and Anne Sullivan would remain friends and work together for the remainder of Anne Sullivan's life. Keller died in 1968 and was only a few weeks short of her eighty-eighth birthday.

Text Questions

1. Which information from the text is an opinion?
   a. Helen Keller's life is one of the most inspirational stories ever told.
   b. Helen Keller was born in 1880 in Tuscumbia, Alabama.
   c. Anne Sullivan moved to Alabama to work with Helen Keller.
   d. Helen Keller graduated from Radcliffe College.

2. What is the first word Anne Sullivan was able to get Helen to truly understand?
   a. Alabama
   b. teacher
   c. mother
   d. water

3. What does the word *mute* mean as it is used in the first paragraph?
   a. unable to see
   b. unable to talk
   c. unable to hear
   d. unable to communicate

4. Summarize the text in two or three complete sentences.

   _____

   _____

   _____

5. What was the author's purpose in writing this text?
   a. to persuade
   b. to explain
   c. to inform
   d. to entertain

Name_____

Harry Houdini

Born in Budapest, Hungary, in 1874, Erich Weisz would later be known as the famous magician Harry Houdini. Houdini was one of seven children. His family moved from Hungary to the United States, and when he was thirteen, he moved with his father to New York to help find a place for the family to live and to begin working.

By 1894, Houdini was beginning to perform his magic for small audiences; however, most were only interested in his escape tricks, such as freeing himself of shackles or from locked prisons. By 1899, Houdini was traveling and living with a vaudeville act that performed around the country.

Houdini's most famous escape trick was the Chinese Water Torture Cell. For this trick, Houdini was suspended by his feet and then lowered into a locked glass cabinet that was filled with water. His body was upside down in the tank. He had to hold his breath for over three minutes to escape from the water-filled prison. Houdini continued to perform until his death in 1926 at the age of fifty-two.

After Houdini's death, his brother was given Houdini's collection of props. Eventually, his brother sold the items and after several different sales, many of his most important pieces—including the Chinese Water Torture Cell—became the property of another well-known magician, David Copperfield.

Text Questions

1. Which paragraph gives the most information about Houdini's childhood?
   a. first paragraph
   b. second paragraph
   c. third paragraph
   d. fourth paragraph

2. Why might David Copperfield want anything that belonged to Harry Houdini?
   a. He wanted to destroy the other magician's props.
   b. He wants to put the items on display in a museum.
   c. He most likely admired the magician and wanted something that belonged to him.
   d. He probably did not realize what he was buying.

3. What can you infer about Houdini's success as a magician?
   a. Everyone loved to watch his performances.
   b. He created all of his own tricks.
   c. His parents gave him money to help get his career started.
   d. His main success came from his skill as an escapee artist.

4. From what you read in the text, which of the following statements is true?
   a. Harry Houdini never married.
   b. Harry Houdini wanted to return to his home in Hungary.
   c. Harry Houdini was eventually a successful magician.
   d. Harry Houdini admired the work of David Copperfield.

5. What does the word *shackles* mean as it is used in the second paragraph?
   a. rope tied into a noose
   b. chains used to imprison
   c. words used to insult
   d. tape used to bind

Name_____

Benjamin Franklin

In 1706, one of America's most well-known historical figures was born: Benjamin Franklin. Franklin was born in the Massachusetts Bay Colony and is considered one of the founding fathers of the United States of America.

Like many children during this time period, Franklin began working at an early age. By the time he was ten, he was already learning to make candles at his father's business. By age twelve, he was apprenticed to work at a print shop, and by age fourteen, he was printing many of his own writings under a pseudonym. Eventually, Franklin would leave his apprenticeship and move to Philadelphia.

Franklin had found his life's passion during his apprenticeship while working with a printing press. He would eventually purchase his own newspaper. He published *Poor Richard's Almanac* by 1732, and during the following years, he would see his success continue to grow. Franklin also began to expand his interests into scientific pursuits during the next few decades. He invented the Franklin stove, and during this time, he also conducted his well-known kite experiments regarding electricity.

Politically, Benjamin Franklin would be part of the colonies rebellion against British rule. He would represent Pennsylvania at the Constitutional Convention. It was here the United States Constitution would be ratified. Franklin also participated in electing George Washington as the new country's first president. These accomplishments and Franklin's many other achievements serve to give him a prominent place in America's history.

Text Questions

1. According to the text, besides his political career, what are two other interests Ben Franklin had as an adult?

   a. science and horticulture
   b. technology and engineering
   c. education and writing
   d. writing and science

2. Which is a synonym for the word *rebellion* as it is used in the last paragraph?

   a. revolt
   b. support
   c. maintain
   d. reveal

3. Which statement is an opinion?

   a. Benjamin Franklin was born in 1706.
   b. Benjamin Franklin is one of America's most popular historical figures.
   c. Benjamin Franklin published *Poor Richard's Almanac.*
   d. Benjamin Franklin was a representative at the Constitutional Convention.

4. What was the author's purpose in writing this text?

   a. to entertain
   b. to persuade
   c. to inform
   d. to state an opinion

5. Why might children who lived during Franklin's time have apprenticeships?

   a. so they did not have to go to school
   b. so they could learn trades or ways to make a living
   c. so they could earn extra money for entertainment and food
   d. so they could share what they learned with others

Name_____

Anne Frank

Anne Frank, a young Jewish girl born in 1929, was eventually a victim of the horrific Holocaust of World War II. She became famous posthumously when a diary she wrote while in hiding eventually became published. Today, her story has been read by millions of people across the globe.

Anne was the youngest child of Otto and Edith Frank. She had an older sister, Margot. Originally, the family lived in Germany, but when Adolph Hitler became Chancellor, Otto Frank knew he had to do something. He moved his family to Amsterdam to try to keep them safe. In Amsterdam, the family was forced into hiding, along with four other people. Their hiding place—where they would stay for over two years—was a place they called the Secret Annex. The Annex was located inside Otto Frank's business. Friends of the family helped get them food and supplies and were the only contact they had with the outside world since they could never leave the hiding place.

During their time in hiding, Anne kept a diary. Once her original diary was full, she wrote on any paper she could find. After August 4, 1944, there are no more entries because Anne and her family were found and captured by the Nazis. To this day, no one knows who gave away their hiding place to the Nazis.

Of the eight people who went into hiding, only Otto Frank survived. Anne and her sister died from typhus while being held at the Bergen-Belsen concentration camp, yet despite her early and tragic death, Anne's words live on even today. After the war, Otto Frank, with the help of friends, collected Anne's writings and had them published into a book. Her story has been made into several movies and is also performed as a play. One can be sure that Anne Frank's story will never be forgotten.

Text Questions

1. What does the word *posthumously* mean as it is used in the first paragraph?
   a. during someone's lifetime
   b. before someone was born
   c. centuries later
   d. after someone's death

2. Which title would be a good alternative for this text?
   a. "The Frank Family"
   b. "The Horror of the Nazi Holocaust"
   c. "Anne Frank: Her Words Live On"
   d. "Nazi Germany"

3. Based on the text, why did Mr. Frank most likely have his daughter's diary published into a book?
   a. He wanted to make a lot of money.
   b. He wanted others to know what Anne's life had been like while in hiding.
   c. He wanted to become an author.
   d. He hoped the diary would be made into a movie.

4. When the war was over, which member of the Frank family survived?
   a. Edith Frank
   b. Otto Frank
   c. Anne Frank
   d. Margot Frank

5. Which statement is an opinion?
   a. Anne Frank was born in 1929.
   b. Anne Frank was the youngest child of Otto and Edith Frank.
   c. Anne Frank and her family moved to Amsterdam.
   d. Anne Frank's story should never be forgotten.

Name_____

Amelia Earhart

Amelia Earhart was born in 1897, in Atchison, Kansas. Amelia spent much of her childhood living with her grandparents due to her parents' unstable financial situation. Perhaps it was this lack of stability as a child that made Amelia determined to succeed on her own. She became extremely independent and wanted to be able to take care of herself rather than relying on anyone else.

During World War I, Amelia volunteered for the Red Cross. Tending to the wounded, she met many pilots. During this period of her life, she became extremely interested in aviation. Then, at an air show in 1920, she took a plane ride. It is at this point she became certain she wanted to become a pilot. By 1923, she was given a pilot's license and was only the sixteenth woman to be issued such a license to fly.

Amelia Earhart would eventually become the first female pilot to fly across the Atlantic Ocean. After her famous flight, she was honored by a reception given for her where she would meet President Coolidge. After this experience, Amelia wanted more of flying. Unlike her first trip, she wanted to fly across the Atlantic Ocean solo. By 1932, she had reached her goal.

Amelia Earhart's love of flying would eventually lead to her death. In 1937, a flight across the Pacific would be her last. Her plane went down somewhere in the Pacific Ocean. Millions of dollars were spent in rescue attempts, but no rescue was ever made. On January 5, 1939, Amelia Earhart was declared legally dead, although her body was never found.

Text Questions

1. Summarize the text in two complete sentences.

   _____

   _____

   _____

2. Which event seems most likely to have made Amelia Earhart extremely independent?

   a. being first-born in her family
   b. learning to fly

   c. having a financially unstable childhood
   d. learning to read at an early age

3. The word *aviation*, as it is used in the second paragraph, most likely deals with which of the following?

   a. the study of birds
   b. the study of ancient artifacts

   c. the study of weather patterns
   d. the study of flight

4. Using information from the text, list in sequential order three things that happened to Amelia Earhart.

   a. _____

   b. _____

   c. _____

5. Based on information from the text, if Amelia Earhart had not died on her last flight, which of the events would have most likely occurred?

   a. She would have never flown again.
   b. She would have continued flying.
   c. She would have begun designing airplanes.
   d. She would have started a school for airplane mechanics.

33

Name_____

Elvis Presley

Elvis Presley was born on January 8, 1935, in Mississippi. Elvis had a twin brother who was stillborn. Elvis eventually became one of the biggest names of all time in music and is often referred to as the king of rock 'n' roll.

Elvis grew up poor but was raised by parents who loved him. As a child, he attended church regularly, and the gospel music he heard there had a great influence on him. By the age of ten, he already owned his first guitar. Later, he would win a talent show at the high school he attended in Memphis, which continued to encourage his love for music. His dream of being a musician became his main goal, and he worked many odd jobs while trying to pursue his dream. He

eventually cut his first record, and he was able to begin touring and recording his music. His first single came in 1954. By 1956, he was on his way to being a singing star and a movie star as he signed a contract with Paramount Pictures.

In 1957, he was drafted and served in Germany for a little over a year. It was in Germany that he would meet his future wife, Priscilla Beaulieu. They would eventually be married in 1967 and would have a daughter, Lisa Marie. Sadly, the marriage would not last.

On August 16, 1977, Elvis Presley passed away from heart failure. To this day, Elvis Presley has remained one of the biggest names in music history.

Text Questions

1. According to the text, what are two interests Elvis Presley had as an adult?
   a. acting in movies and singing
   b. writing and dancing
   c. gospel singing and winning talent shows
   d. cutting records and cooking

2. Which event had an early influence on Elvis Presley's musical career?
   a. listening to gospel music at church
   b. attending many different schools
   c. being drafted into the army
   d. meeting other famous musicians

3. Which events are listed in the correct sequential order?
   a. Elvis won a talent show and received a guitar as a gift.
   b. Elvis was drafted into the army and met Priscilla Beaulieu.
   c. Elvis made his first movie and then recorded his first record.
   d. Elvis's daughter was born, and Elvis recorded his first movie.

4. What was the author's purpose in writing this text?
   a. to entertain
   b. to persuade
   c. to inform
   d. to compare and contrast

5. Which is a synonym for the word *pursue* as it is used in the second paragraph?
   a. hide
   b. follow
   c. stalk
   d. remind

Name_____

Laura Ingalls Wilder

Laura Ingalls Wilder was born in 1867. She and her family lived in Wisconsin at the time of her birth. Her father moved the family often but would eventually settle the family for quite some time in Walnut Grove, Minnesota. Laura and her family were true pioneers of the West. As they moved about, she had many adventures and learned to do many chores that were vital to survival.

Laura had three sisters. She and her sisters learned to do many things to help their father. Despite moving so often, it was important to her family that she receive a good education. Laura's mother had been a schoolteacher, and when they did not live near a school, she made sure the girls were still learning. Whenever possible, though, Laura and her sisters attended school regularly.

When Laura turned sixteen, she became a teacher just as her mother had been. A year later, she married Almanzo Wilder. Their daughter Rose would eventually grow up and work in the publishing industry. Her knowledge of writing would help her mother bring her stories to print in a series of books about her life on the prairie. A television series would later be made based on her popular book series, helping solidify Laura Ingalls Wilder's name as one of the most famous American pioneers.

Text Questions

1. According to the text, which event happens first?
   a. Wilder has a daughter named Rose.
   b. Wilder has a series of books published.
   c. Laura Ingalls marries Almanzo Wilder.
   d. Wilder's books are the basis for a television series.

2. What is one likely result of Laura Ingalls Wilder's education?
   a. She becomes a pioneer.
   b. She marries Almanzo Wilder.
   c. She becomes an author.
   d. She moved a lot as a child.

3. Why was education most likely important to Mrs. Ingalls?
   a. She had been a schoolteacher.
   b. She did not know how to read, and she wanted her children to be able to read.
   c. Her father was a professor at a university.
   d. Her grandmother had been a schoolteacher.

4. Which is a synonym for the word *pioneer* as it is used in the first paragraph?
   a. explorer
   b. immigrant
   c. inventor
   d. parent

5. Which item below is something Laura Ingalls Wilder might have done as a teenager?
   a. She might have churned butter.
   b. She might have published books.
   c. She might have driven a car.
   d. She might have played women's soccer.

Name_____

Rosa Parks

Rosa Parks was born in 1913 in Alabama. As an African-American citizen, she saw that many people were being treated unfairly. All American citizens were supposed to have equal rights, but for Rosa Parks, this was not true. African-American citizens were segregated from white citizens. During her lifetime, African-Americans could not even drink from the same water fountains as other Americans. They could not sit in the same areas of restaurants or movie theaters. The list of inequalities went on and on.

Every day to go to work, Rosa would ride a bus. One rule on the bus was for African-Americans to give up their seats if white passengers wanted them. But one particular day, Rosa decided she'd had enough of the rule. She had paid to ride the bus, and she had paid for her seat; she was not going to give up her place.

Rosa Parks's brave move of defiance led to her arrest. However, many people stood up for her and were proud of her act of courage that day on the bus. The African-American community agreed to a boycott. All of those in favor of Rosa's actions decided to no longer use the bus system, even though for many this meant a long walk to and from work.

As a result of Rosa Parks's actions and a ruling made by the Supreme Court, things began to change for the better. One such change was that African-Americans no longer had to give up their seats for other passengers. The huge Civil Rights Movement that would continue to happen in America would help gain equal rights for all American citizens. Rosa Parks will always be remembered as a true crusader for civil rights.

Text Questions

1. What does the word *segregated* mean as it is used in the first paragraph?
   a. held together
   b. kept separate
   c. hidden
   d. placed in quarantine

2. According to the text, what can you infer is a reason Rosa Parks felt African-Americans were being treated unfairly?
   a. because they were not being treated the same as other citizens
   b. because other citizens were given better seats in public places
   c. because she could not a apply for a job as a bus driver
   d. because her children were being treated different than their classmates

3. What does the word *boycott* mean as it is used in the third paragraph?
   a. to gather up
   b. to stay with others
   c. to stay away from
   d. to invite to go

4. What are civil rights?
   a. rights guaranteed to all adults
   b. rights guaranteed to all children
   c. rights guaranteed to all immigrants
   d. rights guaranteed to all citizens

5. Why did Rosa Parks most likely not give up her seat on the bus?
   a. She was tired and needed to sit.
   b. She was tired of being treated unfairly.
   c. She was unable to stand because she had hurt her leg.
   d. She knew she was about to get off at the next bus stop.

Name_____

Princess Diana

Diana Spencer, best known as Princess Diana, was born July 1, 1961, in Sandringham, England. After attending school, Diana moved to London. She found as a young adult that she loved working with children, and eventually she became a kindergarten teacher.

During this time in her life, Diana began to date Prince Charles. Charles was thirteen years older than Diana. He was also the oldest son of the queen and heir to the British throne. In 1981, the couple married. The royal wedding was shown on television and watched by millions of people. Eventually, the couple would have two sons, William and Harry.

Unfortunately, the royal marriage did not have a fairy-tale ending. By 1996, the marriage was over, and the two divorced. Princess Diana, however, remained popular with the people. Paparazzi followed her wherever she went. On August 30, 1997, while trying to escape photographers, she and her companion died in a car crash. Her sudden death stunned the world. Despite her untimely death, Princess Diana will always be remembered for her devotion to various charities and her determination to help make the world a better place.

Text Questions

1. What was the author's purpose in writing this text?
   a. to entertain
   b. to compare and contrast
   c. to persuade
   d. to inform

2. Based on information given in the text, which word might be used to describe Princess Diana?
   a. selfish
   b. giving
   c. unkind
   d. creative

3. Using information from the text, list in sequential order three events in the life of Princess Diana.

   a. _____

   b. _____

   c. _____

4. What does the word *heir* mean as it is used in the second paragraph?
   a. successor
   b. winner
   c. champion
   d. opponent

5. Why would photographers want to follow Princess Diana?
   a. Even though she was divorced from Prince Charles, people still wanted details about her life.
   b. Photographers thought she was extremely photogenic.
   c. She probably paid them to take pictures for her.
   d. The photographers all worked for the royal family.

Name_____

Levi Strauss

Levi Strauss was born in 1829 in Germany. The name Levi Strauss is now synonymous with jeans. However, it was not always so for the young, American immigrant.

When Strauss was seventeen, he moved from Germany to America. At this time, he supported himself by selling household goods to people who lived in nearby towns, but Strauss was looking to expand his opportunities. When people began moving to California hoping to find gold, Strauss decided to move too.

Levi Strauss would not make his fortune by finding gold. Instead, he would provide something the miners needed: a good pair of work pants. When he arrived in California, he began constructing his first pair of jeans. The pants did not look like the jeans you might find in a store today. They were made out of a brown canvas-like material. The pants were extremely popular, and before long, Levi ran out of material to make the jeans. It did not take him long to discover a new type of material that is like the fabric used today. Strauss dyed the fabric blue and dubbed the new name for his pants "blue jeans."

Text Questions

1. Which title would be a good alternative for this text?
   a. "A Young Immigrant"
   b. "The Dreamer"
   c. "Levi Strauss's Invention"
   d. "The History of Clothing"

2. Why did Levi Strauss most likely not attempt to make his fortune by panning for gold?
   a. He had been a salesman and saw a need for something he could sell to the people in the mining towns.
   b. He loved sewing more than looking for gold.
   c. He was afraid of failing.
   d. He did not have the equipment he needed to look for gold.

3. What does the word *immigrant* mean as it is used in the first paragraph?
   a. someone who moves out of a country
   b. someone who moves into a country
   c. someone who only speaks a foreign language
   d. someone who constantly moves

4. Which question below could be answered using information from the text?
   a. How many siblings did Levi Strauss have?
   b. On what date did Levi Strauss invent his first pair of jeans?
   c. Why did Levi Strauss move to California?
   d. Why did Levi Strauss move from Germany to America?

5. Use the space below to answer the question you circled for question four.

   _____

   _____

   _____

Name_____

Jesse James

Jesse James was born in 1847. By the time the Civil War broke out in the United States, both Jesse and his brother Frank were old enough to serve. Each chose to serve with the Confederate army. Their military careers would soon come to an end as the two became criminals in the area of the country that would become known as the Wild West.

No one knows what made the son of a preacher turn to a life of violence. Historians do know that, in 1863, the James's home was attacked by Union troops. Whatever the cause, James became one of the most notorious outlaws of the times, robbing banks, trains, and stagecoaches. James and the men who followed him became known as the James Gang. This gang of outlaws stole an estimated two hundred thousand dollars and harmed countless people.

Eventually, Jesse James's life of crime came to an end. One of his own men turned against him to collect a reward offered by the Governor of Missouri. Jesse James died at the age of thirty-four, and with his death, the notorious James Gang came to an end.

Text Questions

1. Which statement is an opinion about the text?
   a. James was born in 1847.
   b. James served in the Confederate army.
   c. James became a criminal after his home was attacked by Union soldiers.
   d. James was the most notorious outlaw of all time.

2. What does the word *notorious* mean as it is used in the second paragraph?
   a. popular
   b. infamous
   c. friendly
   d. well-liked

3. Which title would be a good alternative for this text?
   a. "A Life of Crime"
   b. "Turned Against"
   c. "The James Gang"
   d. "Confederate Soldier"

4. Which paragraph provides information about Jesse James's death?
   a. none of the paragraphs
   b. the first paragraph
   c. the second paragraph
   d. the third paragraph

5. Which adjective best describes Jesse James?
   a. villainous
   b. heroic
   c. gallant
   d. brave

Name_____

History

Many students often lament the studying of history. They wonder why they should study something that, in their opinion, has nothing to do with their own lives. That point of view, however, is far from the truth.

History is a culmination of the personal stories and events of people just like you. The men and women who came before you helped shape the country where you live. Their ideas often solved problems and conflicts. Studying the past helps you to understand what your ancestors' lives were like and to see how their experiences have shaped your own life.

Not everything that happened in the past is good. Some of what you study in history helps you understand the mistakes of the past, which will help people to not repeat any injustice that has already occurred. People often learn from the past to have a better future.

Whether you like the subject of history or not, one must appreciate the importance of the events and the people who came before you. The generations who lived before you have impacted your own life in the decisions they made. The decisions of your own generation will eventually affect the generations that come after you. In this unique way, the world is truly connected. History is not just a study of the past; history is the study of people, places, and events that can affect the future.

Text Questions

1. What was the author's purpose in writing this text?
   a. to convince students to like history more than science
   b. to persuade students that studying history is important
   c. to persuade all high school students to take multiple history classes
   d. to show that history is irrelevant to the future

2. Which is a synonym for the word *lament* as it is used in the first paragraph?
   a. consider
   b. grieve
   c. compare
   d. imagine

3. Which paragraph in the text best explains how studying history can help people not repeat the mistakes of past generations?
   a. first paragraph
   b. second paragraph
   c. third paragraph
   d. fourth paragraph

4. Using information from the text, explain why the decisions you make today are important.

   _____

   _____

   _____

5. Which paragraph from the text helps you to explain your answer for question four?
   a. first paragraph
   b. second paragraph
   c. third paragraph
   d. fourth paragraph

Name_____

Slavery

In North America, the thirteen British colonies grew quickly. Farms and industry began to thrive. With this expansion, workers were needed. Some people did work as indentured servants. An indentured servant is different from a slave because this person can earn his or her freedom after an agreed-upon term. Many people came to the New World as indentured servants; someone else paid for their passage in return for a required number of years of service, but eventually the person could earn his or her freedom. This was not so with slavery.

Slavery was introduced in America as early as the 1600s. Slavery expanded in the colonies as the New World began to grow. In fact, the population grew so quickly that many colonists feared they would be overpowered by the slaves. Slave codes were put into place. These codes kept slaves from gathering in large numbers and also from traveling without permits.

The daily life of a slave varied. Some were given jobs as house slaves, while others toiled in fields working long, strenuous hours. Slaves were treated differently depending on their owners. Some were treated very cruelly and punished in barbaric methods, such as being hit with a whip. Others were treated as family such as the life of slave Phyllis Wheatley, who was taught to read and write and was later given her freedom by her owner. Unfortunately, stories like Phyllis Wheatley's did not often occur. The issue of slavery would not be settled in America until 1865 at the end of the Civil War.

Text Questions

1. According to the text, why were slaves needed in the New World?
    a. More people were needed to settle the colonies.
    b. Disease forced them from their own homes.
    c. Farms and industry were rapidly expanding in the New World.
    d. People in Europe had slaves, so people in the New World wanted to continue the practice.

2. What is one difference between an indentured servant and a slave?
    a. An indentured servant could work to earn his or her freedom.
    b. Only males could be indentured servants.
    c. Slaves had free passage to the colonies; therefore, they were unable to be indentured servants.
    d. Unlike a freed slave, an indentured servant could never leave the thirteen colonies even once the person earned his or her freedom.

3. What was the purpose of the Slave codes?
    a. to stop slaves from organizing and trying to be free
    b. to give slaves their own set of laws
    c. to stop slaves from learning to read
    d. to separate slaves from their families

4. Which statement is true about Phyllis Wheatley?
    a. She was the only slave ever taught to read and write.
    b. She was freed from slavery because her owners were afraid of her.
    c. The treatment she received from her owners was not the usual treatment most slaves experienced.
    d. Her life was perfect.

5. Which is an antonym for the word *toiled* as it is used in the last paragraph?
    a. labored
    b. worked
    c. struggled
    d. relaxed

Name_____

Independence

The thirteen colonies wanted independence from British rule. Although the colonists had valid reasons for wanting their freedom, they understood that the act would be considered treason to the crown. Thomas Paine wrote a pamphlet called *Common Sense* that attempted to explain the common-sense reasons why the colonies should no longer belong to England. He felt England was a part of Europe and that the land across the Atlantic Ocean should have no hold over those in America.

The Patriots had already been fighting the British for nearly a year before the document now known as the Declaration of Independence was drafted. The Continental Congress agreed a formal piece of writing was needed to declare the independence of the colonies to British rulers. Thomas Jefferson was chosen to pen the words that would declare the colonies' freedom. July 4, 1776 is the date that the Continental Congress approved Jefferson's document, and thus, the date is the one celebrated each year as the country's Independence Day.

George Washington became the military leader of the Patriots. Believing the Americans could win, the French would eventually join the side of the Patriots and help to win the cause by providing much needed supplies. The war would continue until 1781. The Battle at Yorktown was the victory that gained the final surrender of British troops and gained the colonists their freedom. The original thirteen colonies were now thirteen independent states. The road to a united country would be rocky, but the independent states would eventually form one united country.

Text Questions

1. The first paragraph states the colonists had "valid" reasons for wanting their freedom. Which statement below would be an example of a "valid" reason?
   a. The colonists did not like being in North America.
   b. The colonists did not like being ruled by a country that was not even on the same continent.
   c. The colonists did not want England to have other colonies.
   d. The colonists wanted to be under French rule.

2. How did the French help the colonists win their independence?
   a. by sending threatening letters to the British forces
   b. by giving passage to colonists back to Europe
   c. by giving the Patriots much needed supplies
   d. by providing guards to help protect George Washington

3. Once the colonies won their independence, what happened next?
   a. The colonies became the United States of America.
   b. The colonies turned themselves over to French rule.
   c. The colonies fought amongst themselves and started a Civil War.
   d. The colonies became thirteen independent states.

4. To the original colonists, why was the Declaration of Independence an important document?
   a. The document was written by the famous politician Thomas Jefferson.
   b. The document was the first written work agreed upon by the entire Continental Congress.
   c. The document declared the colonies' wish to be independent from British rule and the reasons for this desire to be free.
   d. The document was used to persuade the French to help the colonists win the war.

5. Which paragraph in the text best explains the reasons the colonists wanted to be free from British rule?
   a. first paragraph
   b. second paragraph
   c. third paragraph
   d. none of the paragraphs

Name_____

The Louisiana Purchase

The Louisiana Purchase occurred in 1803 and was mainly the decision of President Thomas Jefferson. The purchase of what was then known as the Louisiana territory from France more than doubled the land area of the new country. The purchase added 800,000 square miles to America. The entire cost of the Louisiana territory was fifteen million dollars. The purchase was especially important because the new land left control of the Mississippi River in the hands of the United States rather than France. Once the purchase was complete, however, there was much land to be explored. Jefferson hired Meriwether Lewis and William Clark to explore and document this vast new land.

In May of 1804, Lewis and Clark began their now famous exploration from St. Louis. The area west of the Mississippi was basically unknown, and Jefferson hoped the men would be able to return with information including maps of the territory. Forty-five people were a part of this exciting and dangerous expedition.

To help the explorers communicate with the many natives they would encounter, a Shoshone Indian, Sacagawea, was also part of the group. Sacagawea was only seventeen when the explorers began their trip. She traveled with her husband and infant son, and the journals from the trip tell of the times her skill as an interpreter and guide helped save the explorers as they trekked through the unchartered lands.

The entire journey lasted over two years. Many people were surprised by their returning, believing the explorers had most likely perished. Yet Lewis and Clark did return and gave the president many journals filled with details about the new land. They told of plants and animals that most had never seen. The expedition was approximately 8,000 miles round-trip and became a journey that will forever be remembered as the Lewis and Clark expedition.

Text Questions

1. What was the most likely reason Jefferson wanted to purchase the Louisiana territory from France?

    a. to help the French gain funds for future wars
    b. to gain control of the Mississippi River
    c. to be able to send Lewis and Clark on an expedition
    d. to stay on friendly terms with the French

2. Which paragraph from the text helps you to explain your answer for question one?

    a. first paragraph
    b. second paragraph
    c. third paragraph
    d. fourth paragraph

3. What was the main purpose of the Lewis and Clark expedition?

    a. to take notes about the new land and to create maps of the territory
    b. to give Sacagawea a chance to act as guide
    c. to help solidify Thomas Jefferson's place in history
    d. to reach the Pacific Ocean

4. What was the author's purpose in writing this text?

    a. to explain
    b. to persuade
    c. to entertain
    d. to inform

5. If Lewis and Clark had not safely returned, what might have most likely happened next?

    a. No one would have ever ventured back into the territory.
    b. Another expedition would have been sent into the territory.
    c. Lewis and Clark would have lived the rest of their lives with a tribe of Indians.
    d. Sacagawea would have led the next expedition into the Louisiana Purchase.

Name_____

The Wild West

From the mid 1800s to the early 1900s, the land west of the Mississippi River became known as the American Wild West. Much about the Wild West has been romanticized over the years by authors and the entertainment industry. Real life in the West was often very different than these glamorous portrayals. Some well-known figures definitely evolved from this time in America's history. People such as lawmen Wild Bill Hickok and Wyatt Earp or outlaws such as Jesse and Frank James are often written about in American history books. The exploits—some real and some fictitious—of these men and others like them have helped the term "Wild West" to live on.

Another important part of the West was the cowboys and cattle drives. The completion of the railroads helped turn cattle drives into a profitable venture for those living west of the Mississippi. Cattle could be driven to cattle towns located at railroad depots and then shipped by train in stock cars where they could be sold for larger sums of money in urban areas. This profitable business lead to the establishment of railroad towns such as Dodge City and Abilene. Many of the people arriving in these towns spent their money gambling and at local saloons, making the towns unsavory and unsafe for those who lived there; however, the money from the cattle drives was a double-edged sword because the money kept the economy of these towns booming.

One famous cowboy of the Wild West was Nat Love. Love was a former slave from Tennessee. He became a star in the rodeo and was well-known even in his lifetime.

Many former slaves moved away from the South and to the West hoping to find a better way of life. Regardless of anyone's reasons for moving to the West, this unique time in America's history is filled with stories that are worth remembering.

Text Questions

1. What does the word *romanticized* mean as it is used in the first paragraph?

   a. glamorized

   b. belittled

   c. loved

   d. minimized

2. Which paragraph explains how the completion of the railroads helped the growth of the West?

   a. first paragraph

   b. second paragraph

   c. third paragraph

   d. none of the paragraphs

3. Which statement in the fourth paragraph best explains why former slaves might have moved to the West?

   _____

   _____

   _____

4. The second paragraph states that money from the cattle drives was often a "double-edged sword." What does this expression mean?

   a. Spending the money caused people extreme pain.

   b. Spending the money led to both good and bad results.

   c. The money was only spent on buying weapons.

   d. Cowboys stopped using guns and spent money only on swords.

5. What type of figurative language is the phrase "a double-edged sword"?

   a. metaphor

   b. alliteration

   c. personification

   d. idiom

44

Name_____

Early Inventions

After the Civil War and up to the 1900s, industry began to boom in American cities. New industry brought people to the urban areas, and populations boomed. As transportation expanded, so did the cities, and for the first time in American history, people were moving into the suburbs. This economical growth led to many inventions still seen and used today.

During this time period, skyscrapers were new to America's skyline. The name derived from the idea that the buildings were so tall they "scraped the sky." Development of the steel industry helped make these buildings possible. Of course, taller buildings needed another invention: elevators. People needed a way to reach the highest floors of these new, colossal structures. Elevators had been used previously for moving freight. However, earlier elevators were often unsafe, and people did not ride them because they would crash without warning. Elisha Otis created a safety device that would prevent an elevator from crashing even if the cable on the elevator broke. This invention helped move elevators for people into skyscrapers, making the tall buildings practical for everyone.

Electricity was another important invention during this time. Thomas Edison created the first incandescent light bulb in 1879. This first invention led to the creation of the materials needed to generate the power to run electrical lighting. Electrical power led to other inventions, such as trolley cars powered by electricity. The electrical motors in the trolley cars were powered by an overhead wire located above the tracks. People loved the smooth ride of the trolleys, and such economical transportation helped people move outside the busy cities and into the suburbs.

Text Questions

1. What does the term "urban areas" mean as it is used in the first paragraph?
   a. places in the country or rural areas
   b. places just outside the city
   c. places out West
   d. places in the city

2. The first paragraph explains that the population boomed because of increased industry. What does the word *boomed* mean as it is used in this sentence?
   a. increased
   b. decreased
   c. remained stagnant
   d. moved to other areas

3. Write three or four complete sentences comparing how electricity was important in America's early history and why electricity is still important today.

   _____

   _____

   _____

   _____

4. What was the author's purpose in writing this text?
   a. to explain the importance of transportation in America's early history
   b. to remember the importance of Thomas Edison
   c. to entertain the reader with stories of the past
   d. to give information about inventions that were an important part of America's history

5. Which answer best explains how skyscrapers became feasible inventions?
   a. the growth of the steel industry and the invention of trolleys
   b. the growth of the steel industry and the invention of passenger elevators
   c. the invention of passenger elevators and electricity
   d. the invention of electrical power and passenger elevators

Name_____

Women's Suffrage

In the early part of the 1900s, an era of reform began to sweep across America. One important part of this movement was granting suffrage to women. The passage of the fifteenth amendment gave all men the right to vote, as African-American men were given the same privilege as white males. However, women of any race still lacked the same privilege to vote that all males in America had already achieved.

The suffrage movement led by such women as Susan B. Anthony and Elizabeth Cady Stanton was the start of equal rights for women. These early suffragettes helped pave the road to give women the right to vote. Many people were against giving women this privilege—including some women! People during this time often believed women could not handle the responsibility of voting and should leave such decisions to the men. This attitude, however, did not stop the determined women of the suffrage movement.

Gatherings known as suffragette parades were one method used to gain attention for the cause. At first, the parades were greeted with much opposition, but eventually the determined citizens won support for their cause. The passage of the nineteenth amendment finally gave adult women of all races the much deserved right to vote.

Text Questions

1. Why is suffrage for women important?
   a. Women feel important.
   b. The opinion of women can be heard equally with that of men.
   c. People love any reason to have a parade.
   d. People of all ages deserve the right to vote.

2. What does the phrase "pave the road" mean as it is used in the second paragraph?
   a. end
   b. continue
   c. start
   d. finalize

3. Why would the suffragette parades have been met with opposition?
   a. Everyone wanted women to have the right to vote.
   b. Children wanted their mothers at home.
   c. The parades held up traffic in major cities.
   d. Not everyone wanted women to have the right to vote.

4. What was important about the nineteenth amendment?
   a. Women were given the right to vote.
   b. Former slaves were given the right to vote.
   c. Anyone over the age of sixteen was given the right to vote.
   d. Women were denied the right to vote.

5. Which title would be a good alternative for this text?
   a. "Everyone is Equal"
   b. "Women Earn the Right to Vote"
   c. "Suffrage Doesn't Mean Suffer"
   d. "Fight for the Right"

Name_____

The Roaring Twenties

The period after World War I is often referred to as the Roaring Twenties. During this time in American history, much of the younger generation simply wanted to enjoy life after surviving all the horror of the Great War. Much literature, art, and music was produced during this time of cultural change. Jazz music became a favorite among those looking for something different, and the Charleston became all the rage as people danced away their blues.

Many American citizens were able to enjoy an easier lifestyle, which helped create the time known as the Roaring Twenties. Inventions for completing housework made the tasks, which had typically been handled by women, much easier. This freed up time for women, giving them time to enjoy music, poetry, and leisure time. Technology also improved in creating movies. People began going to see films that now had

sound and not just pictures. Through this improved technology, people were able to see what was going on in other parts of the world, and they were able to feel connected to other people living in different areas of the United States as they listened to the same radio programs and watched the same movies.

Sports also saw an upswing in popularity during this time in American history. Crowds began flocking to sporting events, hoping to catch even a glimpse of their favorite players. Baseball legend Babe Ruth and boxer Jack Dempsey became popular during this time as fans followed their every move. People enjoyed attending sporting events and the feeling that the good times of the 1920s would never end. Sadly, the time of economic boom and good times would soon dissolve into one of the worst financial and social disasters of America's history: the Great Depression.

Text Questions

1. Why did people want to have a good time during the 1920s?
   a. Everyone loved to dance and sing.
   b. Everyone was a huge fan of jazz.
   c. Everyone wanted to forget the horror of World War I.
   d. Everyone wanted to spend money in America to help the economy.

2. Which part of the text explains why women were able to enjoy more leisure time during the 1920s?
   a. first paragraph
   b. second paragraph
   c. third paragraph
   d. the title

3. What evidence from the text helps you to explain your answer for question two?

   _____

   _____

   _____

4. What does the word *upswing* mean as it is used in the third paragraph?
   a. a decrease
   b. an increase
   c. a steady drop
   d. to remain the same

5. What would be a primary source a person could use to find out more about Babe Ruth?
   a. an encyclopedia entry
   b. a baseball almanac
   c. a blog about baseball
   d. an autobiography about Babe Ruth

Name_____

The Great Depression

The Great Depression began in 1929, in part, as a result of the crash of the stock market. As stock prices dropped, people lost the money they had invested. Others made a run on the banks to try to take out their money until the banks were forced to close due to lack of funds. Unemployment in America soared, and people found themselves with no way to support their families. Many lost their jobs and their homes.

President Hoover was in office during the beginning of the Depression. Hoover attempted to help the failing economy, but his efforts were not enough. As people were forced to live in makeshift homes, they began calling these places Hoovervilles. Anxious for a new leader and hopes for a better future, Americans voted in Franklin D. Roosevelt, or FDR, as the new president.

Roosevelt was what the American people needed. He communicated to Americans through radio talks known as "fireside chats," and he used these weekly conversations to build confidence in his ideas for America. The president offered his idea of a New Deal for the people. The New Deal was designed to bring relief, recovery, and reform to the struggling country. Roosevelt's programs helped the nation's economy and helped citizens find work. However, the start of World War II would be the eventual turning point in the economy as materials and items were needed as the country went back into war.

Text Questions

1. Which adjective best describes the economy during the Great Depression?
   a. strong
   b. struggling
   c. steady
   d. corrupt

2. What can the reader infer about Roosevelt's ability as a leader?
   a. He elicited confidence in the American people.
   b. He was often unsure of his next move.
   c. He relied heavily on his advisors.
   d. He was not as charismatic as President Hoover.

3. Which event most likely contributed to America's economic growth?
   a. the crash of the stock market
   b. the election of President Hoover
   c. the constructing of Hoovervilles
   d. the start of World War II

4. Which paragraph from the text helps you to explain your answer for question three?
   a. first paragraph
   b. second paragraph
   c. third paragraph
   d. none of the paragraphs

5. Why did people begin calling their makeshift homes Hoovervilles?
   a. They wanted to honor President Hoover.
   b. They hoped President Hoover would help them if they named their makeshift housing after him.
   c. They blamed President Hoover for their lack of jobs and homes.
   d. They believed only President Hoover could help them.

Name_____

World War II

America joined the Allied Powers of Europe to fight against the countries of Germany, Italy, and Japan in World War II. Despite the war already raging in Europe, America attempted to stay neutral. However, on December 7, 1941, that position was no longer possible. Pearl Harbor, Hawaii—which housed a United States naval base—was attacked by the Empire of Japan. America declared war against Japan and was brought into World War II.

During the war, Germany was controlled by the Nazi dictator Adolf Hitler. Italy was also ruled by a dictator, Benito Mussolini. Both leaders held order by using violent and brutal means. Hitler also hoped for a holocaust, or complete extermination, of the Jewish people. Despite their atrocities, many Americans wanted to stay isolated from European problems. President Roosevelt insisted, even before the bombing by Japan, that America could not remain isolated from the events in Europe. After a meeting with Winston Churchill, the British Prime Minister, Roosevelt brought back the idea to the American people that we were fighting for "Four Freedoms," which included freedom of speech and religion, and freedom from fear and want.

For America, World War II was fought on two fronts, both the Pacific and the Atlantic. Ironically, supplying materials for the war effort had one positive effect for the country. The nation was lifted out of the economic depression as jobs became readily available. Women filled in the gaps of workers left by men fighting on both fronts.

Victory in Europe happened before the Pacific front was won. President Truman was in office at the end of World War II and was faced with making the decision to use new atomic weapons on the Empire of Japan. With the support of Great Britain, America dropped two atomic bombs. The first was on the city of Hiroshima; the second bomb was dropped on Nagasaki. Japan surrendered on August 15, 1945, ending World War II for America.

Text Questions

1. Why did Americans want to remain isolated?

   a. to stay out of the war
   b. to keep all spending money inside the country
   c. to stop the growth of factories
   d. to support tourism in America

2. Why did Roosevelt use the idea of fighting for freedoms to convince Americans they could no longer remain isolated?

   a. He wanted to convince America that those in Asia needed to be free.
   b. He wanted to remind Americans how they fought against slavery.
   c. He wanted to convince the American people that freedom was worth fighting for.
   d. He knew that freedom was a gift from Great Britain that America could easily lose.

3. Which event forced America to join World War II?

   a. bombing raids on Great Britain
   b. the two atomic bombs dropped on Japan
   c. the Japanese attack on Pearl Harbor
   d. the continuation of the Great Depression

4. List three things in sequential order that happen in the passage.

   a. _____

   b. _____

   c. _____

5. Based on the text, which statement is most likely true?

   a. Dropping the atomic bombs led to the Japanese surrender.
   b. Roosevelt's meeting with Churchill halted all threat of war.
   c. If Truman had been president at the start of the war, the United States would not have gone to war.
   d. Hitler ended the war after America dropped the atomic bombs.

Name_____

The Iron Curtain

At the end of World War II, many Americans believed the Soviet Union was America's ally. The Soviets had fought on the side of Germany at the beginning of the war but had later left the Axis forces and joined the Allies in fighting against Germany, Italy, and Japan. But by 1946, the Americans realized a friendship between the Soviet Union and the United States of America was not to be the case. Then Soviet dictator Joseph Stalin began a deliberate campaign to spread Communism to other nations in Europe and Asia. In a country ruled by a communist government, the citizens do not have the same freedoms as in a democracy. This act of aggression—the refusal to leave the countries occupied after the war by the Soviet Union—began a conflict with the United States known as the Cold War.

After World War II, Soviet troops refused to leave countries they had liberated, despite America's insistence that the countries be allowed to hold free elections. Winston Churchill, Britain's prime minister, said an "Iron Curtain" had come down on Europe, and behind this curtain people's basic freedoms were disappearing. One clear example of the Iron Curtain was the Berlin Wall—a wall that separated West and East Berlin in Germany. Those on the western side were free, while those in East Berlin were under Soviet control.

President Truman believed the United States should support those people who wanted to be free. This policy and belief would later lead the United States into wars such as the Korean War and Vietnam in an effort to stop the spread of communism.

Text Questions

1. Which adjective best describes America's relationship with the Soviet Union after the start of the Cold War?
   a. friendly
   b. open
   c. affable
   d. hostile

2. Why did the Soviet Union refuse to leave any of the countries occupied by them at the end of World War II?
   a. They wanted to spread communism to other European countries.
   b. They wanted to continue Germany's mission of dominance.
   c. They wanted to go to war with the United States and Great Britain.
   d. They wanted to become a democratic nation.

3. Which statement is <u>not</u> a fact about the story?
   a. After World War II, the Soviet Union attempted to spread communism.
   b. The United States and the Soviet Union engaged in a conflict known as the Cold War.
   c. The Cold War is the most frightening time in America's history.
   d. After World War II, the Berlin Wall separated East Berlin from West Berlin.

4. At the end of World War II, why could the United States no longer remain allies with the Soviet Union?
   a. The Soviet Union wanted to take over the United States.
   b. The Soviet Union's refusal to withdraw from European countries it had occupied near the end of World War II was seen as an act of aggression by the United States.
   c. The Soviet Union's dictator was not friends with the president of the United States.
   d. The Soviet Union was unstable and could not be counted on economically for any help the United States might need.

5. Which part of the text helps you to explain your answer for question four?
   a. first paragraph
   b. second paragraph
   c. third paragraph
   d. the title

Name_____

Civil Rights

One hundred years after the Civil War, African-Americans were still being treated unfairly. In many areas of the nation, but especially in the South, African-Americans continued to be treated as inferior. Everything from water fountains to schools continued to be segregated. This segregation continued to fuel people's prejudices and discrimination towards an entire group of people. Change was needed in the 1960s, and change would require both patience and determination by many different citizens.

One person who stands out as brave enough to fight for civil rights was Rosa Parks. Rosa Parks was an African-American woman living in Montgomery, Alabama. As a passenger on a city bus, Parks refused to give up her seat to a white person. Parks was removed from the bus and arrested for her behavior. An organized protest led to a boycott of the bus system. The Supreme Court eventually ruled that the segregated bus system was, in fact, unconstitutional.

Another famous activist for civil rights was Dr. Martin Luther King, Jr. Dr. King believed in peaceful demonstrations and boycotts to help convince people to change their attitudes and prejudices. His work led to great changes in how African-Americans were treated in America. Sadly, his work eventually led to his death. Dr. King was assassinated in 1968. His name lives on as the country celebrates his birthday each January.

Text Questions

1. Why does the first sentence mention the Civil War?
   a. Many African-Americans were slaves before the Civil War.
   b. The Civil War was the start of the Civil Rights Movement.
   c. Martin Luther King, Jr. was born during the Civil War.
   d. The first organized protests and boycotts for civil rights were held at the start of the Civil War.

2. What does the word *segregated* mean as it is used in the first paragraph?
   a. equal
   b. same
   c. different
   d. separate

3. What are civil rights?
   a. The rights that gave suffrage to all females.
   b. The right to live in any country.
   c. The fundamental freedoms and privileges given to a citizen.
   d. The right to have freedom of speech and freedom of religion.

4. Why are Rosa Parks and Martin Luther King, Jr. both considered important leaders of the Civil Rights Movement?
   a. Both stood up for the rights of African-Americans being treated unfairly and both boycotted unfair treatment.
   b. Both lived in Alabama and were neighbors.
   c. Both organized boycotts of products manufactured in the South.
   d. Both resorted to violent protests.

5. What was the significance of Rosa Parks' decision to stay seated on the bus?
   a. Her refusal to move suggested the law was unfair.
   b. Her refusal to move showed how stubborn the protestors would be.
   c. Her refusal to move caught the attention of the local press.
   d. Her refusal to move sparked riots around the country.

Name_____

The Race into Space

As the Cold War continued between the United States and the Soviet Union, so did the race for technology. Information gleaned from scientists during World War II helped pave the way for an era fueled by the advances in science. The United States, led by the commitment of President John F. Kennedy, worked tirelessly to beat out the Soviets in what would be called the Space Race.

President Kennedy announced to the country in 1963 that before the decade was over, America would have sent a man safely to the moon and back. At this point, the Soviets seemed to be leading the race into space. In fact, as early as 1961, a Russian cosmonaut had already been sent into orbit around Earth. The United States would eventually send John Glenn into orbit in 1962. NASA—the National Aeronautics and Space Administration—knew they would have to step up their game if they were to beat the Soviets.

The culmination of NASA's efforts and Kennedy's dream came to fruition on July 21, 1969, when the *Apollo* astronauts took their first steps on the moon. Neil Armstrong became the first person to step onto the moon's surface. A flag from the United States was left on the surface of the moon to commemorate the events. The astronauts also left a plaque that stated that men from Earth came in peace for all mankind.

Text Questions

1. What was the author's purpose in writing this text?
    a. to persuade people to continue space research
    b. to inform people about the original space program
    c. to explain the origin of NASA
    d. to entertain anyone who likes to read science fiction

2. Which statement is <u>not</u> a fact based on the story?
    a. As early as 1961, a Russian cosmonaut had already been sent into orbit around Earth.
    b. Russian scientists were much smarter than American scientists, who were struggling to keep up with the Soviet's technology.
    c. The United States sent John Glenn into orbit in 1962.
    d. Neil Armstrong became the first person to step onto the moon's surface.

3. What is a problem and a solution found in this text?
    a. America wanted to beat the Soviets in the space race and were able to put the first man on the moon.
    b. The Soviets wanted to beat the Americans in the space race and had a Russian cosmonaut join the American team of astronauts.
    c. Kennedy made a promise to place a man on the moon by the end of the decade, and scientists worked tirelessly to put Kennedy into space.
    d. The Apollo mission flew into space, and NASA was able to retrieve data about previous Soviet missions using satellites in space.

4. The Space Race was a continuation of what war?
    a. World War II
    b. the Korean War
    c. the Cold War
    d. the Vietnam War

5. What does the phrase "step up their game" mean as it is used in the second paragraph?
    a. work harder
    b. work slower
    c. work longer
    d. work cooperatively

Name_____

The American-Indian Movement

In the late 1800s, native tribes in America continued to lose their land to frontier settlers. The United States government often made and broke treaties protecting lands of American-Indians. Using the force of the United States Army, American-Indians were then forced to reside on reservations.

By the 1970s, half of the one million American-Indians lived on reservations. Living conditions, in most cases, were not good. Leaders of the American Indian Movement (AIM) began to get much needed national attention from Washington, D.C. Tribes began to sue for the rights promised to them under treaties originally signed as early as the 1800s but had never been granted.

The courts agreed with the mistreatment of the early American-Indians. For example, in South Dakota, the Sioux were given $100 million for land that had been taken from them in a disreputable treaty deal. Other tribes were also able to make changes. Some stopped large corporations from encroaching on their land and stripping the area of all its natural resources. To honor those early Americans, the American-Indian Day celebration happens each October. This holiday is the second Monday of October each year. The day is set aside to commemorate or remember the crimes committed against the early American-Indians and to learn about and respect the early American-Indian cultures.

Text Questions

1. Why did early native tribes lose land to frontier settlers?
   a. Early settlers wanted the land for themselves.
   b. Early settlers wanted to share the land with the natives.
   c. The natives attacked the settlers and lost the battles, leaving the land unoccupied.
   d. The settlers did not have enough land to grow the needed crops for their families to survive.

2. What is a reservation?
   a. Land set aside by the American-Indians for individual tribes.
   b. Land set aside by the government for the various American-Indian tribes.
   c. Land set aside and paid for by tax dollars.
   d. Land set aside for each generation.

3. Which part of the text best explains the purpose of the American Indian Movement?
   a. the title
   b. first paragraph
   c. second paragraph
   d. third paragraph

4. What evidence from the text helps you to explain your answer for question three?

   _____

   _____

   _____

5. What holiday is celebrated the second Monday of each October?
   a. Martin Luther King Jr.'s birthday
   b. Frontier Celebration Day
   c. American-Indian Day
   d. The birthday of Sitting Bull

53

Name_____

Vietnam

After World War II, America did what it could to stop the spread of communism across the globe. The Cold War continued as America tried to stop the Soviet Union's continuous effort to take over noncommunist countries. The country of Vietnam became part of the struggle between the two powerful nations. The Vietnam War was, in part, a result of America's fear of Soviet occupation and the spread of communism.

In 1964, President Johnson asked Congress to agree to take whatever measures were necessary to stop attacks against the United States' forces. The request came about as a result of reports that North Vietnamese

gunboats had fired at destroyers owned by the United States. President Johnson was given the green light to do what was necessary to stop military aggression by North Vietnamese troops. By 1968, there were more than 500,000 American soldiers in Vietnam.

The country had mixed emotions about America's involvement with Vietnam. Some felt the U.S. had to protect South Vietnam. They believed if one country fell to communism, then others would quickly follow. Others wanted Americans removed from Vietnam as quickly as possible. The Vietnam War finally ended in 1973 with Vietnam still divided.

Text Questions

1. What was the main political goal at the end of World War II?
   a. to spread freedom throughout the world
   b. to stop the spread of communism
   c. to take over the Soviet Union
   d. to take over Vietnam

2. Which sentence best explains why President Johnson wanted to be allowed to use military force, if needed, in Vietnam?
   a. He wanted to start a war with Vietnam.
   b. He wanted to stop attacks against United States' forces.
   c. He wanted to set up military bases in Cambodia.
   d. He wanted to further his own political agenda.

3. What was a direct result of Congress giving President Johnson permission to take whatever measures were necessary to stop attacks against U.S. forces?
   a. The number of soldiers sent to Vietnam increased.
   b. The number of military bases in the Pacific increased.
   c. More soldiers were sent from Canada to join American soldiers.
   d. President Johnson was forced to resign.

4. What does the phrase "mixed emotions" mean as it is used in the third paragraph?
   a. Everyone did not feel the same.
   b. Everyone agreed.
   c. Everyone wanted to go to war.
   d. Everyone wanted to withdraw troops from Vietnam.

5. What was the author's purpose in writing this text?
   a. to entertain
   b. to persuade
   c. to explain
   d. to deny

Name_____

Animal Rights

Do animals have rights? Many people believe they should and do have rights. Animal activists often gather in various organizations to protect animals from being used for things that they consider cruel or unusual. Their work often makes a huge difference in how animals are treated.

Why would people believe animals should have rights? Animal-rights activists believe that since animals can feel pain and distress and since some animals can even reason, then they should not be used for things such as experimental tests, human entertainment, or food. Other activists believe that animals should not be used for clothing. For example, these believers in animal rights are against anyone wearing fur coats or clothing made from leather. Many animal activists fight for the rights of animals in specific categories. For example, some might fight for animal rights in developing medicines, while others might raise awareness against animals being used for food.

One way activists help animals is by operating rescue groups for hurt animals or animals that are in danger. People often give large monetary donations to help these groups run shelters. Major organizations exist all over the world to help fight for animal rights. The popularity of these groups seems to have expanded in the last few decades, in part, because many organizations now have celebrity endorsements to help spread their message. Also, the expanded use of technology has helped spread their message to more and more people.

Text Questions

1. Which sentence best explains why some people believe animals have rights?
   a. Many people believe they should and do have rights.
   b. Animal activists often gather in various organizations to protect animals from being used for things that they consider cruel or unusual.
   c. Animal-rights activists believe that since animals can feel pain and distress and since some animals can even reason, then they should not be used for things such as experimental tests, human entertainment, or food.
   d. Other activists believe that animals should not be used for clothing.

2. Which sentence is an opinion about animal rights?
   a. All animals should be treated with love and care.
   b. Some animals show the ability to reason.
   c. Animal-rights activists often operate shelters for animals that are in danger.
   d. Some celebrities help endorse animal-rights organizations.

3. What are two ways mentioned in the text that animal-rights activists are able to make a difference?
   a. They operate shelters and carry out protests.
   b. They show videos on the internet about animal cruelty, and they offer free legal services.
   c. They run shelters for animals and seek celebrity endorsements for their cause.
   d. They have a strong belief in their cause, and they adopt all animals that are in danger.

4. Which reason is <u>not</u> given for why some people believe in animal rights?
   a. Animals are loving and kind to those who love them in return.
   b. Some animals have the ability to reason.
   c. Animals can feel pain.
   d. Animals are known to show signs of distress.

5. Why might technology be an important tool in helping activists with animal rights?
   a. Animals will often sit still for hours when television shows are being played.
   b. Music helps soothe animals who are in distress.
   c. Activists can spread their message to more people via technology.
   d. People watching videos about animal rights are less apt to send money to organizations wanting to protect animals.

Name_____

Bats

When people think of bats, too often their first thoughts are of vampire movies and creatures who want blood. Bats are so much more than how they are often portrayed in movies and television. These warm-blooded creatures are amazing animals with abilities that both fascinate and awe those who study them.

Most people are not aware that bats are, in fact, mammals. Bats are the only mammals that have the ability to fly. What makes them mammals? They are warm-blooded, their bodies have fur, and they nurse their young. What is unusual, of course, is their amazing ability to fly. Bats use their flying ability to search for food.

There are more than one thousand species of bats known to exist. Because of this, bats can vary greatly in size. The largest known bats can weigh more than three pounds while the smallest species, known as bumblebee bats, can be as small as .07 ounces. Despite their reputation as scary creatures, thanks in part to their connection to vampire stories, these mammals generally try to avoid humans. They are nocturnal creatures who do most of their hunting at night when they should be out of the way of most humans.

One misconception about bats is that these mammals are blind. This is not true. Most bats are only color blind. However, thanks to their excellent sense of smell and hearing, they can use echolocation to gather information about their surroundings. They can use this information to help find their prey and to help keep themselves safe.

Text Questions ••

1. Why are bats unusual mammals?
   a. They use echolocation.
   b. They have fur covering their bodies.
   c. They are warm-blooded.
   d. They have the ability to fly.

2. How does the author feel about bats?
   a. The author believes everyone should be afraid of bats.
   b. The author believes television and movies have accurately portrayed bats in the media.
   c. The author believes most people are unaware of how unique bats are.
   d. The author believes everyone should fight to save bats from extinction.

3. Which is a synonym for the word *misconception* as it is used in the fourth paragraph?
   a. misjudgment
   b. mistrust
   c. mistake
   d. misfortune

4. Which statement is <u>not</u> a fact about bats?
   a. They rise with the sun.
   b. They are warm-blooded.
   c. They have the ability to fly.
   d. They have fur on their bodies.

5. Which paragraph gives details about the physical size of bats?
   a. first paragraph
   b. second paragraph
   c. third paragraph
   d. fourth paragraph

Name_____

Monkeypox

Monkeypox is a disease found in animals that can, in some cases, affect humans. This particular disease was not identified until 1958. The signs of the disease included pus-filled pustules commonly known as pox. These skin pustules were first found on monkeys, and so the disease came to be known as monkeypox.

How can someone become infected with the disease? First, it is important to note that, unlike some other diseases, this particular disease is hard to spread from person to person. To become infected, a person must eat or be bitten by an infected animal.

People in the United States have had symptoms of what was thought to be monkeypox. In 2003, there was an outbreak of the disease, although fortunately no one died. The people who had the symptoms were

quarantined as were any animals thought to have been connected with the virus. This quarantine was initiated to stop the spread of the disease. How did these people contract this unusual sickness? The seventy-one people who were infected were believed to have caught the disease from prairie dogs. These animals had been purchased as pets. The prairie dogs were infected after being housed in a pet shop that had another animal that carried the disease. This animal was a rat imported from Africa to be sold later as a pet.

The best way to prevent being infected by this disease is to stay away from animals that might have had exposure to the disease. When purchasing pets, deal with reputable people. If infected, a person can survive the disease. Sadly, some cases of monkeypox have resulted in death.

Text Questions

1. Which title would be a good alternative for this text?
   a. "Monkeypox, Chickenpox, and Smallpox"
   b. "Diseases Carried by Animals"
   c. "Monkeypox: An Uncommon Killer"
   d. "Pox Rhymes with Fox"

2. Which paragraph best explains how someone can become infected with the monkeypox virus?
   a. first paragraph
   b. second paragraph
   c. third paragraph
   d. fourth paragraph

3. What evidence from the text helps you to explain your answer for question two?

   _____

   _____

   _____

4. What does the word *quarantined* mean as it is used in the third paragraph?
   a. to gather together
   b. to separate from others
   c. to listen carefully
   d. to watch for signs

5. Using information from the text, what is one way to avoid being infected with the disease?
   a. Do not purchase a monkey as a pet.
   b. Wash your hands thoroughly after touching any animal.
   c. Stay away from animals that might have had exposure to the disease.
   d. Only buy monkeys as pets that have first been kept in quarantine.

Name_____

Migration

Why do animals migrate or move? Animals that migrate do so to find a place that will offer better living conditions. Not all animals migrate, but those that do are attempting to help the survival of their species. There are a variety of reasons why animals leave. Some migrate to avoid weather changes. Some leave because of the food supply. Unlike humans who migrate because of relationships, job changes, or other social reasons, animals migrate to survive.

There are different types of migration, but one of the most interesting is the seasonal migration. In seasonal migrations, animals move twice a year. These movements usually occur due to changes in the seasons or in the weather. For example, some birds migrate away from colder regions to warmer weather and then come back to a place once the colder weather has passed.

How do animals know when it is time to migrate? Some animals do not leave an area until the environment changes and becomes a place that is not favorable for them to live. Other animals seem to have inborn systems that tell them when it is time to leave.

Animals that migrate use many different ways to successfully reach their destinations. Scientists believe animals' senses play a huge role in helping them find their way. For example, salmon that migrate are thought to recognize specific odors that help them. Others are thought to use even the sun, moon, and stars to help guide them on their journeys. Although the animals use different methods to migrate, one thing is the same: migration remains an important and vital journey for the survival of many of Earth's most amazing species.

Text Questions ···

1. Why do animals most likely migrate?
   a. to find more food
   b. to find shelter
   c. to find similar species
   d. to find better living conditions

2. Which paragraph best explains how animals know when to migrate?
   a. first paragraph
   b. second paragraph
   c. third paragraph
   d. fourth paragraph

3. How is animal migration different from the migration of some humans?
   a. Humans might migrate for social reasons rather than survival.
   b. Humans migrate based on a twelve-month calendar.
   c. Humans wait for certain species of animals to migrate before leaving a certain area.
   d. Humans do not migrate.

4. Which of the following statements is an opinion?
   a. Animal migration is a fascinating subject that scientists still need to learn about to fully understand.
   b. Some animals do not migrate until environmental changes occur.
   c. Not all animals migrate.
   d. Some animals have inborn systems that tell them when to migrate.

5. What inference can be made about migration?
   a. Seasonal migration is not the only type of migration.
   b. Humans could migrate using the same inborn systems as other animals.
   c. Migration is different for all animals.
   d. At some point in history, all animals migrated.

Name_____

Pythons

When people hear the word *python*, they immediately conjure up images of snakes from horror movies. The python, however, is much more than a snake to be used in fiction; the constrictor is, in fact, a fascinating reptile. Its size alone makes it an amazing creature. The infamous reptile can grow as long as thirty feet. The only other snake that equals the python is the South American green anaconda. These larger pythons can be naturally found in both Africa and Asia. Australia has a much smaller type of python that only grows to be about two feet long. Of course, this type is rarely the star of a horror movie!

Pythons generally eat small mammals and lizards. The larger snakes can, however, kill larger animals, such as pigs. These snakes do not kill their prey with venom.

Instead, they squeeze their prey to death. The constrictor wraps its long body around an animal and then tightens its body until the animal can no longer breathe and blood can no longer flow. To consume the animal, the python swallows its prey whole. Because the animal is consumed in one bite, digestion generally takes several days. Any animal coming after the python has just eaten is generally safe because the creature simply doesn't have room after consuming a large meal.

Pythons are reptiles that lay eggs to produce their young. The females keep the eggs warm by wrapping their bodies around them until the eggs hatch. The amount of eggs varies. However, some pythons can have as many as one hundred eggs!

Text Questions

1. Although the amount of eggs a python can lay varies, how many eggs can a python lay?

   a. one
   b. one hundred
   c. No one has ever gotten close enough to find out.
   d. twenty

2. Which paragraph from the text helps you to explain your answer for question one?

   a. first paragraph
   b. second paragraph
   c. third paragraph
   d. none of the paragraphs

3. What can you infer that the author believes about pythons?

   a. Pythons are unusual.
   b. Pythons are fascinating.
   c. Pythons are horrific.
   d. Pythons are adaptable.

4. What is the purpose of the second paragraph?

   a. to explain how pythons hibernate
   b. to explain how pythons use camouflage for protection
   c. to explain the environment where pythons live
   d. to explain how pythons kill their prey

5. Which of the following statements is an opinion?

   a. A python can grow as long as thirty feet.
   b. The only other snake that equals the python in length is the South American green anaconda.
   c. Pythons are reptiles.
   d. The constrictor is, in fact, a fascinating reptile.

Name_____

Bedbugs

"Sleep tight, and don't let the bedbugs bite," is a familiar phrase said over the years as people prepare for bed. Of course, nothing sounds worse than talking about bugs right before you settle down to sleep, but these creepy critters actually exist! A bedbug is actually a small insect that feeds on the blood of its host.

Bedbugs feed from people but will also feed from other warm-blooded animals. This reddish-brown bug is only about one-fourth of an inch in length. The tiny bug has a sharp beak that it uses to penetrate the skin of the person or animal where it plans to feed. These creatures tend to hide during daylight hours and are most active at night when their victims sleep.

The bedbug is good at hiding. They hide in mattresses, between floorboards, and in carpets—just to name a few of their hiding places. The female will lay her eggs in these places. The female bedbug can lay more than one hundred eggs during her lifetime. The eggs will hatch in as little as two weeks. Bedbugs are considered full-grown after about two months and live for only about six months. The host cannot rely on the bedbugs dying and leaving him or her alone. Areas that are infected must be thoroughly cleaned and in many cases these insects can only be successfully contained by the use of insecticides. Bedbugs irritate their victims by causing bites all over their bodies. Some scientists speculate these bugs might also carry serious diseases. So, the next time someone says, "Don't let the bedbugs bite," you will want to really hope they do not bite you!

Text Questions

1. What is the main purpose of the second paragraph?
   a. to explain the eating habits of a bedbug
   b. to give a physical description of a bedbug
   c. to help people understand and not be afraid of bedbugs
   d. to explain how to exterminate bedbugs

2. Using information from the text, what does the word *speculate* mean as it is used in the third paragraph?
   a. to guess
   b. to remember
   c. to understand
   d. to question

3. From the text, what can you infer about bedbugs?
   a. Most people have them in their homes.
   b. Most bedbugs attack only children.
   c. Most bedbugs are not seen by humans.
   d. Most bedbugs die immediately after biting a host.

4. Which statement is <u>not</u> a fact about bedbugs?
   a. Bedbugs will die without human contact.
   b. The eggs of the bedbug hatch in as little as two weeks.
   c. Bedbugs use a sharp beak to penetrate the skin of its victim.
   d. The female bedbug can lay about one hundred eggs during her lifetime.

5. After reading the passage, what can you infer about bedbugs?
   a. Bedbugs are worse than other pests.
   b. Bedbugs often go undetected.
   c. Bedbugs will attack any type of animal.
   d. Bedbugs are impossible to get rid of once they have inhabited an area.

Name_____

Sleeping Sickness

Sleeping sickness is a disease caused by a single-celled parasite that attacks other animals. This deadly parasite known as a trypanosome attacks humans and other vertebrates, or animals with backbones. The sickness attacks the nervous system of the affected animal. Currently, this unusual disease is only in Africa. The disease is spread by the African tsetse fly. This insect lives on the lake shores and riverbanks in Africa. The fly becomes infected by feeding on the blood of an already infected victim. The trypanosome is in the infected blood consumed by the fly. Once the fly is infected, it can carry the disease to other creatures.

What happens to a victim of sleeping sickness? Fever, headache, and chills are all symptoms of the disease. The infected victim will also have swelling of the lymph nodes, a skin rash, and severe weakness. The attack on the victim's central nervous system can eventually lead to extensive sleeping, and in some cases, a coma and even death.

How can doctors detect this disease? Blood work from an infected victim will show the existence of trypanosomes in the blood. Since the trypanosomes affect the nervous system of their victims, early detection and treatment is critical. Early treatments show a strong success rate with regard to recovery. Unfortunately, if the disease is caught later, the treatments are not as effective, and the trypanosomes often become resistant to the drug used to treat the disease.

Text Questions

1. Where could a person find out more information about sleeping sickness?
   a. a tourist's guidebook to Africa
   b. an atlas with extensive maps of Africa
   c. a book about diseases indigenous to Africa
   d. a website about sleeping disorders

2. What are three symptoms of sleeping sickness?
   a. skin rash, nausea, fever
   b. headache, fever, swelling of the esophagus
   c. nausea, skin rash, severe weakness
   d. headache, chills, skin rash

3. Using information from the text, what can one infer about sleeping sickness?
   a. There is the possibility of sleeping sickness becoming a pandemic.
   b. The Centers for Disease Control and Prevention has no known cure for sleeping sickness.
   c. Sleeping sickness is found only in Africa because the insect that carries the disease only lives on this continent.
   d. Better tests are needed to correctly diagnose sleeping sickness.

4. Think of another disease that is carried by animals, and write one or two complete sentences comparing and/or contrasting the disease to sleeping sickness.

   _____

   _____

   _____

5. Which statement is accurate about the tsetse fly?
   a. The fly spreads the disease by carrying germs through the air as it flies.
   b. The fly becomes infected by feeding on the blood of animals that are already infected.
   c. The fly carries the disease from one continent to another.
   d. The fly's bite causes the sleeping sickness to spread only to humans.

Name_____

Elephants

The elephant is a mammal with many unique traits. This colossal beast is the largest animal to live on land. The elephant also has the largest ears of any other animal. Another fascinating feature about the elephant is its long nose. This long nose actually forms into a long trunk that can be used as a helpful appendage. Just imagine having an extra hand on the middle of your face! Only the elephant has bragging rights to such an extraordinary trunk.

There are basically two main types of elephants living in the world today. The African and Asian elephants live on different continents, just as their names imply. The African elephants are actually larger than the ones that live in Asia. Also, the ears of the Asian elephant are smaller than the African elephant's ears.

Elephants have intricate families. The matriarch is the head of the elephant family. She uses her excellent memory to lead the family over specific migration routes. She knows the best way to travel for survival and memorizes the important locations of certain food and water sources. Adult males rarely live with the females. Generally, there are about ten elephants living together at a time. These small family groups usually have several adult females and their young. The family is then led by the oldest female, who becomes the matriarch. Males leave the group once they become adults; however, they may visit the family group on occasion. These small families often join with other families and some independent males to create a population of these amazing animals.

Text Questions

1. If a diagram were drawn comparing the African elephant and the Asian elephant, which piece of information could be placed on the chart?

    a. information showing the female elephant as the matriarch
    b. information showing the African elephant as a larger type than the Asian elephant
    c. information explaining the population of elephants
    d. information explaining the uniqueness of the elephant's trunk

2. What is the purpose of the second paragraph?

    a. to give more information about the Asian elephant
    b. to give more information about the African elephant
    c. to assure you are not afraid of elephants
    d. to explain the differences between African and Asian elephants

3. What can one infer about the family relationships of elephants?

    a. There is a hierarchy among elephants in each family.
    b. Males are the dominant members of each family.
    c. When young elephants are born, they must be ready to live on their own.
    d. The structural unit of the elephant's family changes every five years.

4. Which statement is a fact from the story?

    a. Elephants have begun to migrate to North and South America.
    b. Elephants have intricate families.
    c. Elephants are trained to use their noses to pick up things but do not mimic this behavior in the wild.
    d. Elephants are ruled by the patriarchs of each family group.

5. Elephants are native to which two continents?

    a. Africa and North America
    b. Asia and Africa
    c. Europe and Asia
    d. Africa and South America

Name_____

Sheep

A sheep was the first animal to be artificially cloned. A cloned animal is a genetically identical copy of another animal. The first cloned sheep was created from cells that were taken from an adult sheep. This scientific breakthrough occurred when the new sheep was cloned from another sheep. Scientists named the result of their experiment Dolly. Dolly lived for approximately seven years, but she had a progressive lung disease, and she eventually had to be euthanized.

Besides being the first cloned animal, sheep are also important animals to people because they can provide both food and clothing to human beings. People who watch flocks of sheep are known as shepherds. Shepherds help keep sheep safe from harm and help protect them against attacks by wild animals.

Today, many sheep are more domesticated than wild. There are more than eight hundred breeds and types of domestic sheep. These domestic sheep can provide people with wool, meat, and milk. Farmers raising sheep are able to use land that is not good for growing crops. Sheep are able to graze on land that would otherwise remain unused by the farmer.

Text Questions

1. What was the author's purpose in writing this text?
   a. to provide information about sheep
   b. to compare and contrast goats and sheep
   c. to encourage people to raise sheep
   d. The author had no purpose.

2. Which statement is a fact about sheep?
   a. Sheep were the first animals to be cloned.
   b. Sheep are the only animal that can provide both food and clothing.
   c. Sheep live for seven years.
   d. Sheep are not domesticated animals.

3. Where could one find a naturally cloned animal?
   a. with the birth of twins
   b. at any farm where sheep are raised
   c. with the birth of animals born in the same year
   d. There are no naturally cloned animals.

4. According to the text, what is one reason sheep are useful to farmers?
   a. They graze on land that cannot be used for crops.
   b. They are the only species that can be cloned to create larger flocks or herds.
   c. They provide wool for the farmer's clothing.
   d. They deter the growth of weeds on the property where they graze.

5. Which is an antonym for the word *domesticated* as it is used in the third paragraph?
   a. tame
   b. cultivated
   c. wild
   d. adapt

Name_____

Jellyfish

Jellyfish are one of the most unique creatures found in the oceans. Their soft bodies are made of a material that is soft and jellylike. This material actually supports the equally soft material that makes up their bodies. This substance is extremely important to the aquatic animals because it allows them to float through the water.

Like most other animals, jellyfish can range in size. Some are microscopic, while the main body of others can grow as large as seven feet. The extensions that hang from their bodies are called tentacles. These tentacles vary in number and length according to the type of jellyfish. Some jellyfish have tentacles that are over one hundred feet long! Another interesting feature about jellyfish is their color. They can be various colors including white, pink, blue, and pale orange.

Jellyfish produce eggs. These eggs go through stages like tadpoles turning into frogs. To protect themselves during their changes, they often attach themselves to hard surfaces underneath the ocean. Once they develop, they detach themselves to join the other jellyfish in the ocean.

Text Questions

1. List three characteristics of a jellyfish.

   a. _____

   b. _____

   c. _____

2. Which part of the text helps you to explain your answer for question one?
   a. the title
   b. first paragraph
   c. second paragraph
   d. paragraphs one and two

3. Which is an antonym for the word *microscopic* as it is used in the second paragraph?
   a. tiny
   b. miniscule
   c. minute
   d. colossal

4. What is the purpose of the third paragraph?
   a. to describe the different types of jellyfish
   b. to explain how jellyfish are reproduced
   c. to inform the reader how unusual jellyfish are
   d. to compare jellyfish to other aquatic animals

5. Which of the following statements is an opinion?
   a. Jellyfish are one of the most unique creatures found in the oceans.
   b. Jellyfish can range in size.
   c. Some jellyfish have tentacles that are over one hundred feet long!
   d. Jellyfish produce eggs.

Name_____

Ticks

Ticks are small animals that belong to the group of animals known as arachnids. Arachnids also include spiders and scorpions. Ticks are different from these other arachnids in that they are parasites. This means they must feed on the fluids of other animals, including humans.

When a tick attaches to a host, it often carries diseases. When they bite into the bodies of animals, the diseases they carry can be passed to the victims. In some cases, these diseases can be deadly. Some ticks even have poisonous bites. This poison has even been known to cause paralysis in humans.

Because ticks carry disease, it is important to remove one, if found, as quickly as possible. Removal is slightly tricky, and the person attempting to remove the parasite must be careful to take out the entire tick and not leave the creature's head inside the victim. Two well-known diseases that can be transferred from ticks to humans are Rocky Mountain spotted fever and Lyme disease. Both diseases are extremely dangerous to those infected.

Like many other animals, ticks lay eggs. The eggs are usually found in dead leaves or other debris. When they hatch, the ticks are born with six legs. These tiny creatures will attach themselves to any animal that passes within their reach. They will stay and gorge themselves on blood and eventually change into eight-legged creatures, going through one more stage until they become adults.

Text Questions

1. According to the text, which statement is false?
   a. Ticks are part of a group known as arachnids.
   b. Ticks are parasites that feed off other animals.
   c. Ticks lay eggs.
   d. Ticks will kill any animals that become their host.

2. Why is it important to remove a tick as soon as it is found?
   a. They carry diseases.
   b. They will multiply quickly.
   c. They will take all of the host's blood.
   d. They are harmless and actually do not have to be removed.

3. Ticks belong to the same group of animals as spiders and are known as what?
   a. arachnids
   b. beetles
   c. reptiles
   d. amphibians

4. What is the purpose of the third paragraph?
   a. to explain how little harm ticks can cause
   b. to explain the dangers that can be caused by ticks
   c. to describe the appearance of a tick
   d. to entertain anyone reading about ticks

5. What is one reason people might want to learn more about ticks?
   a. to help keep themselves safe from disease
   b. to help stop the growth of the tick population
   c. to better understand the group known as arachnids
   d. to help identify the small parasite

Name_____

Chinchillas

Chinchillas are small mammals that are native to the Andes Mountains. They have heavy fur coats that keep them warm in their native areas. In fact, they are best known for their soft, thick fur. Their fur-covered bodies measure anywhere from eleven to eighteen inches in length. Over the years, their fur has been made popular with people who make fur coats.

Because people hunted the chinchillas for their fur, by the 1940s, these small rodents were almost extinct. To save the animals, people began captive-breeding programs to supply the manufacturers with the needed animal hides. Also, laws were passed in some countries to protect the chinchillas that still lived in the wild. Even with these measures, chinchillas are extremely rare and hard to find in their natural habitats.

Today, some people keep these small rodents as pets. Despite the fact that they are classified as rodents, chinchillas are actually relatively clean and gentle. Choosing a chinchilla as a pet requires a lot of responsibility. Chinchillas must eat a special diet that consists of grains and vegetables. Pet owners can buy specially made pellets that contain the nutrients needed by the animal. If treated well, domesticated chinchillas can live close to twenty years.

Text Questions

1. Why were chinchillas nearly hunted to extinction?
    a. People wanted them as pets.
    b. People wanted their fur.
    c. People wanted them to eat.
    d. People wanted to get rid of the rodents.

2. Which part of the text helps you to explain your answer for question one?
    a. the title
    b. first paragraph
    c. second paragraph
    d. third paragraph

3. Which statement is not a fact about chinchillas?
    a. Chinchillas were hunted nearly to extinction by the 1940s.
    b. Chinchillas are native to the Andes Mountains.
    c. Chinchillas can be purchased as pets.
    d. Chinchillas help control the population of certain snakes found in the Andes Mountains.

4. Using the information from the text, what can you infer about hunting chinchillas today?
    a. They are protected in the wild.
    b. They are not protected in the wild.
    c. There are no chinchillas in the wild left to hunt.
    d. There are special weekends set up during the year when chinchillas may be hunted.

5. What was the author's purpose in writing this text?
    a. to inform
    b. to entertain
    c. to persuade
    d. to advertise

Name_____

Animal Experiments

In scientific studies, animals are sometimes used for experiments. Animals are used for experiments because, in many cases, they have such similar internal systems as humans. Advocates of animal testing believe performing experiments on animals can help scientists learn more about the human body. They believe such tests can help lead to medical advances for human beings, and they believe such practices are vital to science and the development of medicines and surgical techniques that can save human lives. However, some people believe such experiments are unnecessary and even cruel to the animals. Therefore, animal experiments are often quite controversial.

For medical research, studying animals can help scientists better understand the human body and how it works. Animals can also be used to test how safe a drug is for humans to use. Even psychologists use animal testing to help humans. They can observe animal behavior under certain conditions. They can also study how animals learn to better understand how the human brain works.

Of course, animal research is met with much controversy. Not everyone believes animal research should be conducted, even if the research helps people. Some, however, feel the benefits are too great to stop the testing on animals. Still, others believe medical research should be allowed, but testing for things such as cosmetics and perfume is something that should not be done. One thing that either party can seem to agree on is that any testing that is done should be conducted so that the pain and distress for the animals involved is at a minimum.

Text Questions

1. Which part of the text best explains why some people are against animal testing?
   a. the title
   b. first paragraph
   c. second paragraph
   d. third paragraph

2. Why are animal experiments met with controversy?
   a. People believe they are cruel and unnecessary.
   b. People believe they occur too frequently.
   c. People believe they are too expensive.
   d. People believe only certain types of animals should be used in the experiments.

3. Which type of experiments seem to be the most controversial?
   a. medical experiments
   b. psychological experiments
   c. experiments done for general research
   d. testing for cosmetics and perfumes

4. Compare and contrast information by listing one reason why animal experiments should occur and one reason why animal experiments should not occur. Use only information from the text.

   a. _____

   b. _____

5. Which is an antonym for the word *advocates* as it is used in the first paragraph?
   a. supporters
   b. believers
   c. opposers
   d. activists

Name_____

Service Animals

Service animals are special animals that are trained to help people who have disabilities. These remarkable creatures can aid those who need help. Their service helps people live longer, fuller lives. People in need of a service animal often form a unique bond with the animal, and they learn to become more independent, thanks to the trained service animal.

Animals that help people can be trained to do a variety of jobs and services. Dogs are often trained to act as guides for people who are blind or have visual impairments. Some of the trained animals simply provide comfort to those who need it the most. Remarkably, there are some animals who seem to be able to sense when a person is about to experience a seizure, and the animal is able to signal for help before the problem occurs.

Service animals are different from other animals that live with people because they are not classified as pets. They may only be available on a temporary basis. Service animals are allowed by law to go where they are needed. These animals are generally given the right to enter any public place, including places of work. Those who are assigned animals are referred to as handlers. The handlers generally do not have to carry identification to prove an animal is a trained service animal. Just looking at one of these amazing animals is generally all the proof that is required.

Text Questions

1. What is the main job of a service animal?
   a. to help those who have poor eyesight
   b. to help anyone with a disability
   c. to assist the elderly
   d. to watch over young children

2. Which statement is not a fact?
   a. Service animals are amazing creatures.
   b. Service animals are not classified as pets.
   c. Service animals are trained to help those who have disabilities.
   d. Service animals can act as guides for people who are blind.

3. Why do you think service animals are not classified as pets?
   a. They have specific jobs to perform.
   b. They do not have a long life expectancy.
   c. They are assigned to the owner on a temporary basis.
   d. They are not good with children.

4. What does the word *disability* mean as it is used in the first paragraph?
   a. a handicap
   b. a promise
   c. a distance
   d. a movement

5. The text presents service animals in a positive light. Take the opposite opinion and write one or two complete sentences arguing against the use of service animals. Be sure to give specific reasons based on what you have read.

   _____

   _____

   _____

Fiction

Contemporary
Realism

Mythology

Fairy Tales
Folklore

Fantasy

Historical

Mystery
Suspense
Adventure

Name_____

Mythology

What is mythology? Mythology is the study of myths or stories. The myths of a society show the people's beliefs during a certain point in their past. Most past cultures have myths, but people today are especially familiar with the myths of the ancient Greeks and Romans.

Why are people today so familiar with the myths and names of the Greek and Roman gods and goddesses? For one thing, their names are often associated with parts of our modern-day culture. For example, Nike—a familiar brand name—was the goddess of victory in one set of myths. Think about the names of the planets and you will find the names of gods and goddesses from Ancient Rome have been used to name the

celestial bodies. Many school mascots also get their names from the myths of ancient Greek or Roman cultures. The professional National Football League's team the Titans is another modern-day example that owes its name to mythology.

Mythology is connected with another word: *theology*. Theology is the study of a group's religion and practices of that religion. Studying the myths of the ancient cultures helps define and explain the group's religious beliefs and practices, even if those beliefs are not still practiced in today's culture. Studying the beliefs and the stories of ancient societies can help us understand the past as well as their appearance in our modern-day world.

Text Questions

1. What does the suffix "ology" most likely mean?
   a. the beginning of
   b. the study of
   c. the ending of
   d. the presenting of

2. Which statement best explains the importance of studying ancient myths?
   a. Myths help explain an ancient culture's religious beliefs.
   b. Myths help people today to understand brand names of products.
   c. Myths give great entertainment.
   d. Myths show us mistakes from the past so we can avoid them in the future.

3. According to the text, which ancient cultures have had a wide impact on modern society?
   a. Egyptian and Greek
   b. Roman and Egyptian
   c. Mayan and Roman
   d. Greek and Roman

4. Which is a synonym for the word *ancient* as it is used in the first paragraph?
   a. new
   b. early
   c. original
   d. mysterious

5. What was the author's purpose in writing this text?
   a. to compare and contrast
   b. to entertain
   c. to persuade
   d. to inform

Name_____

Echo

Have you ever yelled out a word or phrase and had your words echo back to you? Maybe you have shouted "hello" or perhaps you have said your name, and you were able to hear the words resonate all around you. When this happens, people today say they are listening to their echo. But where did the word *echo* come from?

In Greek mythology, Echo was a nymph or goddess of the mountains. Echo was also considered to be very beautiful and extremely talkative. Her voice is what is known most about her because this is what caused her to be cursed.

According to one ancient myth of Echo, the nymph talked so much to the goddess Hera, the wife of Zeus, that she could not concentrate. Hera, who was a jealous wife, spent much of her time keeping an eye on her husband. By watching him, she hoped to keep him faithful to her. Echo's constant talking made it impossible for Hera to keep an eye on her husband. In her anger over her inability to stop her husband from being unfaithful to her, Hera cursed the beautiful Echo. Hera's punishment was to change Echo's speaking ability. Hera cursed Echo to a life where the only way she could speak was to repeat someone else's words.

Today, when we hear our own words repeated, we instantly recognize the sound as our echo. The next time you hear your echo, remember the curse of Echo, and listen carefully as "she" repeats your words!

Text Questions

1. In mythology, what quality is Echo most known for possessing?
   a. She is extremely kind.
   b. She is extremely evil.
   c. She is extremely talkative.
   d. She is extremely humorous.

2. Why is the myth of Echo most likely important to us today?
   a. It explains a natural phenomenon.
   b. It explains that the goddesses were often jealous of each other.
   c. It helps us see people in the past were often vindictive.
   d. It helps explain Hera's jealous behavior.

3. Which of the following words would best explain Hera's behavior to Echo?
   a. jealous
   b. vindictive
   c. friendly
   d. encouraging

4. If you wanted to know more about Echo, which would be the best source to use?
   a. an atlas of ancient Greece
   b. an encyclopedia entry about Hera
   c. a book of myths related to the Greek nymphs and myths about Echo
   d. a personal website by someone who loves mythology

5. Which paragraph best explains why we call the repeating sound of our words an echo?
   a. first paragraph
   b. second paragraph
   c. third paragraph
   d. fourth paragraph

Name_____

Greek Mythology

There is a plethora of ancient Greek myths for people to read and study today that help one to understand the culture of the ancient Greeks. Many of the Greek myths attempted to explain the origins of the world, or they gave guidance to the people on how they should have conducted themselves in life. The deities in these myths were often given very human reactions; however, they also had powers that went far beyond that of the Greek people.

In ancient Greece, the culture perpetuated the belief of many deities. These deities lived in many places, but the major gods and goddesses of Greece made their home on Mount Olympus. Mount Olympus is the highest point of land in Greece. Thus, this majestic mountain was the perfect home for the major deities.

According to the ancient myths of Greece, twelve gods and goddesses ruled the universe from the top of Mount Olympus. These gods, or Olympians, had control over many different aspects of life on Earth. Three of the most well-known Olympians include Zeus, Poseidon, and Hades. Zeus was the ruler over all the lands as well as the gods and goddesses. His brother, Poseidon, ruled the seas, and their brother, Hades, ruled the Underworld. Also powerful were the goddesses of Mount Olympus. Hera was the queen of the gods, while Aphrodite was the goddess of love and beauty. The final seven gods and goddesses represented the remaining civilization of the world.

The stories found in Greek mythology are entertaining for us to read. For the ancient Greeks, the stories of the gods were an important part of their lives. The Greeks' beliefs would, in fact, heavily influence later cultures, including the mighty Roman Empire.

Text Questions

1. What is the meaning of the word *plethora* as it is used in the first paragraph?
   a. shortage
   b. overabundance
   c. miniscule
   d. colossal

2. After reading the text, what can you infer about the importance of the myths to the ancient Greeks?
   a. The myths helped them explain their world and how they should conduct themselves.
   b. The myths were simply used to entertain the ancient Greeks.
   c. The myths were used to keep people from attempting to climb Mount Olympus.
   d. The myths were copied from those of the Roman culture.

3. Which statement is a fact about the story?
   a. Poseidon was the most powerful of the Greek gods.
   b. Zeus was the king of the gods and goddesses.
   c. Aphrodite ruled the seas beside Poseidon.
   d. As god of the Underworld, Hades was not allowed on Mount Olympus.

4. According to the text, how many major deities are there in the ancient Greek culture?
   a. There is an unlimited amount.
   b. There are twelve.
   c. There are no major deities.
   d. There are six.

5. Which of the following is true about the Greek myths?
   a. They attempted to explain the beginning of the world.
   b. They attempted to explain when the world will end.
   c. They explained the importance of societies learning from each other.
   d. They were written purely for entertainment.

Name_____

Hephaestus

Hephaestus was one of the many gods of the ancient Greek culture. In mythology, he is the god of fire and is known for his skills in metal work. The Roman god, Vulcan, is similar to Hephaestus, which is not unusual, since many of the Roman gods are almost exact duplicates of the earlier deities of the Greeks. One can understand that, as the god of fire, Hephaestus's home was inside a volcano.

When Hephaestus was born, he was an embarrassment to his mother Hera because he was born lame. The myths explain that Hera threw him into the sea, but his deformity made it difficult for him to swim. He was rescued by the nymphs who lived there. They are the ones who taught him much of his craft as he lived in a cave to stay safe from Hera.

Eventually, Hephaestus would become a skilled craftsman. He would build palaces for the gods and goddesses, but those creations are not what he is best remembered for making. Hephaestus is credited with the creation of Pandora who would later open the box that would let evil out into the world. The only thing in the box Pandora is able to save from escaping is hope. The importance of the myth is, of course, to explain why there is such wickedness in the world, but that people can always hope and try for things to be better. Hephaestus's role in Pandora's creation gives him a permanent place in the ancient Greek myths.

Text Questions

1. According to the text, what is the most important story about Hephaestus?
   a. that he lived in a volcano
   b. that he created fire
   c. that he fell in love with a mortal
   d. that he created Pandora

2. Which culture copied many of the myths created by the ancient Greeks?
   a. the Egyptian
   b. the Roman
   c. the Sumerian
   d. the European

3. What does the word *lame* mean as it is used in the second paragraph?
   a. unable to walk normally
   b. unable to speak normally
   c. unable to see normally
   d. unable to hear normally

4. What is the significance of "hope" being left inside Pandora's box?
   a. Even though there is evil in the world, people can hope that things will always get better.
   b. Someday, a girl named Hope will be born, and she will bring with her peace for the world.
   c. There is no significance of "hope" being left inside the box.
   d. Pandora would someday have a daughter, and she knew she should name the daughter Hope.

5. Why did Hera throw her own child into the sea?
   a. She had wanted a girl instead of a boy.
   b. She did not like the name his father had given him.
   c. She was embarrassed that she had a son with a deformity.
   d. She wanted to give a sacrifice to Poseidon, who ruled the ocean.

Name_____

Creation

In ancient cultures, such as those of the Greeks and Romans, mythology played an important role in explaining the beginning of all things. Creation myths were explanations to the people living during those times as reasons for such things as man's existence on Earth, the beginning of the universe, as well as many other various themes of creation.

In the Greek myths, the world began with Chaos. Chaos was the gap between Earth and sky. Our own word, *chaos*, comes from this ancient Greek myth and refers to things being in a state of confusion, which would be an appropriate description of the Greeks' beginning for the world. During the beginning of Earth, the Greeks believed there were twelve Titans who helped to create the world as we know it. These twelve Titans would later be defeated by their own children. Their children would be the gods and goddesses who would eventually rule on Mount Olympus.

Cronus, one of the original Titans, is often seen in modern-day stories that reference characters from Greek mythology. According to the legend, Cronus is captured underneath Earth, and his release would cause the end of the world. The fact that these creation myths are still used today in movies and literature show how important the Greek myths were and are to the people who have heard them over the years.

Text Questions

1. What is important about Chaos?
   a. Chaos is considered the first god to ever exist in Greek mythology.
   b. According to the ancient Greeks, Chaos is the space between Earth and sky where the universe began.
   c. Chaos is the father of all the ancient deities.
   d. Chaos has no part in the original creation myths.

2. From this text, what can the reader assume about ancient cultures?
   a. Most ancient cultures had some type of creation myths.
   b. All cultures that came after the ancient Greeks copied the original ideas of the Greeks.
   c. Those who lived in ancient times did not like the idea of creating stories to explain the origins of the world.
   d. All ancient cultures were afraid of the Titans.

3. Which paragraph explains how the ancient Greeks' creation myths have had an influence on modern-day society?
   a. first paragraph
   b. second paragraph
   c. third paragraph
   d. none of the paragraphs

4. Explain why you chose the answer for question three.

   _____

   _____

   _____

5. Which title would be a good alternative for this text?
   a. "Life of the Ancient Romans"
   b. "The Beginning"
   c. "Ready, Set, Go!"
   d. "The Romans and the Greeks"

Name_____

Poseidon

According to Greek mythology, Poseidon was the ruler over all the seas. As a brother to Zeus and Hades, Poseidon was given reign over all its waters when the three gods divided up the world. Quick to anger, this god was given credit for the tsunamis and other terrible storms that often raged within Earth's waters.

Poseidon had many powers. He could use his trident to cause earthquakes and make islands appear out of the sea. He also used his trident to cause the waves of the sea. Rather than swim everywhere, he rode in a chariot that was pulled by giant sea horses across the waters. Poseidon also used his powers to help. The Greeks believed Poseidon could do many good things for them. Many times he is described as protecting sailors at sea and helping fishermen by filling up their nets with bounty from the sea.

There are numerous stories that involve Poseidon and his many adventures—both good and bad. The ancient Greeks generally believed Poseidon was a god with a fierce temper. The country of Greece has always relied on its oceans for both food and economic success. Since Poseidon was one of the original twelve deities to rule on Mount Olympus, it is no wonder there are so many varied myths about this Greek god.

Text Questions

1. How did the ancient Greeks feel about the god Poseidon?
    a. They both admired and feared him.
    b. They feared him.
    c. They blamed him for all their problems.
    d. They thought of him as their favorite deity.

2. Explain why you chose the answer for question one.

    _____

    _____

    _____

3. According to Greek mythology, what did Poseidon control?
    a. Earth
    b. the Underworld
    c. the seas
    d. the earth and the seas

4. Which symbol is most often associated with Poseidon?
    a. a lightning bolt
    b. a giant hammer
    c. a golden shield
    d. a trident

5. What does the word *numerous* mean as it is used in the third paragraph?
    a. none
    b. many
    c. few
    d. minority

Name_____

The Titans

The Titans were the original twelve rulers in Greek mythology. They existed before the twelve deities that ruled on Mount Olympus. According to the various myths, in the beginning there was Chaos. From Chaos came Heaven and Earth, and from these came the Titans.

According to the myths, the Titans had other children besides the twelve deities on Mount Olympus, but these children would be the ones they would fight with for power over Earth. For ten years, the Titans fought their children. Eventually, the Titans would lose and be banished. The Olympic gods and goddesses had the Titans banished to Tartarus, a place below the Underworld. Here they were to remain imprisoned forever.

Although there are many myths about the Titans, and some modern-day books and movies deal with the Titans, one of the most important myths relates to one of the Titans' children, Prometheus. Prometheus was not one of the twelve Olympians. The myths state that Prometheus played an important role for mankind. Prometheus liked mankind and wanted to help them. To help make their lives easier, Prometheus stole fire from Zeus and shared it with mankind.

The Titans are portrayed as harsh rulers and often as cruel parents in the many myths about them. Yet it is through their descendent Prometheus that mankind was able to have fire. Thus, to the ancient Greeks, the Titans were a vital part of mankind's history.

Text Questions

1. Who were the Titans?
   a. the gods and goddesses who lived on Mount Olympus
   b. the children of Chaos
   c. deities who were created for modern-day books and movies
   d. the parents of the twelve deities who lived on Mount Olympus

2. Which statement is a fact from the story?
   a. The Titans had other children besides the twelve deities on Mount Olympus.
   b. The Titans were the strongest deities of all the Greek gods and goddesses.
   c. There are more myths about the Titans than any other Greek deities.
   d. The Titans could never escape from the Underworld.

3. Why is Prometheus considered an important figure in Greek mythology?
   a. He saved mankind from severe punishment from the rulers of Mount Olympus.
   b. He let mankind live on Mount Olympus.
   c. He was the father of all the Titans.
   d. He gave fire to mankind.

4. What does the word *vital* mean as it is used in the fourth paragraph?
   a. unimportant
   b. frivolous
   c. desperate
   d. essential

5. Write a summary of the text in two or three complete sentences.

   _____

   _____

   _____

   _____

Name_____

Cyclops

The Cyclops were definitely one of the most interesting creations of Greek mythology. The creatures were considered to be giants, but what made them stand out, other than their size, was one unusual feature. Each Cyclops only had one eye right in the middle of its forehead.

Most people think of Cyclops as monsters, but in mythology, they did have some good qualities, too. They are said to have been skilled workers. They are even given credit for building the walls of several cities in ancient Greece. Some myths claim the giants created the thunderbolts used by the god Zeus on Mount Olympus. The Cyclops also make an appearance in Roman culture and are workers who help Vulcan, the god of fire.

The Cyclops, however, are probably best remembered for their role in an epic poem written by the Greek poet Homer. In the story, the brave Odysseus is captured by a Cyclops, the son of Poseidon. The Cyclops eats several of the crew from his ship before Odysseus is able to trick the Cyclops, blind his one eye, and free himself and the rest of his men.

Text Questions

1. According to the text, which statement best describes the Cyclops?
   a. To the ancient Greeks, the Cyclops were vicious giants.
   b. To the ancient Greeks, the Cyclops were gentle giants.
   c. To the ancient Greeks, the Cyclops were deities.
   d. To the ancient Greeks, the Cyclops could be both good and evil.

2. Which sentence is an opinion?
   a. The Cyclops were definitely one of the most interesting creations of Greek mythology.
   b. Each Cyclops only had one eye right in the middle of its forehead.
   c. In mythology, the Cyclops did have some good qualities.
   d. The Cyclops also make an appearance in Roman mythology.

3. Which paragraph best describes the physical appearance of the Cyclops?
   a. first paragraph
   b. second paragraph
   c. third paragraph
   d. none of the paragraphs

4. After reading the text, which adjective best describes the Cyclops?
   a. magical
   b. fearsome
   c. timid
   d. mysterious

5. Explain why you chose the answer for question four.

   _____

   _____

   _____

   _____

Name_____

Horus

The ancient Greek and Roman cultures were not the only ones greatly influenced by their myriad of deities. Ancient Egypt also has its share of gods and goddesses. One god who was especially important to the ancient Egyptians was the god Horus.

Horus was an extremely powerful deity. His physical description was a mix of human and bird, although at one point, he was simply seen as a hawk or falcon. Later, the image of the god changed. He became a man with the head of a bird. The eyes of Horus were extremely important. According to the myths, his right eye represented the sun, and his left eye was the moon.

Many of the myths surrounding Horus involve his constant struggle with the god Set. Set is said to have killed Horus's father, and Horus spends much of his time attempting to avenge his death. In various myths, the two gods fight for control and engage in constant contests of strength. In one epic battle, Set blinds Horus, but his eyesight is healed by mystical forces who want Horus to win against Set.

Horus eventually is asked by the gods to rule—just as Zeus is the head of the deities on Mount Olympus in the ancient Greeks' culture. Horus is able to make amends with the god Set. He even invites him to live in the sky and become the god of storms.

Text Questions

1. Which pair of words are synonyms for the word *culture* as it is used in the last paragraph?
   a. bacteria, germ
   b. civilized, refined
   c. society, civilization
   d. coddle, protect

2. Which paragraph best describes the physical appearance of Horus?
   a. first paragraph
   b. second paragraph
   c. third paragraph
   d. fourth paragraph

3. According to myths, what did Horus's right eye represent?
   a. moon
   b. stars
   c. planets
   d. sun

4. According to information in the text, which statement is correct about the two gods Horus and Set?
   a. Horus and Set remained enemies.
   b. Horus and Set were able to settle their differences.
   c. Horus had Set imprisoned in the Underworld.
   d. Horus never forgave Set for attempting to blind him.

5. If someone wanted to know more about Egyptian mythology, what would be a good source to use?
   a. an encyclopedia entry about gods and goddesses
   b. an atlas with maps of ancient Egypt
   c. a website by someone who currently lives in Egypt and has seen the pyramids
   d. a nonfiction book about ancient Egyptian deities

Name_____

Dragons

Dragons are one of the best-known mythological creatures. Ancient cultures throughout the world wrote about these fire-breathing, mythical animals. Usually the beasts were described as having wings, reptile-looking features, and massive claws. Not only could they fly, but they could also breathe fire.

In some cultures, the dragon was portrayed as an evil monster. Heroes of Greek and Roman myths were often portrayed in battles fighting dragons. However, in other cultures, the dragon was a symbol of good. In ancient China, for example, the dragon was seen as a symbol representing good fortune, wealth, and happiness.

Dragons are still used as symbols today. They appear on everything from cartoons to jewelry. Many types of children's toys feature various types of dragons. Some mythological creatures are only mentioned today if someone is studying ancient cultures, but the dragon has infused itself into modern-day culture. The dragon is one myth from the past that will not be forgotten.

Text Questions

1. Which statement from the text is an opinion?
   a. Ancient cultures throughout the world wrote about these fire-breathing, mythical animals.
   b. In some cultures, the dragon was portrayed as an evil monster.
   c. Dragons are still used as symbols today.
   d. The dragon is one myth from the past that will not be forgotten.

2. According to the text, which statement is true about dragons?
   a. In some cultures, they are a symbol of evil, but in other cultures, they are a symbol of good.
   b. Dragons can disappear and breathe fire.
   c. In ancient Greece and Rome, dragons were considered symbols of happiness and good fortune.
   d. Dragons became popular in modern times after several young-adult novel series were written about the mythical creatures.

3. Dragons are described as a symbol representing different things in various cultures. Give an example of another symbol and explain what the symbol represents.

   _____

   _____

   _____

   _____

4. Which sentence is an example of a compare-and-contrast statement?
   a. Dragons are used as symbols in everything from toys to television shows.
   b. In some cultures, dragons were a symbol of good, while in other cultures, dragons were a symbol of evil.
   c. Dragons are fire-breathing creatures.
   d. The mythological dragon will never be forgotten.

5. What was the author's purpose in writing this text?
   a. to compare and contrast
   b. to entertain
   c. to persuade
   d. to inform

Name_____

Set

When you hear the word *set*, you might think about setting the table for dinner or playing a game and hearing someone call the words "ready, set, go!" However, in ancient Egypt, the word *set* had an entirely different meaning. Set was, in fact, a powerful deity in Egyptian mythology.

Set's personality changes throughout ancient Egypt's history. At first, in the myths, he is seen as a god filled with goodness and heroic qualities. Later, he is portrayed as a jealous god filled with evil. In several myths, he even murders his own brother.

Why is Set such an important god in Egyptian history? Set comes to represent evil in the world much as Satan represents evil in the Christian religion. Eventually, Set battles the god Horus. According to mythology, this battle is considered an epic battle between good and evil. Horus defeats Set, and Set becomes an enemy of the gods, with his name and image removed from various artifacts in ancient Egypt.

Text Questions

1. Which is <u>not</u> a definition for the word *set*?
   a. to place something in a specific spot or position
   b. a group or collection of something
   c. to arrange in advance
   d. to maintain an upright position

2. According to the text, what is one reason Set most likely became an evil god?
   a. He was afraid.
   b. He was jealous.
   c. He was insane.
   d. He was worried.

3. Why is the battle between Horus and Set important?
   a. The battle lasts for exactly twenty-four hours.
   b. The battle happens over and over again.
   c. As a result of the battle, Set is able to rule all of Egypt.
   d. It is an epic battle between the forces of good and evil.

4. Which is an antonym for the word *epic* as it is used in the third paragraph?
   a. multitude
   b. heroic
   c. larger than life
   d. minor

5. Based on this text, which other god could a person study to learn more about Set?
   a. Zeus
   b. Egypt
   c. Horus
   d. Mythology

Name_____

Persephone

In ancient mythology, Persephone was known as the queen of the Underworld. The daughter of Zeus and Demeter, she was not always part of the Underworld. As a child, Persephone spent much time with her mother Demeter, the goddess of agriculture. They would travel together all over the world.

Hades, the god of the Underworld, wanted Persephone to be his wife. Persephone's own father helped with a scheme to have her kidnapped and given to Hades. Zeus caused a beautiful flower to grow, knowing that when Persephone saw the blossom, she would stop to admire the unusual plant. When she did, Hades seized her and carried her to the Underworld. Demeter knew nothing of this plan; she only knew her daughter was missing. She spent all of her time searching for her daughter. This led to the crops dying, and famine threatened the people. Zeus became worried all of mankind would die if Demeter did not stop looking for

Persephone. If mankind died, there would be no one to give sacrifices to the gods. So, he finally decided to bring Persephone out of the Underworld and back to her mother.

Hades did not want to lose Persephone. Knowing she was about to leave, he offered her a pomegranate. Persephone ate part of the seeds but did not eat them all. As a result of eating the pomegranate seeds, she was cursed to always return to the Underworld for part of each year because anyone who eats food from the Underworld can never be totally free.

So, Persephone would stay with her mother part of each year. She would then return to the Underworld for the remaining months. During the months she was in the Underworld, Demeter would make the world cold and bleak. When her daughter returned, she would once again tend to the earth. For the ancient cultures, this myth explained the cycle of the seasons.

Text Questions

1. Which sentence best proves Demeter loved her daughter?
   a. As a child, Persephone spent much time with her mother Demeter, the goddess of agriculture.
   b. They would travel together all over the world.
   c. Demeter knew nothing of this plan; she only knew her daughter was missing.
   d. She spent all of her time searching for her daughter.

2. Explain why you chose the answer for question one.

   _____

   _____

3. Why was the myth about Persephone's life important to ancient cultures?
   a. The myth made Hades seem kinder.
   b. The myth taught daughters to have a strong bond with their mothers.
   c. The myth helped explain the cycle of the seasons.
   d. The myth showed Zeus's love for mankind.

4. What happened as a result of Persephone's eating the pomegranate?
   a. She could never leave the Underworld.
   b. She could leave the Underworld, but she had to return for several months each year.
   c. She cursed all of mankind.
   d. She could never see her mother again.

5. Why did Demeter most likely make the world cold and bleak when she was separated from Persephone?
   a. Demeter loved only warm weather, so she saved the good weather for her return.
   b. Demeter was too busy watching over Persephone in the Underworld to worry about the weather.
   c. Demeter wanted Zeus to be miserable.
   d. The weather was a reflection of her mood when she was separated from her daughter.

Name_____

The Underworld

According to ancient Greek mythology, Hades was the ruler of the Underworld. Along with his brother Zeus, who ruled the earth, and his brother Poseidon, who ruled the seas, he helped keep order by ruling the world of the dead. Hades' world was separated from his brothers' worlds by various rivers.

One important fact about the Underworld is no one could enter without crossing the River Styx. This crossing was an important part of the journey for the newly dead. To cross the river, the passengers had to ride a ferry, but the ride was not free. Every passenger would have to pay the ferryman a coin. To provide for this passage, people of the ancient world were often buried with a coin placed in their mouths so they would have the money they needed when they reached the river.

Another important part of the Underworld was the guard dog Cerberus. Cerberus was a three-headed watchdog. Once the dead entered the Underworld, the creature's job was to make sure they never left.

Finally, those who entered the Underworld were separated by the judges of the dead. Every soul would be sent to spend eternity based on these judgments. Those who were rewarded were sent to the Elysian Fields. Those who did not deserve rewards in the afterlife were sent to Tartarus, a place of eternal punishment.

Text Questions

1. Why were the myths about the Underworld an important part of ancient mythology?
   a. The myths explained what happens to people after their deaths.
   b. The myths of the Underworld provided scary stories for the ancient cultures.
   c. The myths explained the creation of Cerberus.
   d. The myths assured humans they would not suffer in the afterlife.

2. Which paragraph explained the crossing of the River Styx?
   a. first paragraph
   b. second paragraph
   c. third paragraph
   d. fourth paragraph

3. Which title would be a good alternative for this text?
   a. "Life After Death for the Greeks"
   b. "Myths of Ancient Greece"
   c. "The God of Death"
   d. "Eternal Punishment"

4. What was one way those who were still living aided those who had died?
   a. They hid a coin on their body for passage at the River Styx.
   b. They held candlelight vigils for those who had died.
   c. They tried to distract Cerberus to help them escape.
   d. They built pyramids for all their dead.

5. Based on the passage, what can one assume about the Elysian Fields?
   a. The Elysian Fields were for those people who had committed severe crimes on Earth.
   b. The Elysian Fields were a place of rewards for those who had lived a good life.
   c. The Elysian Fields were set up as a playground for the deities.
   d. The Elysian Fields allowed people to have passage back to Earth.

Name_____

Medusa

Medusa was one of three creatures in Greek mythology known as Gorgons. Gorgons were hideous monsters, and Medusa was no exception. Her hair was made of snakes, and her face was so deadly that any person who looked directly at her would immediately be turned to stone.

In ancient mythology, Medusa is best known for her death. Medusa was not immortal, even though she possessed unusual powers. Anyone who went against Medusa usually died. This would not be the case for the Greek hero Perseus.

Perseus was called upon by his king to bring him the head of Medusa. The king did not like Perseus and felt he was sending the young man off to certain death. However, Athena, Hermes, and Hades approved of Perseus and offered to help him survive the encounter with the Gorgon. They gave him several gifts, including a cap of invisibility, sandals with wings, and a shield, which he polished until he could see his reflection. This way he could look at Medusa's reflection rather than look directly at her and turn to stone.

Using the gifts, Perseus was able to behead Medusa, ending her life. He placed her head in a bag and then used the winged sandals to escape from her two sisters. Perseus was not finished, though. He showed the head of Medusa to the king who had sent him on the death mission and, using the head, turned the evil ruler into stone. To thank Athena for her help, he gave the head to the goddess to use as she saw fit. However, Medusa's legend does not end with her death. Drops of her blood would later become her two sons, and so the legend of the Gorgon sister continued on in mythology.

Text Questions ....

1. What was Medusa's greatest power?
   a. the poisonous snakes that made up her hair
   b. the support of her two evil sisters
   c. the sons that were born from her drops of blood
   d. the ability to turn anyone who gazed at her into stone

2. Which gift helped Perseus to escape?
   a. the cap of invisibility
   b. the bronze shield
   c. the winged sandals
   d. Medusa's head

3. Which paragraph explains what Perseus did after he beheaded Medusa?
   a. first paragraph
   b. second paragraph
   c. third paragraph
   d. fourth paragraph

4. Why did the king want Perseus to bring him back the head of Medusa?
   a. He thought he was sending Perseus to his death.
   b. He wanted Medusa's head to use against his enemies.
   c. He wanted to see if Athena would help Perseus.
   d. He needed Perseus to prove his bravery.

5. List three things in sequential order that happen in the story.

   a. _____

   b. _____

   c. _____

Name_____

Athena

Athena was the daughter of Zeus in Greek mythology. She was born from his skull and dressed in complete armor at her birth. With such an unusual birth, it is no wonder this goddess was known as the goddess of war. Athena also had other attributes. She was known for her arts and crafts and for her great wisdom. Because of her wisdom, there were times when the goddess preferred peace over war.

As a goddess, she guarded over certain ancient cities. One city she looked after was Athens. The Parthenon was built in the city as a temple to Athena. A replica of the temple can be found today in Nashville, Tennessee, at Centennial Park. The Parthenon in Nashville also houses a statue of Athena that is based on the original and is forty-two feet tall. Both the replicas of the Parthenon and the statue are amazing architectural accomplishments.

The Greeks celebrated their great admiration of the goddess Athena by holding a huge festival known as the Panathenaea. This was an annual celebration that took place in Athens. At the celebration, there were many activities including both athletic and musical events. Sacrifices were also offered up to the goddess during the festival. All the events surrounding the celebration were to honor the goddess of war and wisdom, a deity seemingly admired by most of the ancient Greeks.

Text Questions

1. Which statement is <u>not</u> a fact about the story?
   a. The Parthenon was built in the city as a temple to Athena.
   b. A replica of the temple can be found today in Nashville, Tennessee, at Centennial Park.
   c. The Parthenon in Nashville also houses a statue of Athena that is based on the original and is forty-two feet tall.
   d. Both the replicas of the Parthenon and the statue are amazing architectural accomplishments.

2. Explain why wisdom would be an important quality for the goddess of war to possess?

   _____

   _____

   _____

3. Which line from the text helps you to explain your answer for question two?
   a. She was born from his skull and dressed in complete armor.
   b. Because of her wisdom, there were times when the goddess preferred peace over war.
   c. The Greeks celebrated their great admiration of the goddess Athena by holding a huge festival known as the Panathenaea.
   d. All the events surrounding the celebration were to honor the goddess of war and wisdom, a deity seemingly admired by most of the ancient Greeks.

4. Which is <u>not</u> a synonym for the word *attributes* as it is used in the first paragraph?
   a. qualities
   b. characteristics
   c. standards
   d. traits

5. What was the purpose of the Panathenaea?
   a. to raise money for the temple
   b. to show admiration for the goddess Athena
   c. to rally everyone for peace instead of war
   d. to gather workers to complete Athena's temple

Name_____

Zeus

Zeus, according to Greek mythology, was the son of the Titan Cronus. Cronus believed that one of his children would eventually overthrow him for power, so he ate each one that was born. To protect Zeus, his mother Rhea wrapped a stone in baby blankets and fed the stone to her husband, thus saving Zeus. Zeus would later trick Cronus to get all of his brothers and sisters back. Cronus was right to be afraid of his children. With Zeus as their leader, they would eventually overthrow the Titan and become the gods and goddesses of Mount Olympus.

As the ruler of the heavens and Earth, Zeus became a symbol of power. His most famous weapon was the thunderbolt, which he used as needed to maintain control. Zeus was quick to reward those who deserved praise and punish those who were evil.

The legend of Zeus continues today in books and movies. Even today, the god is generally portrayed much as he was in the time of the ancient Greeks. He is seen as a powerful being, quick to anger but usually just to those who deserve his mercy. No wonder he was given the power to rule over the heavens and Earth.

Text Questions

1. How was Rhea able to protect Zeus from her husband?
   a. She sent him away to live with her sister.
   b. She fed her husband a rock instead of the child, Zeus.
   c. She made Zeus appear invisible whenever Cronus was near him.
   d. She could not find a way to protect Zeus.

2. Which sentence from the passage explains the importance of Zeus's weapon?

   _____

   _____

   _____

3. What does the word *just* mean as it is used in the third paragraph?
   a. fair
   b. ridiculous
   c. barely
   d. exactly

4. Why was Cronus afraid of his offspring?
   a. They were all born with unusual gifts and powers.
   b. He believed one of his children would eventually overthrow him and become ruler.
   c. They were born with physical afflictions that frightened him.
   d. He was a timid and easily frightened deity.

5. What symbol of power is generally associated with Zeus?
   a. a thunderbolt
   b. a bronze shield
   c. a cap of invisibility
   d. a triton

86

*Name*_____

A Messed-Up Fairy Tale

A long, long time ago—last week to be exact—there lived a beautiful girl named Tiffany. Tiffany was the princess of her family, or at least she thought she was, because her father always called her his little princess. Tiffany knew it was important to act like a princess at all times, which was why she was so good at bossing around her little brother, Tommy.

"Get me some chocolate milk!" Tiffany screamed at Tommy when she was thirsty. "Get me a bowl of grapes!" Tiffany screamed at Tommy when she was hungry. "Get me whatever I want!" Tiffany screamed . . . because she believed she should have exactly that.

One day, Tiffany became extremely sick. She had the flu and was quite miserable, but even being sick didn't stop her from screaming at her little brother. "Get me some tissues! Get me some hot tea! Get me more blankets!"

By the time her father got home from work and checked on her, she had worked herself into quite a state. "What's the matter with my princess?" Her father's look of concern was Tiffany's undoing, and she burst into tears. "I have been stuck here all day, and Tommy won't even come to see me. No matter how much I called, he wouldn't come."

Knowing how his daughter was, the father asked, "Did you ask him nicely?"

Puzzled, Tiffany asked, "What do you mean?" Her father explained that even a princess needs to be kind when asking for help.

The next morning, Tiffany yelled for her brother, "Tommy! Get me some chicken noodle soup, get me some medicine, and get me a fluffy pillow!" Tommy's sigh could be heard throughout the house. He threw the pillows at his sister and walked out the door. What? You didn't really think Tiffany would suddenly become nice, did you?

And so, Tiffany's poor little brother Tommy lived unhappily ever after . . . or at least until Tiffany moved out and went to college.

Text Questions ••

1. Which adjective best describes Tiffany's personality?

   a. narcissistic   b. conscientious   c. friendly   d. generous

2. Write an example from the text that would support your answer to question one.

   _____

   _____

3. In the story, why does Tommy not come and help his sister?

   a. Tommy is selfish.
   b. Tommy does not want to catch the flu.
   c. Tommy does not want to help his sister because she is not nice to him.
   d. Tommy is too clumsy to help.

4. Why is Tiffany mean to her younger brother?

   a. She believes Tommy is her parents' favorite.
   b. She is jealous of Tommy because he gets everything he wants.
   c. She believes she is acting like a princess.
   d. She always wanted a younger sister instead of a younger brother.

5. What does the phrase "quite a state" mean as it is used in the sentence, "By the time her father got home from work and came to check on her, she had worked herself into quite a state"?

   a. Tiffany was unusually calm.   c. Tiffany's illness had become progressively worse.
   b. Tiffany was extremely upset.   d. Tiffany wanted to move to another state.

Name_____

Dragon Achoo

"Achoo!" The sound of the dragon's sneeze reverberated through the cave. "Oh, me," the dragon said to no one in particular, since he was all alone except for a few skeletons. "I think I have a nasty cold coming on."

Whenever the dragon got sick, he knew there was only one thing to do. He would have to go to the village and ask for help. When a dragon has a cold, the strangest thing happens: instead of the fire shooting out, the fire shoots in. Talk about a case of heartburn!

The dragon first came across a small rabbit. "Don't run," he shouted. "I'm sick, and I need help. If you can give me some of your carrots to chase away my cold, I would owe you a big favor." The rabbit looked at the behemoth dragon and then looked back at the safety of its hole before saying, "Sorry, can't help you." Then he scurried away to hide inside his home.

The dragon moved on. The heartburn was getting worse. He needed some fruits or vegetables to get better, and he knew just where he could find some. Three knocks on the door of the three little pigs' brick home was all it took to get one of the pigs to the door.

"Excuse me," said the suffering dragon, "but I was hoping you might be able to help me. I need some fruit or vegetables, if you please, and if you will help me get well again, I will owe you a huge favor." The pig looked over his shoulder at his brothers, and then he looked at the dragon before slamming the door shut as he shouted, "Sorry, I can't help you!"

Sighing, the dragon moved on. He came across just what he needed: a man selling fruits and vegetables on the side of the road. "Excuse me, Sir," the dragon said to the man. "I need your help. I am sick, and the only thing that can help is to eat fresh fruits or vegetables. If you could help me, I would owe you a huge favor."

The man did not hesitate; he gave the dragon three giant watermelons that he swallowed in three giant gulps. Grinning at his good fortune, the grocer said, "Now you owe me."

"Indeed I do," said the dragon, and he blew his fire all over the man's grocery stand until there was nothing left but ashes.

"Why did you do that when I helped you?" the man asked the grinning dragon.

"I gave you something in return," explained the unrepentant dragon. "A reminder that if a deal seems too good to be true, it probably is."

Text Questions

1. What does the word *reverberated* mean as it is used in the first paragraph?
   a. ricocheted   b. echoed   c. squashed   d. engulfed

2. Why did the rabbit most likely not help the dragon?
   a. He did not know the dragon.   c. He did not want the dragon to come to his house.
   b. He did not have what the dragon needed.   d. He did not trust the dragon.

3. Why did the man most likely agree to help the dragon?
   a. He wanted the dragon to owe him a favor.
   b. He once had a pet dragon, so he was not afraid.
   c. He knew the dragon was in a lot of pain and wanted to help.
   d. He wanted to trick and capture the dragon.

4. Which adjective best describes the dragon?
   a. boring   b. tricky   c. shy   d. considerate

5. Which sentence shows the grocer believes he is making a good bargain with the dragon?
   a. Grinning at his good fortune, the grocer said, "Now you owe me."
   b. "If you could help me, I would owe you a huge favor."
   c. "Why did you do that when I helped you?"
   d. "I gave you something in return," explained the unrepentant dragon.

Name_____

The Tortoise and the Snail

Once upon a time, there was a tortoise and a snail. I know what you're thinking. You think I have it wrong. You think that the story should say the tortoise and the hare. Well, it's right, and you're wrong. This is a story you have probably never heard before, so pay attention, okay?

Let's try this again, shall we? Once upon a time, there was a tortoise and a snail. The two were arguing about who was faster. The tortoise was bragging that he was extremely fast. After all, he had just recently bested a rabbit in a small 5K run. No one, he argued, was as fast as him. Imagine his surprise when a small snail spoke up. "I'll race you, Mr. Tortoise, and I'll beat you," stated the tiny snail.

Smiling at the chance to prove once again what a great racer he was, the tortoise agreed to race the snail. When the race began, the tortoise took the lead, leaving the snail only inches from the start line. The race looked as if it was over before it had even begun.

As the determined snail slowly inched its way forward, the crowd all left to follow the progress of the tortoise. A bird flying overhead spotted the snail all by itself, and it swooped down and grabbed up the snail for a tasty snack. The snail was held tightly in the claw of the bird. The bird flew across the sky. The snail could see through the cracks of the bird's claws and knew just what it needed to do. Using its tiny antennae, the snail tickled the feet of the bird, causing the claws to lose their grip. The snail fell to the earth, protected by its hard shell. He landed right on the finish line, where he sat patiently waiting for the tortoise to come into view.

When the tortoise saw the snail already at the end of the race, he didn't know what to say. He was that surprised. "Don't worry," the snail said to his new friend. "Slow and steady can still win the race, but luck and circumstance don't hurt either."

Text Questions

1. In the second paragraph, what does the sentence mean when it states the tortoise had "bested" a rabbit?
   a. The tortoise had befriended a rabbit.
   b. The tortoise had ignored a rabbit.
   c. The tortoise had done better than a rabbit.
   d. The tortoise had hidden from a rabbit.

2. Which sentence best shows the tortoise's attitude about the new race?
   a. Let's try this again, shall we?
   b. Imagine his surprise when a small snail spoke up.
   c. Smiling at the chance to prove once again what a great racer he was, the tortoise agreed to race the snail.
   d. The race looked as if it was over before it had even begun.

3. Why was the tortoise surprised to see the snail at the finish line?
   a. because he had left the snail behind him
   b. because he didn't think the snail would finish the race
   c. because he thought the bird would eat the snail
   d. because he thought the snail would quit

4. List three events in sequential order that happen in the story.

   a. _____

   b. _____

   c. _____

5. What does the snail mean when he says, "luck and circumstance don't hurt either"?
   a. It is important to plan.
   b. Determination is the key to winning.
   c. Sometimes things happen at just the right time.
   d. Finding a four-leaf clover or other talisman can help.

Name_____

Let Down Your Hare

Once upon a time, there was a girl named Rafunzel. Rafunzel had been trapped in a tower by an evil queen. Rafunzel had been in the tower for such a long time that she had never had a haircut. Her hair was so long that it dragged across the floor of the tower. It was extremely dirty and greasy. I know; I know. That's so gross, right?

Poor Rafunzel had very few friends. Well, really, she had no friends because there was no one else locked in the tower with her. However, Rafunzel seemed to attract the attention of the forest animals where her tower was hidden. In fact, she seemed to attract a lot of attention from the animals. It probably had something to do with the wonderful aroma that rose from her hair.

In between visits from the wicked queen, and when she was very bored, Rafunzel would hang her long hair out the window of the tower, and all the hares from the woods would climb up her long hair as though it were a rope ladder. They would come into the tower where Rafunzel lived, and they would keep the poor, lonely girl company.

One day, a handsome prince rode his mighty steed into the depths of the forest and found the tower. He spied Rafunzel from the window. He wanted to save the beautiful girl even if she did have greasy, dirty hair. Realizing he could use those tresses as a ladder, he asked the girl for her name and then hollered in his best hero voice, "Rafunzel, Rafunzel, let down your hair!"

Now Rafunzel, having lived alone, wasn't the brightest of girls. She thought he meant all of her rabbit friends, and so she began throwing down the hares one by one. The poor rabbits bounced off the head of the unsuspecting prince, who was eventually knocked unconscious by the unexpected surprise. The queen found the poor prince and was forced to move Rafunzel out of the tower and into a condominium at the beach.

Text Questions

1. This story is an example of which type of writing?
   a. a limerick
   b. a parody
   c. a metaphor
   d. a pun

2. Which of the following statements is <u>not</u> accurate?
   a. Rafunzel was trapped in the tower by an evil queen.
   b. Rafunzel had extremely long hair.
   c. Rafunzel's tower was discovered by a prince riding in the forest.
   d. Rafunzel threw down her hair for the prince to use as a ladder.

3. What is the meaning of the word *aroma* as it is used in the second paragraph?
   a. atmosphere
   b. perfume
   c. odor
   d. language

4. Which title would be a good alternative for this text?
   a. "The Handsome Prince"
   b. "To the Rescue"
   c. "Hidden Secrets"
   d. "The Rescue Attempt"

5. What is implied in the story?
   a. Rafunzel has long and dirty hair.
   b. Rafunzel does not always understand everything.
   c. Rafunzel has been trapped in the tower for a couple weeks.
   d. Rafunzel's tower is discovered by a prince.

Name_____

Beauty and the Bear

Once upon a time, there was a beautiful princess named Ella. She had long, clumpy hair; a hooked nose; a wart on her plump, little cheek; and black, rotted teeth. Okay, okay. Maybe she was only beautiful to her parents, but she had a good heart, and that is what really matters.

Ella loved taking long, leisurely walks through the woods, but the villagers were all scared of the forest. They knew a large bear lived in the woods. This man-eating bear had dragged off many of the villagers for his midnight snacks. Ella, however, was not scared. She could spend hours in the woods, unafraid, spying on the animals that lived there. She loved watching them all scurry away whenever she came near. Her favorite thing to do was to scare the birds from their nests and crack their eggs on the nearest rocks. She would spend hours chasing the rabbits back into their holes and swinging her lucky rabbits' "feet" from a chain on her wrist whenever she knew no one was watching. Okay, okay. Maybe she wasn't so beautiful on the inside either.

One day, Ella was taking her customary walk through the woods when she heard a sudden growling noise. The sound came from behind her. She turned to see a behemoth creature standing only a few feet away. Its massive paws and furry body quickly helped her to identify the animal as a grizzly bear. Ella was not afraid. She stood her ground and growled back. The bear was not used to people refusing to run away. He tilted his head in confusion and stared straight into Ella's beady, little eyes. Neither Ella nor the bear looked away from the other. The two stood that way for days with neither willing to give in.

After two weeks, Ella was starting to get hungry. Her stomach gave a mighty growl, so loud in fact, that the bear was startled. He yelped like a puppy and ran off to hide in the woods. In fact, he kept running until he was never heard from again. All of the villagers were so happy that they decided to give Ella a special crown. They christened her as the greatest queen of all times, and she lived happily ever after and never bothered the creatures in the forest again.

Text Questions

1. Which paragraph in the story gives a physical description of Ella?
   a. first paragraph
   b. second paragraph
   c. third paragraph
   d. fourth paragraph

2. In which point of view is "Beauty and the Bear" written?
   a. first person
   b. third person
   c. second person
   d. first person limited

3. What does the word *customary* mean as it is used in the phrase, "her customary walk" in the third paragraph?
   a. unusual
   b. usual
   c. varied
   d. atypical

4. Why were the villagers happy with Ella?
   a. She stopped the rabbits from eating their gardens.
   b. She would go in the woods each day and leave them alone.
   c. She helped everyone anytime she could.
   d. She scared away the bear that had been plaguing the villagers.

5. What can one infer will happen to Ella since she scared away the bear?
   a. She will continue to be cruel to all the animals and people in the village.
   b. She will become a beloved member of the community where she resides.
   c. She will become a veterinarian.
   d. She will start a sanctuary for bears.

Name_____

Let Me In!

Once upon a time, there were three little wolves. That's right, I said three little wolves. The three little wolves lived in three little houses. Why didn't they live in the woods, you ask? Would you want to live in the woods all the time with no roof over your head; no nice, comfy bed; and no television? Well, as you can imagine, neither did the wolves.

The three wolves, unfortunately, didn't have a lot of money, so buying groceries and fancy clothes was a bit out of their budget, but they had saved up enough money to build their houses. They'd gotten some money from their days of modeling for some fairy-tale books. The author needed to work with wolves that weren't quite as feral as some other wolves. Anyway, the wolves had taken the money they did have and invested their savings into three homes. The first wolf made his home entirely out of straw. The second wolf made his home entirely out of sticks. The third wolf made his home entirely out of recycled fur. After all, wolves do shed a lot, so there was plenty of fur to be found.

One day, all of the wolves were hanging out in the third wolf's furry abode when a knock came at the door. It was a soft knock with little noise because it's hard to make a loud noise when someone's knocking on fur. But, with their excellent sense of hearing, the wolves realized within minutes that someone was at the door. The third wolf opened the door and found standing on his doorstop a very large pig. The pig was sniffling and crying and attempting to apologize. "I'm so sorry," he began, "but I have terrible allergies and when I walked by the houses of your two brothers, I sneezed and when I sneezed, their houses collapsed."

The third wolf invited the distraught pig inside the house where he retold the story to the other two wolves. The other two wolves seemed a little upset, but by the time dinner was over and they had feasted on bacon, they were just fine with the idea of staying with their brother for a while.

So now, as you've guessed it, it's time for the moral of the story—the lesson to be learned from this tale: "The true nature of a beast is hard to change." Or, then again, maybe it's "never say no to a free meal." I think the wolves would agree both are probably true.

Text Questions

1. Why is the pig knocking on the door of the wolf's home?
   a. He is lost and needs directions.
   b. His car has broken down, and he needs to use a telephone.
   c. He wants to rob the house if no one is home.
   d. He wants to apologize to the wolves.

2. What does the word *feral* mean as it is used in the second paragraph?
   a. wild
   b. tame
   c. domesticated
   d. international

3. Which paragraph best explains what happened to the homes of two of the wolves?
   a. first paragraph
   b. second paragraph
   c. third paragraph
   d. fourth paragraph

4. What does the story imply happened to the apologizing pig?
   a. He was invited to dinner with the wolves.
   b. He was the dinner for the wolves.
   c. He went out and bought everyone dinner.
   d. He cooked dinner for everyone.

5. What do you think the moral of the story is? Explain your answer. (You do not have to choose from the two given.)

_____

_____

Name_____

The Curse

There once was a handsome prince named Roberto. Roberto spent all of his time looking in the mirror and saying to himself, "I am so handsome. I love my beautiful face." In fact, he was so narcissistic that he had no time do anything else because that would take away from his time of sitting around each day and admiring his handsome face. He didn't care about the people in his kingdom or the problems they faced. As long as he had his mirror, he was happy.

One day, a servant in the house of the prince was cleaning his room, and she accidently broke his beloved mirror. When the prince came in from his morning swim (he hadn't carried the mirror because he could see his reflection in the water) and when he saw what she had done, he was furious. He banished her from the castle. Much to his surprise, the servant girl was more than she seemed. In fact, she was actually a witch! Angered by the prince's pride and refusal to accept her apology for breaking the mirror, she transformed into the true version of herself. Then she raised her wand full of dark and evil magic, and she cast a spell upon the unsuspecting prince.

By the time she left the room, the only sign of life left was a frog wearing a tiny, gold crown. The frog was hopping from one shard of glass to another, trying desperately to see his image in the pieces that were scattered across the floor.

When the prince finally saw his reflection, he gasped. The noise reverberated through the room. The frog prince tilted his head to the left and then tilted his head to the right. He craned his frog neck as far as he could to get a better view, and then he said to the empty room, "Why, even as a frog I'm amazingly handsome!" Then he scooped up a tiny sliver of the mirror and hip-hopped away, smiling the entire time.

Text Questions ••

1. At the end of the story, which phrase best fits the attitude of the prince?
   a. He made lemonade out of lemons.
   b. He didn't bite off more than he could chew.
   c. He didn't put the cart before the horse.
   d. He didn't count his chickens before his eggs hatched.

2. Which line from the text helps you to explain your answer for question one?
   a. When the prince finally saw his reflection, he gasped.
   b. The noise reverberated through the room.
   c. The frog prince tilted his head to the left and then tilted his head to the right.
   d. He craned his frog neck as far as he could to get a better view, and then he said to the empty room, "Why, even as a frog I'm amazingly handsome!"

3. In the first paragraph, the prince is described as being narcissistic. Which set of words below best defines the word *narcissist*?
   a. someone who is angry all the time
   b. someone who is extremely vain and selfish
   c. someone who always thinks of others
   d. someone who has little care for the feelings of others

4. Why did the prince gasp when he saw his reflection?
   a. because even as a frog, he thought he still looked good
   b. because he could not believe he was wearing a crown
   c. because he was upset the witch had turned him into a frog
   d. because he was so small

5. Which paragraph gives the most details about the personality of the prince?
   a. first paragraph
   b. second paragraph
   c. third paragraph
   d. fourth paragraph

Name_____

The Cat's Meow

There once was a family who had fallen on hard times. The family was out of money and needed food, so the father sent off his oldest son with the family's only cow and asked him to sell it in the market for a good price. As the son walked away from the family's cottage, pulling the cow along behind him with a rope, the father called out from the porch steps, "Remember, trade for a good price. Don't let any of the villagers trick you!"

As the young boy arrived at the village, he discovered there was a fair going on, and there were many villagers in the small town. As the young boy walked through the crowded streets, vendor after vendor called to him to trade the cow for a service. "Let me read your palm!" "Come and see a show!" "Find out how strong you are for the price of your cow!" However, the good boy continued to ignore their shouts and kept moving toward the market area where he could trade the cow for food for his family.

At the market, he found a vendor who was willing to make a trade. He could trade the family cow for a magical cat. Now the boy knew he needed food for the family, but a magical cat was too good to pass up. So, he quickly made the trade, put the cat down into his bag, and went home to share the new fortune with his family.

When the father saw what his son had done, he could not believe it. He sat down at the table and looked stunned. There was no food, and now they had no cow. "Don't worry, Papa," the young boy said. "You haven't seen just what this cat can do." He stroked the fur of the cat, and the cat started to purr. When he did, food magically appeared on the table. When he stroked the cat's fur harder, more and more food appeared. The boy's father could not believe his eyes. The boy had not made a foolish trade after all. From here on out they would have plenty of food to eat and a helpful pet to keep away any nasty vermin. From that point on when people asked the family how they were doing, there was only one way they could describe their new situation: everything was absolutely . . . *purrfect.*

Text Questions

1. What does the phrase "fallen on hard times" mean as it is used in the first paragraph?
   a. having a hard time financially
   b. unable to keep one's balance
   c. having trouble with friends
   d. unable to travel

2. As the boy entered the fair, what temptations did he encounter?
   a. People wanted to buy his cow.
   b. People wanted him to work at the fair.
   c. People wanted to trade their services for his cow.
   d. People wanted him to set up his own booth and sell milk from the cow.

3. Which statement will be true about the boy and his family?
   a. They will never own another cow.
   b. They will go back and try to find the man who traded the cat for a cow.
   c. They will never be hungry again.
   d. They will buy several more cats to try and find more magical cats.

4. What does the word *foolish* mean as it is used in the fourth paragraph?
   a. wise
   b. imaginative
   c. unwise
   d. important

5. What lesson could be learned from the story?
   a. Everything is not always what it seems.
   b. A penny saved is a penny earned.
   c. There's no time like the present.
   d. Curiosity killed the cat.

Name_____

All That Glitters

Many years ago, there lived a beautiful princess. All she ever wanted was to marry a handsome prince. Yes, that was her only goal. She didn't want to go to college or to seek her own fortune. She wanted only to get married, buy pretty dresses, and attend parties for the rest of her life. Not that there's anything wrong with that. I'm just letting you know she was serious about getting married. Her father advised her to wait, but she would listen to no one, so ready was she to find true love.

To find a husband, she held a gala at her father's summer home at the beach. She invited as many people as she could from miles around, hoping to find her handsome prince. She bought the most beautiful dress she could find and had her hair and makeup professionally done so that, on the night of the ball, she was completely ready to meet her future husband.

As the guests poured into the home, the beautiful princess searched the crowd for her future beau. She believed in love at first sight and felt sure the minute their eyes met, she would know that he was the one. As one particularly handsome young man entered the house, the princess could feel her heart pounding swiftly. His eyes scanned the room and then locked with hers. Bingo! She had found him. The princess rushed over to meet the new guest and found that he was as charming up close as he had been from afar. His eyes were the deepest shade of blue, his smile lit up the room, and his voice was like music to her ears.

One week later, the two married. However, the princess soon learned that looks were not everything. Her true love had no manners. He burped out loud, interrupted people whenever he pleased, chewed his food without closing his mouth, and seemed to be unaware that he should lower the lid on the toilet! The princess was now married, and her handsome prince no longer seemed so handsome.

When the princess went to beg her father for help, he shook his head sadly. He reminded her that she would not listen to his advice, and now she had to live with the decisions she had made. Then he let out a huge burp and smiled just a little as he watched her leave the castle.

Text Questions

1. What does the title of the story "All That Glitters" most likely mean?
   a. The title refers to how happy the princess was the night of the party and how she was practically glowing with excitement.
   b. The title refers to the proverb "all that glitters is not gold," which means that just because something looks good from the outside, it does not mean it will be good on the inside.
   c. The title refers to the smile of the prince lighting up the entire room.
   d. The title has little or no connection to the story.

2. What could the princess have done to have had a happily-ever-after ending as in most fairy tales?
   a. She could have had more than one party.
   b. She could have waited to get married.
   c. She could have asked her father for his blessing on the marriage.
   d. She could have realized there is no such thing as love at first sight.

3. Which literary device can be found in the last paragraph of the story?
   a. irony   b. repetition   c. alliteration   d. foreshadowing

4. What does the word *gala* mean as it is used in the second paragraph?
   a. ceremony   b. meeting   c. party   d. conference

5. List three things in sequential order that happen in the story.

   a. _____

   b. _____

   c. _____

Name_____

Little Miss

There once was a little girl who refused to eat her breakfast. Every morning, she made everyone's life miserable because no matter what was offered to her, she did not want it. Her parents tried pancakes, cereal, bacon, eggs, sausage, biscuits, oatmeal, and any other breakfast food you can think of, but nothing would please the little girl.

One day, her father decided that enough was enough. He was tired of trying to eat his own breakfast with all of her screaming and crying. He was tired of his wife's unhappy face because she could find nothing her daughter would eat. He had often told her to let the child go hungry, but the wife would refuse, reminding him that breakfast was, after all, the most important meal of the day. And so, the once happy couple was starting to grow cross and negative with each other because every day began with the young girl's tantrums.

Waiting until his wife was out of the room, the father grabbed a pillow off the couch, threw it outside, grabbed his daughter and her bowl of porridge and her spoon and quickly threw them all outside and into the yard. So strategic was his throw that she landed, sitting upright, on the pillow with her bowl and spoon in her hand and not a drop of porridge spilled on her pajamas. He shut the door and was ready to eat in peace.

The daughter was so stunned that she did a most amazing thing. She stopped crying. She looked down at the bowl of porridge in her lap, and she did another most amazing thing. She took a bite and then another and another and another and . . . well, you get the idea. She ate until it was all gone.

The next day, the father cooked her porridge for breakfast again, and she began to scream. He threw her outside where she ate in peace and quiet and again finished the entire bowl. Each day, the father fed her the same way, and each day she finished her food. He tried putting a table outside, but she screamed.

And so you ask, what is the moral of this story? You can't teach an old dog new tricks? Be kind to others and they'll be kind to you? No, no, no. Neither of these is the moral of this story. The lesson learned from this, dear friends, is the grass is always greener on the other side of the closed door.

Text Questions

1. What is the problem in this story?
   a. The daughter is a picky eater.
   b. The daughter screams each afternoon at lunch.
   c. The parents do not listen to their child.
   d. The porridge is too hot.

2. Why does the father most likely wait for the mother to leave the room before taking any action with the child?
   a. She would not have approved of his actions.
   b. She would not want food taken outside the house.
   c. She would not want her pillows used outside.
   d. She would have wanted to go outside with their daughter.

3. What does the word *moral* mean as it is used in the last paragraph?
   a. story   b. trick   c. lesson   d. nightmare

4. Why did the mother want to make sure the child had breakfast each day?
   a. She believed if she cooked the food, the family had to eat it.
   b. She worked for a bakery and made delicious treats for her family that she did not want wasted.
   c. She believed breakfast was the most important meal of the day.
   d. She wanted to listen to her child scream each morning.

5. What is the main idea of the second paragraph?
   a. to explain how clever the father was
   b. to explain how the child was making everyone in the house miserable
   c. to describe the child's appearance
   d. to help the reader understand why the child cried each day

Name_____

Little Blue Riding Hood

Once upon a time—for this is how all good stories begin—there was a girl named Little Blue Riding Hood. Now Blue was a very friendly sort of girl, and she looked forward to visiting her grandmother every Sunday afternoon. So, when Sunday rolled around, she waited patiently while her mother filled up a basket full of delicious baked treats, and then Blue headed off through the woods to visit her grandmother.

As Blue was walking through the woods, she heard an unusual noise. She froze and listened. She heard the noise again, only this time the sound was closer. Being especially brave, Blue walked towards the noise. When she got to the spot where she was sure the noise was coming from, she pushed back the limbs and leaves that blocked her view. To her surprise, there was an elf caught in a trap.

The elf looked at her and seemed relieved that someone had finally found him. He spoke to Blue and said, "Thank goodness someone has come at last! I seem to have gotten myself tangled up in this trap. If you release me, I'll grant you one wish for freeing me, but be careful with the wish because wishes can be quite dangerous if not used correctly."

Blue thought seriously about the elf's words, for she was a serious type of girl. She thought of her loving parents, her wonderful grandmother, her great life. She looked at the basket of goodies and knew she always had plenty to eat, and she had a good place to live. She could think of nothing she would want to wish for. She told the elf, "I will release you on one condition. Use the wish yourself for I already have everything I need." Then Blue released the elf and went on her way.

The elf was shocked but then smiled and made a wish. He didn't look like himself as he walked out of the woods, but the handsome, young man knew his destination that day. He went in search of a young girl like none other, and the rumor is he found her, and they most likely lived happily ever after.

Text Questions

1. How is Blue best described in the first paragraph?

   a. as a mean-spirited girl
   b. as a self-centered girl
   c. as a content girl
   d. as a friendly girl

2. What problem occurs in the second paragraph?

   a. Blue realizes she's forgotten the basket of goodies for her grandmother.
   b. Blue hears a wolf hiding in the woods.
   c. Blue discovers an elf ensnarled in a trap.
   d. Blue finds a genie's bottle and accidently releases the genie.

3. Why is the elf shocked by Blue's wish?

   a. because she wants to give the wish to her grandmother
   b. because she asks for more wishes before she'll release him
   c. because she steals her wish and then refuses to help him
   d. because she wants him to have her wish

4. What can one assume the elf does with the wish he is given?

   a. He changes himself into a handsome, young man.
   b. He changes himself into a handsome elf.
   c. He gives the wish back to Blue.
   d. He uses the wish and causes himself much trouble from the wish.

5. List three things in sequential order that happen in the story.

   a. _____

   b. _____

   c. _____

Name_____

The Old Woman and the Doctor

An old woman became almost totally blind from a disease of the eyes. After consulting a doctor, she made an agreement with him in the presence of witnesses that she would pay him a high fee if he cured her. However, if he failed, he would receive nothing. The doctor prescribed a course of treatment and visited her on a regular basis to apply ointment to her eyes. With each visit, he took away with him some article from the house, until at last, when he visited her for the last time and the cure was complete, there was nothing left. When the old woman saw that the house was empty, she refused to pay him his fee. After repeated refusals on her part, he sued her before the magistrates for payment of her debt. On being brought into court, she was ready with her defense. "The claimant," she said, "has stated the facts about our agreement correctly. I promised to pay him a fee if he cured me, and he, on his part, promised to charge nothing if he failed. Now, he says I am cured; but I say that I am blinder than ever, and I can prove what I say. When my eyes were bad, I could see well enough to know that my house contained a certain amount of furniture and other things. But now, when according to him I am cured, I am entirely unable to see anything there at all."

Text Questions

1. Why did the woman refuse to pay the doctor?
   a. She claimed he charged her nothing.
   b. She claimed he had received his payment.
   c. She claimed he did not cure her.
   d. She claimed he stated the agreement incorrectly.

2. What role does the magistrate play in this story?
   a. He will determine the best way to fix the woman's eyes.
   b. He will perform a marriage ceremony.
   c. He will judge if a crime has been committed.
   d. He will determine if payment is due.

3. What does the word *prescribed* mean as it is used in the text?
   a. wrote down ahead of time
   b. wrote directions
   c. advised a medical treatment
   d. imposed rules

4. What is the moral of the story?
   a. Through evildoing, one loses any reward for the good he has done.
   b. We would often be sorry if our wishes were gratified.
   c. Wealth unused might as well not exist.
   d. Things are not always as they seem.

5. How would you rule if you were the magistrate? Give reasons to support your answer.

   _____

   _____

   _____

   _____

Name_____

The Unusual Mice

Once, in the small town of Hospitality, there lived a clockmaker named Gonzales. Gonzales loved working with his clocks and figuring out what made them tick. He truly loved his job, but he had one little problem. Every night, when he went to sleep, mice would come out in his shop.

Gonzales had tried mice traps, getting a cat, and even staying up late trying to capture the pesky critters, but he never had any success. As he slept, the rodents would run through his shop and spread out the parts for the clocks with their tiny mouse feet, causing Gonzales a lot of extra work each day as he had to put everything back in order.

One night, determined to stop the mice from causing such havoc, Gonzales hid yet again in his shop and tried to stay awake so he could catch the pesky critters. As the main clock in his shop began to chime the hours of midnight, Gonzales watched fascinated as three mice climbed out of the clock and onto the shop's counters. They stumbled and stammered, knocking into nearly everything as they began scurrying about the shop.

Gonzales grabbed an empty wire trashcan and threw it over the unsuspecting mice. At last, they were trapped.

As Gonzales came closer to the pesky creatures, he shined his flashlight inside the trashcan. Imagine his surprise when he shined the light on the rodents only to discover all three were wearing dark glasses and carrying tiny canes. In seconds, he realized the mice were blind! Huddling close together, the three mice could not see but knew they were trapped.

Gonzales, who was a kind man, knew he would have to help the mice. He scooped up the three frightened creatures, speaking words of comfort to them the best he could, and then put them out in his shed where he knew they would be safe but no longer in his shop. He knew his wife would want proof the creatures were dead, so he took three pieces of leathery rope and cut off three strips that looked much like the tails of the three mice. The next morning, when shown the proof of the mice's demise, the wife was ecstatic. Gonzales checked on his new friends later that day and found they had settled in nicely, and as all good fairy tales should end—everyone lived happily ever after.

Text Questions

1. What problem was Gonzales having?
   a. Mice were messing up his shop each night.
   b. He was having a major fight with his wife.
   c. He did not want to hurt any living creature.
   d. He had lost his ability to fix clocks.

2. What does Gonzales decide to do about his mouse problem?
   a. He puts out several traps.
   b. He stays up late to try again to catch the mice.
   c. He calls in an exterminator.
   d. He and his wife set a trap for the mice.

3. What does the story reveal about Gonzales's personality?
   a. He is a kind man.
   b. He has little patience.
   c. He cares only about his work.
   d. He is extremely selfish.

4. Why does the mice being blind change Gonzales's feelings?
   a. He realizes they cannot see where they are going, so they are not messing up his shop on purpose.
   b. He realizes someone was probably mean to them once before.
   c. He is reminded of something that happened to him in the past.
   d. He, too, is blind, so he understands how things are hard for the mice.

5. Why does Gonzales most likely not tell his wife what he has done with the mice?
   a. She would still want him to get rid of them.
   b. She would want to bring them inside and keep them as pets.
   c. She would want him to leave them in the clock shop.
   d. She would want to get another cat.

Name_____

The Sweet Touch

Long ago, there lived a king who loved chocolate more than anything else in the world. He had statues carved out of chocolate. He had a pantry in his kitchen filled with nothing but chocolate. He even had a fountain in his garden that ran with pure chocolate.

One day, a visitor came to the castle and begged shelter from the king. The king was a kind man and immediately offered the traveler his hospitality. Unbeknownst to the king, the traveler was, in fact, a fairy creature. When she revealed her true form to the king, he was amazed. Because he had been so kind, she told him she would give him all the chocolate he could ever want. The king, overwhelmed with the idea of such a gift, asked if she could make everything he touched turn to chocolate. She tried to warn him that his gift would have unusual consequences, but he could not be deterred. Wanting only to help the kind king,

the fairy left with a heavy heart knowing what would happen next.

The next morning, the king's little dog came running up to jump into the king's outstretched arms, as he did every morning. The minute the king's hands touched his dog, the faithful pet turned to chocolate. The king was horrified! He grabbed a nearby servant to try and get help, and the servant immediately turned to chocolate. Everything he touched was quickly changing to chocolate. He sank to his knees and called out for the fairy to help him. Without hesitating, the fairy took away the king's first wish and changed everything back. The grateful king thanked the fairy and invited her to dinner. At the end of the meal, the king exchanged smiles with the fairy as he offered her dessert . . . vanilla ice cream and peach cobbler. Both the fairy and the king agreed that dessert that night was delicious!

Text Questions

1. Which adjective best describes the king?
   a. impoverished
   b. obsessed
   c. controlling
   d. disrespectful

2. How does the fairy wish to reward the king for his kindness?
   a. She wants to give him three wishes.
   b. She wants to give him silver and gold.
   c. She wants to give him wisdom in making decisions.
   d. She wants to give him all the chocolate he could ever want.

3. What is the consequence of the king's selfish request?
   a. He becomes overwhelmed by his ability to turn everything into chocolate.
   b. He begins to dislike chocolate.
   c. He is able to sell the chocolate he creates and get money for the kingdom.
   d. He is able to turn his enemies into chocolate statues.

4. Which literary term best describes this short story?
   a. The story is a parody.
   b. The story is a metaphor.
   c. The story is a pun.
   d. The story is a simile.

5. What lesson did the king learn from his experience?
   a. Many things are better in moderation.
   b. It is better to bend than to break.
   c. There are two sides to every truth.
   d. Those who seek to please everybody please nobody.

Name_____

What Is True?

There once was a young boy who could never quite tell the truth. When his teachers asked him if he had his homework, he would quickly lie. When his mother would ask him if he had finished his chores, he would lie and say they were done. Even when the truth would not have hurt him if it were told, he still preferred to tell lies instead of the truth. So, for the most part, people avoided him because no one could stand to hear all of his lies.

One day, the young boy was playing near the edge of the woods when he saw a fire begin near the edge of town. He tried to put out the flames with a few buckets of water he saw near the town's well, but the flames quickly spread, and he was unable to contain them with the small amount of water he had.

The boy ran into the town and began asking for help from the townspeople, telling everyone he met that a fire was quickly spreading towards the town. Had the people been able to believe the boy, they might have glanced in the direction he pointed. They might have seen the smoke moving closer to the town, but no one believed him, so no one bothered.

When it was too late to stop the deadly blaze, the townspeople began to realize the boy had been telling the truth. Everyone gathered together to fight the blazing inferno, but in truth, their actions were too little, too late. Before the fire could be brought under control, many lost their businesses and their homes.

The boy hung his head and cried. He knew he could have stopped the tragedy if only he could have convinced someone to believe him. That day he learned the painful truth—no one believes a liar, even once he finally speaks the truth.

Text Questions

1. What fault exists in the boy's character?
   a. He doesn't tell the truth.
   b. He doesn't tell lies.
   c. He doesn't have friends.
   d. He doesn't sympathize with others.

2. What happens right after the boy sees the fire?
   a. He runs away because he is scared that he will be blamed for the fire.
   b. He tries to put out the fire but cannot.
   c. He runs straight into town and tries to get help.
   d. He does nothing.

3. Which paragraph best shows the townspeople's reaction to the boy's news that a fire is getting close to the town?
   a. first paragraph
   b. second paragraph
   c. third paragraph
   d. fourth paragraph

4. Which adjective best describes the boy's feelings after much of the town is destroyed by the fire?
   a. remorseful
   b. anxious
   c. gleeful
   d. nervous

5. Which line best explains the moral of the story?
   a. The boy hung his head and cried.
   b. When it was too late to stop the deadly blaze, the townspeople began to realize the boy had been telling the truth.
   c. There once was a young boy who could never quite tell the truth.
   d. That day he learned the painful truth—no one believes a liar, even once he finally speaks the truth.

Name_____

An Unusual Friendship

There once was a giant who lived in the deepest part of the woods. He tried to stay away from the people who lived in the nearby village. It was not that the giant was unfriendly. In fact, he enjoyed the company of others, but too many times he had accidently frightened the young children who lived close to his woods. When the bravest of children would dare to enter the edge of the woods to try to see the giant, they would nearly faint when they got their first glimpse of the colossal man. Before he could even speak to them or try to convince them he was friendly, the children would go running and screaming back to the village.

The giant's strange encounters with the children of the village caused the giant to move deeper into the woods. He did everything he could to stay away from the village. He might wish for someone to talk to, but he was kind enough that he never wanted to see the frightened faces of the children again. So, he stayed in the woods and away from everyone else.

One day, a small boy from the village managed to escape the watchful eyes of his mother. Before she even knew where he might have gone, the child had disappeared into the area of the woods that belonged to the giant. The giant was not aware that the small boy had entered his forest because he had problems of his own. He had fallen and could not get up!

When the young boy saw the giant's house, he was more curious than afraid. He was just about to walk up and knock on the giant door of the giant house when he heard someone moaning. The boy rounded the corner of the house and spied the giant on the ground and in distress. Thinking only about helping the poor soul, the young boy grabbed a piece of wood that was nearby on the ground. He used the plank as a lever and managed to apply pressure to one end of the wood and slide the other piece just underneath the body of the giant. Using the lever, he managed to help the giant regain his balance. The giant, now standing, was overwhelmed by the boy's kindness. He helped the young boy find his parents and was surprised by how kind they were to him and how grateful they were that he had helped their son find his way back home. The giant left the village with a much lighter heart than he had before, and he smiled as he heard the boy holler that he would visit him again very soon.

Text Questions

1. What is most likely the reason the story is called "An Unusual Friendship"?
   a. because the giant usually scared the children in the village
   b. because the giant only wanted to be friends with other giants
   c. because the children from the village never talked to strangers
   d. because no one ever wanted to see the giant

2. How did the young boy help the giant?
   a. He helped him find his lost puppy.
   b. He helped him make friends with the villagers.
   c. He helped him get off the ground.
   d. He helped him make his dinner.

3. What does the phrase "watchful eyes" mean as it is used in the third paragraph?
   a. The mother's eyes could keep up with the time.
   b. The mother was blind in one eye.
   c. The mother kept a close watch on her child.
   d. The mother was a night watchman for the village.

4. Which event in the story happened first?
   a. The children would run screaming whenever they saw the giant.
   b. The young boy helped the giant when he had fallen.
   c. The giant met the young boy's family.
   d. The young boy disappeared into the woods.

5. What was one effect of the boy helping the giant?
   a. He realized he was extremely strong.
   b. He knew he wanted to become a doctor when he grew up.
   c. He helped the giant by befriending him.
   d. He was no longer afraid to go into the woods.

Name_____

The Great Inventor

Mattie was excited. Today, her father was taking her to visit one of his friends, Mr. Edison. Her father had told the family last night at the dinner table that his friend was an amazing inventor. He had entertained them at dinner with stories of all of Mr. Edison's inventions. Mattie had been captivated by the tales. She wanted very much to make a difference in the world someday. She wondered if, perhaps, she could be an inventor, too. However, what Mattie was most excited about was the fact that just she and her father were going to visit her father's new friend. Her brothers and sisters all had to go to school. For once, she would have something special to talk about at supper instead of only having to listen to all the things they did while they were gone for the day.

The next morning, Mattie and her father walked to Thomas Alva Edison's home. Mattie immediately felt at ease with the kindly older man. His wife had made cookies, and Mattie thought they were delicious. She sat on a small stool beside her father and listened as the two men discussed various news. When she was finished with her treat, she followed the two men into another room. It was there that she learned just how great an inventor her father's friend was.

In the corner stood something she had never seen. Later, she would learn it was called a phonograph. Mr. Edison showed them how the machine could record voices and play the sounds back. Mattie giggled in delight when he recorded her voice. She recited her favorite nursery rhyme about Mary and her little lamb. Mr. Edison laughed and said he had recorded the same words the first time he had used the machine.

The morning seemed to go much too quickly, and eventually it was time to leave. Mattie waved goodbye to her new friend and hugged her father and thanked him for bringing her with him. As she held fast to her father's hand, she wished her brothers and sisters would get home soon. She had so much she wanted to share with them. She hoped her father would take them soon to meet Mr. Edison, but she was certainly glad she had been able to meet him first.

Text Questions ....

1. List three things in sequential order that happen in the story.

   a. _____

   b. _____

   c. _____

2. Which paragraph best explains how Mattie felt after her visit with Mr. Edison?
   a. first paragraph
   b. second paragraph
   c. third paragraph
   d. fourth paragraph

3. Why is Mattie glad she got to meet Mr. Edison before her brothers or sisters?
   a. The day was something special that only she had shared with her father.
   b. The others would have been rude to Mr. Edison.
   c. Her mother could not spare the other children for them to be able to go and visit Mr. Edison.
   d. She knew he would not like her brothers and sisters if he met them.

4. How do the Edisons help Mattie feel at ease?
   a. They take her to see all of Mr. Edison's inventions.
   b. They give her homebaked cookies for her to eat.
   c. They invite her brothers and sisters to come and visit.
   d. They name one of Mr. Edison's inventions after her.

5. Which adjective could best be used to describe Mattie's feelings about meeting Mr. Edison?
   a. excited   b. frustrated   c. nervous   d. remorseful

Name_____

Saying Goodbye

Tom was dressed in his best clothes. He was not going to a party or to any type of celebration. Instead, he was going to stand with the hundreds of others to watch the train pass—the train that held the body of the country's beloved president, Abraham Lincoln.

As Tom put on his shoes, he could not stop thinking about the assassination of President Lincoln. After four years of war, the country had already been through so much. Losing the president seemed liked the final straw. He felt especially sorry for Mrs. Lincoln. He imagined how things would be for his mother if something happened to his father. She relied on his strength just like he was sure Mrs. Lincoln had relied on her own husband. He hoped the country could pull together and be there to help her and her family.

Tom's parents were ready to go when he walked outside to join them. He held tight to his mother's hand as the three began to make their way up the street and toward the train station. He knew he would never forget this day, even if he wanted to. He wasn't sure what would happen when they arrived or if they would even be able to see the president, but he knew they all needed to go to show their respect for the man who had tried so hard to preserve the Union.

As they continued their walk, Tom thought a lot about what he might want to do someday. No answer came to him as he made the slow and steady walk with his parents, but one thing did become clear to him. He wanted to make a difference in the world, just like President Lincoln had.

Text Questions

1. What can you infer about Tom's family's feelings for President Lincoln?
   a. They respected the president.
   b. They disagreed with the president's political views.
   c. They had no strong feelings regarding the president.
   d. They felt nothing wrong had happened.

2. Which sentence shows that Tom admired President Lincoln?
   a. As Tom put on his shoes, he could not stop thinking about the assassination of President Lincoln.
   b. Tom's parents were ready to go when he walked outside to join them.
   c. He wanted to make a difference in the world, just like President Lincoln had.
   d. Tom was dressed in his best clothes.

3. What is the main idea of the second paragraph?
   a. Tom was worried about how the president's death would affect his own family.
   b. Tom was worried about how the nation could heal after such a tragic event.
   c. Tom was worried about what would happen to the Southern states now that the president was dead.
   d. Tom was worried about how Mrs. Lincoln would handle the death of her husband.

4. Which paragraph explains why Tom is putting on his best clothes?
   a. first paragraph
   b. second paragraph
   c. third paragraph
   d. fourth paragraph

5. Which sentence from the text helps you to explain your answer for question four?
   a. Tom was dressed in his best clothes.
   b. He was not going to a party or to any type of celebration.
   c. Instead, he was going to stand with the hundreds of others to watch the train pass—the train that held the body of the country's beloved president, Abraham Lincoln.
   d. Tom's parents were ready to go when he walked outside to join them.

Name_____

The Land of the Free

"Why do we have to leave our home?" Andrea's question hung in the air waiting for an answer. Her mother, with tears in her eyes, leaned down and kissed young Andrea on the cheek before answering. Andrea noticed her mother was no longer wearing the yellow star she had worn for days. She looked at her own coat and saw that her star was absent now, too.

"Andrea," her mother's voice was steady despite the tears in her eyes. "We are thankful to be going to our new home in America. Your uncle has gone to so much effort to help us join him in New York. We are going to have a wonderful new life there with him; I promise you."

"But, you still haven't answered my question, Mother," Andrea persisted. "Why do we have to leave our home? Why can't Uncle join us where we live instead?"

Andrea watched as her father knelt down to her level and began to talk. She loved the smooth cadence of her father's voice. She noticed his eyes were shiny, too. She couldn't imagine her father crying, so she had no idea what made his eyes shine so bright. "Andrea," he began in way of explanation, "we no longer have a home in Europe. We have been exiled from our homeland because there are people there who do not want us to stay. But in America, everyone is welcome. You will see."

Andrea hoped her father was right. She had heard her friends talk about America, but she had never thought much about it because she had never believed she would see it. Standing on the edge of the deck of the ship, she began to understand that her world was changing. She could see the outline of a lady, a statue, in the distance. Even from where she stood, Andrea could tell she was beautiful.

"What does the statue mean?" she asked her parents.

"Freedom," they said in unison.

Suddenly, Andrea wasn't afraid anymore. There was a plethora of reasons she was anxious to reach the shore. In fact, she couldn't wait to see America.

Text Questions

1. What is a main problem in the story?
   a. Andrea has left her doll and is sad because her parents will not go back and get the toy for her.
   b. Andrea has become separated from her parents and cannot find them on the ship.
   c. Andrea is sad because she believes she will never make friends again.
   d. Andrea is upset because she doesn't understand why her family has been forced to leave their home.

2. Which sentence helps the reader know Andrea and her family were Jews fleeing from Europe during World War II?
   a. Andrea noticed her mother was no longer wearing the yellow star she had worn for days.
   b. "Freedom," they said in unison.
   c. "Andrea," he began in way of explanation, "we no longer have a home in Europe."
   d. "We are thankful to be going to our new home in America."

3. What monument does Anna see as the family gets closer to America?
   a. Plymouth Rock
   b. the Statue of Liberty
   c. the Eiffel Tower
   d. the Empire State Building

4. What does the word *cadence* mean as it is used in the fourth paragraph?
   a. orbit
   b. sequence
   c. rhythm
   d. severity

5. What will make things easier for Andrea and her family when they reach their new country?
   a. having removed the yellow stars they were wearing
   b. having family already in America who are expecting their arrival
   c. having plenty of luggage
   d. having a good attitude about the move

Name_____

Everyone's Dream

Paula stood in the huge crowd, amazed at how calm and polite everyone was being. For days, she had heard everyone talk about their worries of violence and fights breaking out among the crowds that were determined to march on Washington, but now that Paula was among those waiting to hear Dr. King speak, she saw no hint that things might turn violent. In fact, the entire March on Washington had been peaceful, just as Dr. King would want it to be.

The crackling noise of the speaker brought Paula's attention back to the podium. She was close enough that she could see Dr. King as he walked up to the microphone. He had such a presence about him that the entire crowd immediately fell silent. His words rang out through the crowd loud and clear. She watched, mesmerized, as he seemed to push his speech away and begin talking as though straight from his heart. King's voice carried over the crowd as he spoke of his dream for all the people of America. The crowd could not look away as his words echoed so eloquently their own thoughts and hopes. He had said in his speech what everyone in the crowd believed and wanted.

When the day finally ended and Paula was back at her hotel room, she could not go to sleep because she was so excited about the possibilities of what might be next in America's future. Could those of different races ever live in peace and harmony? She knew she was only one person, and she wasn't sure how much difference she could make, but when she thought about all those people who marched today, she knew that together they could be unstoppable. Paula couldn't wait for tomorrow to arrive.

Text Questions ••

1. How does Paula feel about Dr. King's ideas?
   a. She does not support his ideas.
   b. She is indifferent to his ideas.
   c. She fully supports his ideas.
   d. She has not yet made up her mind if she supports his ideas or not.

2. What surprises Paula most about the March on Washington?
   a. There have been no acts of violence from the large crowd.
   b. There are not as many people there as she thought there would be.
   c. She does not see anyone she recognizes in the large crowd.
   d. She cannot hear Dr. King when he begins to speak.

3. Which paragraph best explains Paula's commitment to Dr. King's ideology?
   a. first paragraph
   b. second paragraph
   c. third paragraph
   d. none of the paragraphs

4. What does the phrase "his words echoed so eloquently their own thoughts and hopes" mean as it is used in the third paragraph?
   a. Dr. King had said exactly what they were feeling.
   b. Dr. King was speaking for everyone who did not have a voice.
   c. There was an echo when he spoke to the crowd.
   d. The microphones were not working, so each person was having to tell everyone else whatever they could hear of Dr. King's speech.

5. What will Paula most likely do next?
   a. Go home and never mention she heard Dr. King's speech.
   b. Follow Dr. King around the country, so she can hear all of his speeches.
   c. Give up and not try to make any changes.
   d. Try to bring about the changes Dr. King talked about in his speech.

Name_____

Making a Difference

"Mother, why can't we have suffrage like father does?"

Elizabeth Walters looked at her inquisitive daughter Rosalyn and wondered how best to answer her child's queries.

"Dear, sweet Rosalyn," she sighed and then bent down and wrapped her daughter in a tight hug. "In our country, women currently are not allowed to voice their opinions by casting their own votes. Many women feel they do have a voice because their husbands listen to their opinions and cast their votes for their entire family's beliefs. But, it's not enough. By the time you are a grown woman, hopefully things will be much different, and you'll be able to vote yourself and for your own beliefs. This fight for suffrage will be nothing your children should ever have to worry about."

Rosalyn watched her mother stand and walk over to the corner of the room. She picked up two wooden signs and brought one to Rosalyn and kept one for herself. The signs had words painted on them. Rosalyn asked her mother what they said.

"'Women's Suffrage' and 'Everyone Deserves the Right to Vote' are what I painted on our signs. We will carry these signs as we march in the parade. Your father will be there, too, cheering us on."

Rosalyn took the smaller of the two signs and held it tightly in her hands. She loved her mother and wanted to please her, but deep down she knew even if her mother hadn't agreed, Rosalyn would be marching for women's rights on her own. Her father had taught her, along with her mother, that women should be treated equally and fairly. Rosalyn was not afraid. She was determined.

As Rosalyn and her mother stepped out into the streets and into the line of protestors, Rosalyn felt extremely proud of her parents. She had friends whose parents would not allow them to voice any opinions. Rosalyn knew she was lucky. She smiled to herself as she walked beside her mother.

She stood a little taller as a wonderful thought came to her. Maybe someday a woman might even become president, and it would all be possible because people were willing to help make a difference.

Text Questions

1. Why is Rosalyn so proud of her parents?
   a. They have just told her they will pay for her to go to college.
   b. They have given her everything she has always wanted.
   c. They are willing to stand up to others and try to make changes to things they believe are unfair.
   d. They are both going to the parade.

2. What does the word *suffrage* mean as it is used in the text?
   a. the right to free speech
   b. the right to freedom of worship
   c. the right to vote
   d. the right to protest

3. Why is it significant that Rosalyn's father will also be at the parade?
   a. because his presence shows he likes parades
   b. because he is a journalist and will be reporting about the protest
   c. because he has lost his job and needs something to do during the day
   d. because his attending shows he supports his wife and daughter

4. What can the reader infer about Rosalyn's future?
   a. She will continue to fight for women's rights.
   b. She will no longer fight for women's rights.
   c. She will rebel against her mother and father.
   d. She will become president someday.

5. What lesson could be learned from the story?
   a. A person must believe to help make change happen.
   b. Parades are a good way to protest.
   c. No one person can ever make a real difference.
   d. Mothers and daughters should spend more time together.

Name_____

Disaster in the Sky

Connie was anxiously awaiting the arrival of her sister. She was flying in today on a zeppelin, the *Hindenburg*. The ticket had been expensive but according to her sister Ann, well worth the exorbitant price to be able to experience the opulent trip across the ocean while high in the air. Connie had never flown before, so she could only imagine what the world must look like from Ann's eyes so high above the clouds.

Within minutes of waiting, Connie could see the massive airship making its way in for a landing. Crew members on the ground rushed in as the massive ropes were dropped, ready to tether the airship to its landing spot. Everything seemed to be going smoothly despite the few rumbles of thunder the waiting crowd could hear in the distance.

Then, without warning, the airship became a ball of fire in the sky. Screams erupted all around. Connie felt her knees grow weak, and she nearly fainted as she watched the zeppelin go up in flames. How would anyone survive such an explosion?

Within seconds, the ship was gone. Connie tried to rush in, but security pushed her and others trying to get through back and away from the wreckage. Her eyes, filled with tears, scanned the area, hoping for any signs of survivors. It did not take long to realize that in fact, many of those on board had survived. Although many were hurt, others seemed to be walking away from the wreck without any assistance.

"Connie!"

Connie heard her sister's voice calling out her name. She turned, and there was Ann. Her dress was in tatters, and she looked scared and frightened, but she was alive. She was alive!

The people who had been holding Ann back let her run past them and grab Ann into her arms. She held her sister tightly, knowing only a miracle could have saved her.

"I was so afraid," Connie sobbed.

"Me, too," Ann said, "but I'm okay. Somehow, I'm okay."

Ann and Connie linked arms and watched the scene unfolding before them. They knew there would be others who weren't so lucky, and as much as they wanted to leave, they knew they wouldn't. They wanted to be able to help in any way they could.

Text Questions ••

1. Why is Connie watching the landing of the zeppelin?
   a. She is fascinated by air travel.
   b. She has never seen a zeppelin before.
   c. She wants to get a job on one of the great airships.
   d. She is waiting for her sister to arrive.

2. What does the word *exorbitant* mean as it is used in the first paragraph?
   a. inexpensive   b. economical   c. excessive   d. embarrassing

3. Why do the sisters decide to stay even after they have found each other?
   a. They want to see if they can find Ann's luggage.
   b. They want to stay to file a lawsuit against the owners of the airship.
   c. They want to see if any other ships are landing.
   d. They want to stay to see if they can help any of the other passengers or families.

4. Which paragraph best describes the explosion of the airship?
   a. first paragraph   c. third paragraph
   b. second paragraph   d. fourth paragraph

5. Why is Connie fascinated by the zeppelin?
   a. She is impressed by anything made by the Germans.
   b. She is only interested because her sister is on board the airship.
   c. She has never flown and wonders what it must be like to be aboard the airship.
   d. She is not interested at all.

Name_____

A Twist of Fate

"What do you mean, you couldn't get the tickets?" Sally Peterson was extremely upset. For months, she and her husband had been planning to go to America to visit her mother and father. Now all their plans were going to be put on hold because her husband had come back without the tickets.

John looked at his wife and tried to reason with her. "Sally, it's not like I did this on purpose. You know we have the money for tickets, and I am as anxious as you are to get started on the trip, but there were no more tickets to buy when I arrived. I am afraid we won't be sailing on the *Titanic* after all, but the man at the port assures me we can get another ship to take us if we can wait until next week.

Sally knew her husband had tried, and she could not be upset with him any longer. He loved her parents as much as she did and was just as anxious to see them. They would have more time to get ready for the trip now. She knew that many times things had a way of

working out the way they should. She gave him a quick hug and assured him everything was fine. She had just been disappointed, but they would still get to America.

Good news came to the couple in only a few days. Another ship was sailing for America, and they would be able to buy passage on this one without any problems. Before long, Sally and John were sailing to America.

After days of travel, they were thankful to finally reach shore. As they walked off the ship and reached land, they were quickly engulfed in the arms of Sally's parents.

"Mom, I knew you'd be happy to see us, but please don't cry. We're here. Everything is fine."

"So, you haven't heard the news then?" her father's voice spoke up. He then held out a newspaper with the shocking headline that the *Titanic* had sunk only a few days earlier.

Text Questions

1. Which title would be a good alternative for this text?
   a. "Something Surprising"
   b. "The Shocking News"
   c. "The Big Trip"
   d. "The Lost Ticket"

2. Why was the newspaper headline shocking to Sally and John?
   a. They knew people who were onboard the *Titanic*.
   b. They had wanted to get tickets to be on the *Titanic*.
   c. They believed the *Titanic* was unsinkable.
   d. They could not read the headline.

3. Which paragraph best shows that Sally is a forgiving and understanding person?
   a. first paragraph
   b. second paragraph
   c. third paragraph
   d. fourth paragraph

4. Which sentence from the text helps you to explain your answer for question three?
   a. Sally knew her husband had tried, and she could not be upset with him any longer.
   b. He loved her parents as much as she did and was just as anxious to see them.
   c. She had just been disappointed, but they would still get to America.
   d. They would have more time to get ready for the trip now.

5. How might Sally and John feel when they sail back home?
   a. anxious
   b. happy
   c. indifferent
   d. relieved

Name_____

The Man on the Moon

Katie was watching the live broadcast with her parents. Their black-and-white television showed the details as if they were there with the astronauts. Katie could not believe how real everything seemed. She felt she could reach out and touch the moon. Everyone in the room seemed to be holding their breath as astronaut Neil Armstrong made his first step on the moon.

When her father finally turned the knob and shut off the television, Katie's mind was filled with thoughts about space. If men could land on the moon, what would stop them from landing on other planets? What if there were other people out there in space who might come and land on Earth? Suddenly, it seemed as if everything she knew about the universe could change.

"That was pretty exciting, wasn't it?" Katie's father's words interrupted her thoughts.

"Yes, Daddy. I don't think I will ever forget it."

"You won't," her father assured her. "Someday, when people talk about a man landing on the moon, you will remember exactly where you were when it happened.

This memory will stay with you when others have faded away."

Katie believed her father. She couldn't imagine ever forgetting what it was like to see something so exciting happen. Her grandfather had not been as impressed. In fact, throughout the entire broadcast, he had claimed the entire event was faked and that someone in Hollywood was trying to trick everyone into believing man had really landed on the moon. Katie had looked at her mother when he said that, but her mother had only winked at her before turning her head to continue watching the television. Katie might not agree with her grandfather, but she did not want to be disrespectful and argue with him.

That night, when Katie looked at the stars, she thought about what it would be like to go into outer space. She knew she would not want to do it, but she secretly hoped that someday a woman would join the list of men's names who went to the places men were just starting to explore.

Text Questions

1. What are the grandfather's feelings about the television broadcast in the story?
   a. He believes the story is all a hoax.
   b. He is as excited as the rest of the family.
   c. He does not understand what is happening.
   d. He is proud of the astronauts who have landed on the moon.

2. How are Katie and her family experiencing the historical event?
   a. They are listening to the event on the family radio.
   b. They are watching the sky to see what happens next.
   c. They are watching the event on a television.
   d. They are streaming the event on the family's home computer.

3. What does Katie's father assure her about that day's events?
   a. that she will live to see many more such events
   b. that she will never forget that day's event
   c. that she will grow up and experience space travel
   d. that she will someday forget what she has seen

4. Does the event in the story affect how Katie views the world?
   a. Yes, the event changes Katie's views.
   b. No, the event has no effect on Katie's views.
   c. It is not certain whether the event affects Katie's views.
   d. Katie does not think about the event anymore once she is finished watching it.

5. Which sentence from the text helps you to explain your answer for question four?
   a. Katie believed her father.
   b. "This memory will stay with you when others have faded away."
   c. Katie might not agree with her grandfather, but she did not want to be disrespectful and argue with him.
   d. Suddenly, it seemed as if everything she knew about the universe could change.

Name_____

The British Are Coming

Cal heard the words announcing the coming of the British ringing through the night wind. He watched as everyone around him moved into action, shutting up businesses and locking doors, readying for the arrival of the expected but uninvited guests.

Cal was more excited than afraid. His own father had left months earlier to help any way he could the Patriots whom he believed were fighting for a new way of life. Cal had been left with his mother to help run the small printing press, which released news about the many changes and events that were destined to shape the future of the colonies.

Hurrying home, Cal wondered if his father knew what was happening and if he was safe. He hoped so. Cal's mother was waiting for him at the door of their house. The minute he arrived, she shut the door behind him and asked him what news he had heard. He quickly relayed the words he had heard shouted from the rider as he made his way through the streets of the town.

The meal that night was sparse—only bread and cheese—as both mother and son were too anxious to eat. A knock on the door brought them both abruptly to their feet. Who could be at their door at this late hour, Cal wondered.

Before his mother could stop him, Cal unlocked the wooden door and pulled it back. He could not contain the smile that broke across his face when he saw who the visitor was.

"Father! You're home!"

His mother ran to the door, tears sliding down her cheeks. "George, is everything alright?" Cal's mother questioned him.

"I do not know how things will turn out, but mark my words, tonight is the start of a revolution. There is no turning back from tonight's events."

Text Questions

1. Why is Cal most likely excited about the announcement that the British are coming?
   a. His family supported the Patriots.
   b. He had always wanted to meet a British soldier.
   c. He knew the British coming would give him plenty to write about for his paper.
   d. He had an excuse to go home early from work.

2. Which word best describes the reaction of Cal's mother when Cal arrived home?
   a. surprised
   b. anxious
   c. upset
   d. happy

3. What does the word *sparse* mean as it is used in the fourth paragraph?
   a. plentiful
   b. bare
   c. typical
   d. unusual

4. What can one infer about Cal's father and his feelings about the British coming?
   a. He is hoping for change that will be in favor of the Patriots.
   b. He is hoping the arrival of the British will increase business for his family.
   c. He is convinced the British will punish everyone who lives in the area.
   d. He understands the Patriots are in serious trouble.

5. List three events in sequential order as they happen in the story.

   a. _____

   b. _____

   c. _____

Name_____

The Unending Dust

"Quickly, children! Quickly!" Mrs. Hatcher's voice could barely be heard over the noise of the wind. "Go back into the school, now!"

Jake looked back over his shoulder at the cloud of dust that was descending with deadly stealth across the plains. The swirling mass of destruction was headed straight for the students and the schoolhouse. Jake did not hesitate to move from the playground and follow Mrs. Hatcher's order to hurry to the relative safety of the one-room schoolhouse. Jake waited at the door and held it open until he saw all of the students safely inside. Mrs. Hatcher stood with him and helped him hold the door steady until the very last student was in, and they shut the door together.

"Thank you, Jake," Mrs. Hatcher said. There were tears in her eyes as she gazed at him.

After several close calls with the great clouds of dust, the students knew what to do. They huddled near the floor and covered their noses and mouths with cloths they kept wrapped around their necks.

Suddenly, little Suzy Hatcher began to cry. "I can't find Molly," Suzy cried. Molly was Suzy's doll. She went everywhere with her precious toy. Suzy was even allowed to bring her to school. "I think I left her outside."

Mrs. Hatcher's eyes met Jake's. They both knew if the doll was outside, then it would be long gone. Jake's eyes frantically scanned the room to try to find something that might appease the already terrified child. His eyes latched on to something sticking out from beneath the bench. He crawled over to the object and pulled, and to his relief, he found Molly hidden underneath the wood.

"Don't cry, Suzy. Molly was just a little scared, that's all. She was hiding, but now she wants to be with you."

Suzy's happy laugh filled the room, and some of the tension the others felt seemed to melt away. Even in a time of crisis, it was good to know happiness could still be found.

Text Questions

1. Which sentence from the text shows Jake is a responsible, young man and cares about others?
   a. Jake looked back over his shoulder at the cloud of dust that was descending with deadly stealth across the plains.
   b. Jake did not hesitate to move from the playground and follow Mrs. Hatcher's order to hurry to the relative safety of the one-room schoolhouse.
   c. Jake waited at the door and held it open until he saw all of the students safely inside.
   d. "Thank you, Jake," Mrs. Hatcher said.

2. What natural disaster is threatening the children?
   a. a tornado
   b. a dust storm
   c. a hurricane
   d. an earthquake

3. What has happened to upset Suzy?
   a. She is afraid of the storm.
   b. She misses her parents.
   c. She has lost her doll.
   d. She cannot find her homework.

4. What lesson could be learned from the story?
   a. A little kindness goes a long way.
   b. Pay attention to the small details.
   c. Don't ask others to do for you what you can do for yourself.
   d. Don't count your chickens before they hatch.

5. Which adjective best describes Jake?
   a. clever
   b. dependable
   c. wise
   d. nervous

Name_____

A Time for Hope

"I found a job, but I'll have to leave for a while."

Elijah froze at his father's words. Since the stock market had crashed in 1929, his family had struggled to make ends meet. His father had lost his job and had been unable to find work. His mother had been doing odd jobs to try to help the family make money, and the entire family had spent their hard-earned cash only when absolutely necessary, trying to keep the family fed and to not lose their home. To hear his father say he had a job was remarkable news, but no one wanted him to leave.

Elijah realized his mother must have already known the news because the eyes of both his mother and father were trained on him, waiting for his reaction.

"That's great news, Dad," Elijah managed to say. "What will you be doing?"

Looking relieved at his son's reaction, his father began to explain. "I will be working at a park in Tennessee.

Along with other men from around the country, I'll help build needed walkways and bridges and make other improvements to the national park that is located there."

Elijah's eyes grew wide in surprise. "Tennessee! But, that's so far away."

"It's far, but we are lucky I've found a job. You know that, son."

Elijah knew this decision was necessary, but he also knew it was hard for his father. He did not want to make it any harder.

"I'll miss you a lot, but I'm proud of you, Dad. Mom and I will hold down the fort here until you get home."

When Elijah saw the relief that crossed his father's face, he knew he had said the right thing. The Depression definitely wasn't over, but for the first time in a long time, Elijah thought things might get better soon.

Text Questions

1. Which sentence near the start of the story helps the reader to know the story takes place during the Great Depression?
   a. "I found a job, but I'll have to leave for a while."
   b. Since the stock market had crashed in 1929, his family had struggled to make ends meet.
   c. His father had lost his job and had been unable to find work.
   d. To hear his father say he had a job was remarkable news, but no one wanted him to have to leave.

2. What can the reader infer about Elijah's relationship with his parents?
   a. He is not very close to his parents.
   b. He is closer to his friends than he is to his parents.
   c. He and his parents are very close to each other.
   d. He has no relationship with his parents.

3. Which line helps the reader know that Elijah's opinion matters to his father?
   a. Elijah realized his mother must have already known the news because the eyes of both his mother and father were trained on him, waiting for his reaction.
   b. Looking relieved at his son's reaction, his father began to explain.
   c. "It's far, but we are lucky I've found a job."
   d. "I'll miss you a lot, but I'm proud of you, Dad."

4. What is the cause of Elijah's father having to move?
   a. He and Elijah's mother are having trouble with their relationship.
   b. Elijah and his father need some time apart from each other.
   c. Elijah's father is going to visit family friends in Tennessee.
   d. The only job Elijah's father could find is in Tennessee.

5. Which adjective best describes the family's relationship?
   a. caring
   b. self-centered
   c. remorseful
   d. disengaged

Name_____

The Teddy Bear

"What do you have there, Gabe?" Martin asked his nephew.

"Mom bought it for me at Mr. Partridge's toy store. She said they call it a teddy bear," Gabe replied.

"A teddy bear, huh?" Martin raised his eyebrows as he looked at the furry, stuffed bear his eight-year-old nephew was hugging close. There was something familiar about the new toy, but he couldn't remember what. Then it hit him.

As his nephew went outside to play, Martin found the newspaper he was looking for sitting on the kitchen table. He skimmed through the pages until he found the article he had been trying to find.

The headline read, "New Toy Named After Softhearted President."

Martin quickly scanned the article. Apparently, after a hunting trip, the country's beloved president, Theodore Roosevelt, had opted not to shoot a small bear he saw while out on one of his expeditions. The small bear was the inspiration for a new toy, which was pegged with the name Teddy after Theodore, himself.

Martin folded up the pages of the paper and placed it back on the table. He smiled as he watched his nephew lugging the small bear across the backyard and saw him place the new toy in the center of the tire swing before giving the bear the ride of his life. Martin knew he wouldn't even bother to explain the article to Gabe. To his nephew, it didn't matter where the bear had come from or who it was named after. He would love his new toy regardless, and that was all that really mattered.

Text Questions

1. Which sentence best shows that Gabe loves his new toy?
   a. He would love his new toy regardless, and that was all that really mattered.
   b. The headline read, "New Toy Named After Softhearted President."
   c. "Mom bought it for me at Mr. Partridge's toy store."
   d. There was something familiar about the new toy, but he couldn't remember what.

2. What can one infer about Martin's feelings for his nephew?
   a. He does not have any strong feelings for his nephew.
   b. He cares about him and wants him to be happy.
   c. He rarely talks to his nephew.
   d. He is only interested in him because of the teddy bear.

3. Which sentence from the text helps you to explain your answer for question two?
   a. He smiled as he watched his nephew lugging the small bear across the backyard and saw him place the new toy in the center of the tire swing before giving the bear the ride of his life.
   b. Martin raised his eyebrows as he looked at the furry, stuffed bear his eight-year-old nephew was hugging close.
   c. The small bear was the inspiration for a new toy, which was pegged with the name Teddy after Theodore, himself.
   d. "What do you have there, Gabe?" Martin asked his nephew.

4. Which title would be a good alternative for this text?
   a. "The Wonderful Gift"
   b. "A President's Furry Legacy"
   c. "Fuzzy Wuzzy Was a Bear"
   d. "Go and Play"

5. Why is the new toy called a teddy bear?
   a. The toy is named after Theodore Roosevelt.
   b. The toy is named after the inventor.
   c. Gabe named his toy teddy bear.
   d. The story does not explain why the toy is called a teddy bear.

Name_____

Gone Too Soon

It is a true tragedy that the nation has lost such a beloved American heroine. The announcer's voice came across the radio as Mariann finished washing the dishes. She was stunned by the news the announcer had given and could hardly believe that the nation's beloved Amelia Earhart was missing and believed to be dead.

Standing at the kitchen sink, Mariann looked out the window and up at the beautiful, blue sky. The day was clear, without a cloud in the sky. It was hard to believe that the same sky had swallowed up an American legend.

This news made Mariann emotional. She had never met Amelia Earhart. She didn't know her personally, but it felt like she had. So many people had followed her career, but Mariann had especially. How many times had she dreamed of doing what Amelia was brave enough to do? She had been in a plane one time, and ever since, she had longed for the chance to fly one on her own.

The fact that Amelia was now missing should have been enough to make her dream go away, but instead, it had the opposite effect. Mariann was now more determined than ever to fly.

Text Questions

1. Why is Mariann so stunned by the news on the radio?
   a. She cannot believe that Amelia Earhart might be dead.
   b. She cannot believe that the announcer interrupted her favorite radio show.
   c. She cannot believe that the plane Amelia was flying is now missing.
   d. She cannot believe that Amelia's name is the only one they are mentioning on the radio, when she was not alone on the plane.

2. Which paragraph best shows how Mariann feels about the news that Amelia Earhart is missing?
   a. first paragraph
   b. second paragraph
   c. third paragraph
   d. fourth paragraph

3. Why is Mariann most likely now more determined than ever to learn how to fly?
   a. She wants to be famous like Amelia Earhart.
   b. She knows the company Amelia Earhart flew for will be looking for another pilot.
   c. She already has all of the things she needs to be ready to pilot an airplane.
   d. She wants to be successful to honor the person who inspired her.

4. What can one infer about Mariann's desire to fly?
   a. She is not very committed to the idea of learning to fly.
   b. She is determined to learn to fly.
   c. She is uncertain if she wants to learn to fly.
   d. She never wants to learn to fly.

5. Which is a synonym for the word *tragedy* as it is used in the first paragraph?
   a. heartbreak
   b. joy
   c. monument
   d. gala

Fiction: Historical

Daily Warm-Up 14

Troubling Thoughts

Name_____

Benjamin Franklin had always endeavored to help people. He was thrilled when he had created bifocals that could help others to see so much better and without any inconvenience. If only he could figure out a way to help England see what the colonies wanted was fair and just, then maybe he could help stop the war that was coming. His sigh was long and loud. He did not think he could stop the inevitable from happening, no matter what he tried.

Thaddeus Martin looked sharply at the man who was sitting alone at the small table waiting for his food to be served. Thaddeus knew Mr. Franklin, but he was surprised to see the normally jovial Franklin all alone and looking so concerned. Thaddeus knew whatever was bothering Franklin was surely something monumental as his trademark smile was nowhere to be seen.

With his dinner ready to be served, Thaddeus grabbed the order and hurried over to set the meal in front of the elderly statesman.

"Mr. Franklin, sir," Thaddeus said respectfully, "I have your order, ready. Is there anything else at all I can get for you, sir?"

Franklin looked up and was startled to see such concern for him expressed on the boy's face. He quickly smiled and responded, "No, lad. I'm fine, really. This wonderful food is all I need to get my thoughts straight. This is truly the best help you could give me on this night."

Thaddeus walked away feeling a little better. He knew the colonies were about to be involved in changes even those living here could barely even begin to imagine. But, with leaders like Franklin, he felt sure that whatever came to pass would be for all the right reasons.

Text Questions

1. What does the word *jovial* mean as it is used in the second paragraph?
   a. friendly
   b. selfish
   c. respected
   d. annoying

2. Which sentence best shows that Franklin is troubled about something?
   a. Benjamin Franklin had always endeavored to help people.
   b. His sigh was long and loud.
   c. Franklin looked up and was startled to see such concern for him expressed on the boy's face.
   d. "This wonderful food is all I need to get my thoughts straight."

3. Why does Franklin most likely believe he cannot stop the inevitable?
   a. He knows he cannot control the actions of a country as powerful as England.
   b. He knows he cannot persuade Thaddeus's family to sell the restaurant.
   c. He knows he does not have the respect of the colonists, so no one will listen to him.
   d. He thinks he is too old to make a difference.

4. How does Benjamin Franklin make Thaddeus feel?
   a. ashamed
   b. embarrassed
   c. important
   d. useless

5. Why does Thaddeus most likely want to help Benjamin Franklin?
   a. He is loyal to England.
   b. He wants to receive a good tip from Franklin.
   c. He owes Franklin a favor.
   d. He has great respect for Franklin.

Name_____

Forgiving

The bell rang to signal the beginning of lunch. Juanita rushed out of the classroom and headed straight for the library. There was no way she was going to eat in the cafeteria today. Not after what happened in class. She would be too embarrassed to face everyone so soon afterwards.

Juanita couldn't believe her luck. No one noticed she'd gone missing. Even the teachers, in their rush to have their own thirty-minute break, hadn't noticed she'd slipped away from the rest of the class. If her luck would only hold, she could slip past the eyes of Mrs. McGuire, the librarian, and hide out in the corner of the fiction section of books where there's a nice, minute cubbyhole just large enough for her to sit and go undetected.

It didn't take long for Juanita to solve her next dilemma. She waited for another student to reach the circulation desk and begin a conversation with Mrs. McGuire, and then she slipped past her eagle eyes and into the place she planned to spend the next thirty minutes. However, when she rounded the corner, she was shocked to see her entire class, including her teacher, standing in her way. They must have entered through the other set of double doors while Juanita was trying to sneak past the front desk.

"I can explain," Juanita's voice sounded worried even to her own ears.

"You don't need to," her teacher interrupted. "We are like a family, Juanita. Sometimes we do things we wish we hadn't done. Sometimes we get embarrassed. Sometimes we get upset. Sometimes we even make mistakes. But, what we don't do, what we never do, is not be there for each other." She smiled at Juanita, and all the other students began to cheer.

Juanita knew she would never forget today. No matter what happened from this point forward, she would always remember how kind everyone had treated her, and she hoped she could pay the kindness forward.

Text Questions

1. What has Juanita done that causes her to try and hide from the rest of her class?
   a. She made fun of some of her classmates as they were giving their speeches.
   b. She slipped and fell in front of the entire class.
   c. The passage never reveals what she has done.
   d. She was disrespectful to the teacher.

2. The first sentence in the second paragraph states that Juanita couldn't believe her luck. What does this expression refer to?
   a. Juanita was always winning contests.
   b. Juanita had earned a good grade in the class.
   c. Juanita was in class with many of her best friends.
   d. Juanita had slipped away without anyone seeing her.

3. The last sentence in the story states that Juanita hopes she can pay the kindness forward. What does this statement mean?
   a. She hopes one day she can be as kind to someone else as the class was to her.
   b. She hopes she can get enough money to give some to everyone in the class.
   c. She hopes to get a job after school.
   d. She hopes to complete volunteer hours at the school.

4. What does the phrase "eagle eyes" mean as it is used in the third paragraph, when the words are used to describe the librarian Mrs. McGuire?
   a. Mrs. McGuire has great eyesight and rarely misses seeing anything.
   b. Mrs. McGuire has eyes the color of an eagle.
   c. Mrs. McGuire has eyes that are set close together and look mean.
   d. Mrs. McGuire has golden-colored eyes.

5. List three things in sequential order that happen in the story.
   a. _____
   b. _____
   c. _____

Name_____

The Lucky Break

The ballgame was tied, and time was running out. Mark Thomas knew he would have to do something fast if the Ravens were going to beat their rivals, the Knights. He knew the coach was counting on him as quarterback to lead the team to victory. He only hoped he could make the right decision.

The crowds on both sides of the football field were all standing on their feet. With only one minute left, there was very little time for mistakes. The Ravens had the ball on their own ten-yard line, but they were also facing a fourth down. Normally, they would have brought in their kicker and scored the three points given from a field goal to take the lead. But last week's game had badly injured their field-goal kicker, and the coach couldn't be certain he was ready yet to kick the winning points. Instead, he was counting on Mark to throw the touchdown pass that would win the game and send the Ravens on to the playoffs.

Mark knew which play he was going to call. The team made a quick huddle and then broke up and walked to the line. Mark could see the defense adjusting to line up against their offense. As the play began, Mark could see it all happening in slow motion. The player he had planned to throw the ball to was being blocked by one of the Knights' defensive players. He glanced to his left and saw no help there. He swallowed the panic he was feeling and searched the field, looking for the answer in the play that was unfolding.

Then he saw it: a whole setup for him to run through. He abandoned the plan to throw for the winning touchdown and, instead, tucked the ball securely against him as he ran through the opening and crossed the line for the winning touchdown. The crowd went wild as the team scored and the clock ticked down until all the time was gone. The Ravens had won!

As everyone cheered Mark, he knew the moment he could talk, he would make sure everyone knew he had not won the game for the team. It took all the players to win. He had simply carried the ball for the entire team.

Text Questions

1. Which title would be a good alternative for this text?
   a. "The Last-Second Win"
   b. "The Boy Hero"
   c. "Winning Isn't Everything"
   d. "Hold Your Horses"

2. What can you conclude about Mark after reading the story?
   a. He is extremely self-centered.
   b. He is a team player.
   c. He loves receiving accolades.
   d. He is the best quarterback the Ravens have ever had.

3. Which paragraph best explains Mark's feelings about winning the game?
   a. second paragraph
   b. third paragraph
   c. fourth paragraph
   d. fifth paragraph

4. What is the main idea of this text?
   a. It often takes a team to be successful.
   b. One person can make all the difference.
   c. One person who is not a team player can ruin everything for everyone else.
   d. Everyone wants the chance to be a hero.

5. What does the word *abandoned* mean as it is used in the following sentence: "He abandoned the plan to throw for the winning touchdown and, instead, tucked the ball securely against him as he ran through the opening and crossed the line for the winning touchdown."
   a. gave up
   b. tried again
   c. remained
   d. explained

Name_____

Lost and Found

Meg couldn't find her phone anywhere. She knew her parents were going to be so upset with her. They hadn't wanted to buy her a phone for her birthday because they thought she wasn't responsible enough to keep up with one. But she had begged and pleaded and tried to convince them she was responsible until finally they had given in and purchased the phone for her.

Now, she knew she was proving them right.

She and her friends had been at the waterpark for only an hour when she realized her phone was nowhere to be found. She wanted to take pictures using the camera, but when she went to get her phone, it was gone. Despite her best search of the area, she couldn't find the phone anywhere.

Meg sat down on the chair beside the pool. She could feel the tears sliding down her cheeks. She hoped the others thought it was just water from the pool. She didn't want them to know she was crying.

Suddenly, she heard a familiar tune. The ring was coming from her phone, but where was it? She jumped up from the chair and began frantically searching through bags and under towels. When she looked up, a guy about her age was walking toward her with her phone in his hand and a grin on his face.

"I knew eventually I would find the owner this way. The relief that went across your face when you heard your ringtone was so obvious. I believe," the stranger said as he held out her phone, "that this belongs to you."

Meg couldn't stop grinning as he explained he worked at the snack bar and had found her phone there. She remembered now having it with her when she went to get a drink, but when she left, all she had in her hands was her purchase. Meg thanked him for finding her phone. She wasn't sure if she'd tell her parents about losing her phone, but she was definitely sure that she had learned a lesson about being responsible.

Text Questions

1. In what way is Meg irresponsible?
   a. She begs her parents for a phone for her birthday.
   b. She talks to strangers.
   c. She loses her cell phone.
   d. She cries when she can't find her phone.

2. Which of the following statements can be inferred about Meg once she has found her phone?
   a. She will most likely be more responsible.
   b. She will probably still continue to lose her things.
   c. She will probably have to get a new phone from her parents.
   d. She will probably keep asking her parents for new things.

3. Which sentence from the text helps you to explain your answer for question two?
   a. Meg couldn't stop grinning as he explained he worked at the snack bar and had found her phone there.
   b. She remembered now having it with her when she went to get a drink, but when she left, all she had in her hands was her purchase.
   c. Meg thanked him for finding her phone.
   d. She wasn't sure if she'd tell her parents about losing her phone, but she was definitely sure that she had learned a lesson about being responsible.

4. What is the main problem in the story?
   a. Meg wants her parents to buy her new things all the time.
   b. Meg is too scared to ask her friends for help.
   c. Meg cannot find her phone, even though she promised her parents she would be responsible if she had one.
   d. Meg is afraid of the water and will not do any of the activities at the water park.

5. Why does Meg most likely not want her friends to know she is crying?
   a. She doesn't want to be embarrassed.
   b. She doesn't want to upset them.
   c. She doesn't want everyone to look for her phone.
   d. She doesn't want her friends to see her not wearing her makeup.

Name_____

Don't Stop the Music

"What's wrong?" Kevin asked his sister Janelle as she stormed into the house, slamming the door behind her.

"Everything!"

"Can you be more specific?" Kevin tried to joke, but his sister was not in the mood to smile.

Janelle looked at him and rolled her eyes before answering. "They want to get rid of the band at our school to save money. I don't know what I'll do if that happens."

Kevin listened intently, surprised when he heard the news. The high school band was Janelle's life. She loved everything about it. He suddenly felt just as upset as his sister did.

"They can't do that," he protested.

Janelle poured herself a glass of tea from the kitchen refrigerator and then turned to face her brother. "Mom and Dad are going to a meeting tonight to see what can be done. Hopefully, they can get everyone to listen to how important the program is for so many students at our school."

There wasn't much else Kevin could do to help, but he hated seeing Janelle so sad. "Why don't we make some signs and posters to take to tonight's meeting, and then I can drive you over there tonight if you want to go."

Janelle smiled for the first time since she'd walked through the door. "That would be great, Kevin. At least then I know I'm doing something to help."

Kevin smiled back at Janelle. He knew what they were doing might not make a difference, but he would always be there for Janelle. He hoped, no matter how things turned out, that she knew that.

Text Questions

1. Which sentence best shows that Kevin wants to help his sister?
    a. "What's wrong?" Kevin asked his sister Janelle as she stormed into the house, slamming the door behind her.
    b. Kevin listened intently, surprised when he heard the news.
    c. "They can't do that," he protested.
    d. "Why don't we make some signs and posters to take to tonight's meeting, and then I can drive you over there tonight if you want to go."

2. Which title would be a good alternative for this text?
    a. "Stop, Look, and Listen"
    b. "Something Strange"
    c. "Let the Beat Go On"
    d. "Brothers and Sisters"

3. What can the reader infer about Kevin's relationship with his sister?
    a. They rarely get along.
    b. They care what happens to each other.
    c. They do not have much of a relationship.
    d. They do not go to the same schools.

4. From the story, what can the reader conclude will most likely happen to the band program?
    a. There is not enough information to know.
    b. The band program will most likely be canceled.
    c. The band program will most likely be saved.
    d. The students will have to change schools if they want to be in band.

5. What is the main idea of the last paragraph?
    a. Janelle can only rely on her brother for help.
    b. Janelle's brother will always try to help her if he can.
    c. Janelle is closer to her friends than to her family.
    d. Janelle does not want help from anyone.

Name_____

The Unexpected Gift

Max stood at the window, watching the taillights on his brother's car slowly disappear down the driveway. He stood by the window until he could no longer see them. His parents were both outside, still waving at his brother, even though he knew his brother was too far away to see them now. He couldn't believe that his brother had just left for college. In four years, it would be his turn, but that didn't matter right now. What mattered was that Camden was gone.

He turned away from the window and sighed. He and Camden had always been close despite the differences in their ages. Sure, Camden had given him the occasional hard time, but then that's what big brothers were supposed to do. But most of the time, his brother had always invited him along. Even when he was going to games or other events at the school or with his friends, he hadn't minded most of the time if Max came, too. He knew from talking to his friends that he was lucky to have a brother like Camden. And now, Camden was gone. Max knew Camden would come home and visit, and they'd talk all the time, but he also knew it would never be the same as it was.

As the door to the outside opened, and his parents came in, Max could hear his mother crying. His parents were going to miss Camden just as much as he was. He needed to remember that and try to be there for them, but right now, he just wanted a moment alone.

Opening the door to his room, he was surprised to see a package sitting on his bed. He went over and saw a card sticking out. He opened it and immediately recognized Camden's handwriting even with just the one word he'd written . . . *surprise*!

Max ripped into the paper and laughed out loud when he saw what it was. He ran downstairs to show his parents. Camden had written a manual on what they should do for the first ten days after he left so they wouldn't miss him so much. Max quickly saw that day one involved going to a movie and getting pizza and then calling Camden at least three times while they were out. Max was glad to see his parents were smiling as they left the house to begin enjoying the ideas Camden had given them.

Text Questions

1. Which adjective best describes Max and Camden's relationship?
   a. antagonistic
   b. bitter
   c. unusual
   d. friendly

2. Why is the gift Camden leaves so important to Max?
   a. Max has been wanting to go out and see a movie.
   b. Max now has a reason for his parents to give him some attention instead of his brother.
   c. Max sees that Camden knew they would miss him and was trying to be supportive of his family.
   d. Max knows Camden spends a lot of money on gifts for the family.

3. What can one infer about the relationship between Max and Camden?
   a. They will most likely remain close.
   b. They will most likely stop being close.
   c. They will most likely never speak to each other again.
   d. They will most likely remain close until Max goes to college.

4. Which paragraph best explains how Camden treated Max when he still lived at home?
   a. first paragraph
   b. second paragraph
   c. third paragraph
   d. fifth paragraph

5. Why does Max most likely want some time alone at first?
   a. so his parents won't see how upset he is
   b. so he can take a nap
   c. so he can talk on his phone without being interrupted
   d. so he doesn't have to talk to his mother

Name_____

Winter Blues

"I know we wanted some snow days, but this is ridiculous!" Todd Frank stood out in his yard and looked at the three feet of snow that blanketed the front area of his house. He and his friend, Paul, were out with their sleds, trying to find something new to do since they had been out of school now for two weeks due to the inclement weather.

"I know what you mean, Todd," Paul said. "At first, it was fun getting to sleep in late, drink lots of hot chocolate, and play in the snow. But now," he sighed, "well, I hate to admit it, but I'm starting to miss school."

Todd nodded in agreement. "Don't tell anyone, but I feel the same way. It's bad enough with me that I'm even starting to miss my teachers!"

Paul laughed and said, "Okay, I promise. I won't tell anyone you said that!"

The two boys kept walking, pulling Todd's sled behind them. "Maybe we could make some money while we're off school," Paul spoke up. "We could offer to take people's pets on sled rides for $1.00 each. Since people can't get out and walk their dogs, they might be willing to pay for them to ride."

Todd shook his head. "I don't think that's going to work, but it would be a good idea if we figured out a way to fight our boredom while making some money." Just then, Todd saw his neighbor Mr. Mundy shoveling the snow from his driveway. When he saw how hard the work was for his neighbor and how he had to keep stopping to rest between each shovel, both boys had the same idea at the same time.

Two hours later, when the driveway was shoveled and they had extra money in their pockets, they were both changing their minds about wishing the snow would go away.

Text Questions

1. What does the word *inclement* mean as it is used to describe the weather in the first paragraph?
   a. unfavorable
   b. favorable
   c. changeable
   d. unusual

2. What is the most likely reason the boys are starting to wish they could go back to school?
   a. They are getting bored.
   b. They are tired of being cold.
   c. They are wishing for summer.
   d. They want to have work to do.

3. What do the boys decide to do to help relieve their boredom?
   a. go skating
   b. get a job
   c. go back to school
   d. go take a nap

4. How does the reader know the boys took the job shoveling the driveway?
   a. The story states the driveway was shoveled and the boys now have money.
   b. The boys stated they shoveled the driveway to help their neighbor.
   c. The neighbor thanks the boys for doing such a nice job shoveling his driveway.
   d. The reader cannot determine if the boys did or did not shovel the neighbor's driveway.

5. Which part of the story helps you to explain your answer for question four?
   a. the title
   b. the introduction
   c. the body of the story
   d. the conclusion

Name_____

High in the Sky

The view from up above the treetops was unbelievable. Sandra smiled at her best friend. She could not believe they were both riding in a hot-air balloon, high above the treetops and the rooftops of all the buildings they could see.

Two weeks ago, Sandra had called in to a radio station, trying to win tickets to a concert. She didn't win the concert tickets, but instead was given the second-place prize, which included breakfast and two tickets to ride in a hot-air balloon. As she gazed in wonder at all they were seeing, she found it hard to believe that this prize was considered second place. It was amazing!

The hardest part about the entire experience had been trying to decide who she would invite. She didn't want to hurt any of her other friends' feelings, but when she really thought about it, she knew the choice was easy. She had to choose Theresa. They had been friends since kindergarten—long before she had met any of her other friends.

Sandra looked over at Theresa and could tell she was having a great time just like she was, when all of a sudden everything started to become blurry. Sandra could feel herself getting hotter and hotter as the heat rose from inside the balloon. Before she knew it, she felt her legs buckle underneath her, and she lost all consciousness. When she woke up, Theresa's concerned face was hovering over her as were the faces of the two men who had taken them out in the hot-air balloon. Sandra was shocked when she realized they were already on the ground. She must have been passed out longer than she realized.

"Are you okay?" Theresa asked.

"I guess I just got too hot," Sandra explained. "I can't believe I passed out and missed the landing!"

Theresa grinned, now that she knew Sandra was okay. "Don't worry," she said, holding up her phone, "I videoed the entire thing. Not only did we have a spectacular landing, but there's some great sleeping princess video that you aren't going to want to miss!"

Text Questions

1. Which title would be a good alternative for this text?
   a. "The Greatest Gift of All"
   b. "High, Higher, Highest"
   c. "Adventure in the Sky"
   d. "On the Ground"

2. List three things in sequential order that happen in the story.

   a. _____

   b. _____

   c. _____

3. Why does Sandra feel as if the prize was just as good as the first-place concert tickets?
   a. because she is having an amazing time
   b. because she loves traveling
   c. because she decided that she no longer liked the singer whose concert tickets she was trying to win
   d. because she did not have to spend any extra money

4. What does Theresa mean when she says she has a video of a sleeping princess?
   a. She has a video of Sandra before they arrived.
   b. She has a video of a cartoon about princesses.
   c. She has a video of Sandra when she was unconscious.
   d. She is only joking because she did not take any video.

5. Which part of the story best explains why Sandra passed out?
   a. the title
   b. the introduction
   c. the body
   d. the conclusion

Name_____

Unexpected Help

"I can't believe I have a flat tire!" Tom Shepherd looked at the front tire of his car and sighed. The last words his father had said to him before he left the house for school was to be sure to be careful with his car. He was only letting Tom borrow the Mustang because Tom's car was still in the shop. Now, he would have to call him to come and fix the tire. He knew his father wouldn't blame him for the flat tire, but he still dreaded making the call because something had happened to his father's vehicle while he had it.

"You need some help?" a man's voice brought Tom away from his musings. He looked up and saw his friend Jeff's father. He was looking at the tire and then at Tom.

Tom responded, "I was just about to call my dad, but I remembered he's in a meeting this afternoon. I'm not sure what to do next."

Jeff's dad nodded his head in understanding before speaking up. "I tell you what, Tom. I'm going to have to wait for Jeff for at least another hour while he gets

out of practice. Why don't we take this tire off and run it over to the tire shop and see what can be done."

Tom's eyes lit up with hope. It didn't take them long to remove the tire and throw it in the back of the truck. Once they arrived at the tire shop, Tom realized he knew the owner. He lived only a few houses down from where Tom lived. The owner of the shop quickly looked over the tire and assured Tom that he could remove the nail they had found and plug the tire. When he was finished with the repair, Tom pulled out his wallet, hoping he would have enough money to pay for the repairs.

"It's on the house," the man said, surprising Tom. "I just hope in the future, you'll bring me your business." Tom shook his hand and assured him he would definitely come again when he needed help. Jeff's dad drove Tom back to the school, and they had just finished putting the tire back on when Jeff came out of practice. Tom knew he could never have managed everything without such amazing, unexpected help.

Text Questions

1. Why does Tom most likely not want to call his father for help with the car?
   a. His father will be very disappointed in him.
   b. His father would never let him borrow his car again.
   c. His father would take away his privilege to drive.
   d. His father trusted him with the car, and Tom doesn't want to take it back to him with something wrong.

2. What does the word *musings* means as it is used in the second paragraph?
   a. thoughts
   b. lies
   c. rumors
   d. dreams

3. Which adjective best describes Tom?
   a. concerned
   b. irresponsible
   c. reckless
   d. euphoric

4. What is the main purpose of the first paragraph?
   a. to explain what has happened to the car
   b. to explain how Tom always gets what he wants from his parents
   c. to explain how Tom fixes the flat tire
   d. to explain what Tom will do once he gets home

5. What will Tom likely do in the future if he has a flat tire?
   a. He will call his father.
   b. He will take his car back to the same tire shop.
   c. He will call Jeff's father.
   d. He will stop driving.

Name_____

The Day Off

Devon had a huge chemistry test, but he had forgotten to study. He could not believe it was now time for bed, and he had not put any time into studying all the notes and study guides that he had in his binder.

He knew he should stay up late and study for at least an hour, but if his mother saw him studying, she would know he forgot, and he knew she would only be upset with him. He didn't want that either.

Devon sighed. He had spent the night helping his mother get ready for their yard sale for this weekend. It wasn't as if he had been playing games or watching television. They had both been working hard for hours. He knew his mother would have wanted him to study instead of working with her. None of this was her fault. He had just simply forgotten.

Devon didn't know if he would ever fall asleep; he was that worried, but the next morning, the sound of the alarm was loud in the small space of his bedroom. His hand reached out and smacked at the offending noisemaker, hoping to hit the snooze and gain a little more sleep. As he rolled over, he saw his chemistry book on the floor beside his bed. Reality came rushing back to him, and he sat up quickly. He definitely didn't have time for the snooze button. In fact, he needed to get ready as quickly as he could, so he could at least study a little bit this morning.

Just as Devon was about to go downstairs and get his breakfast, he heard his mother's voice hollering up the stairs for him to hurry down. He wondered what could be wrong this early in the morning. When he got down the stairs, his mother was looking at the television.

"You are not going to believe this, Devon. Something has happened with the water at your school. The news just reported it will be at least a day before everything is fixed, so you don't have to go to school today. Looks like you get to enjoy an unexpected day off!"

Devon couldn't believe his luck, but much to his mother's surprise, he didn't go back to bed. He decided not to waste another second. He opened his chemistry book and started to study.

Text Questions

1. What problem does Devon have?
   a. He is not prepared for school.
   b. He has no more time to help his mother.
   c. He cannot finish what needs to be done for the yard sale.
   d. He has failed his chemistry test.

2. Why does Devon believe he will have trouble falling asleep?
   a. He is worried about his mother.
   b. He is worried about his grades in school.
   c. He is worried about the test that he has the next day.
   d. He is worried about a disagreement that he had with his friends.

3. What will Devon most likely do with his unexpected free day?
   a. He will continue to help his mother get ready for the sale.
   b. He will study for his chemistry test.
   c. He will go back to bed and sleep.
   d. He will call his friends and hang out with them.

4. What does the story's title mean?
   a. Devon almost breaks his arm.
   b. Devon is lucky because his uncle gives him some money.
   c. Devon gets an extra day to study that he isn't expecting.
   d. Devon and his mother have won a large sum of money.

5. Why is school canceled for the day?
   a. There is a problem with the electricity.
   b. It is Saturday.
   c. There is a problem with the water line.
   d. School is canceled so Devon has more time to study.

Name_____

Tastes Like Chicken

Makenzie's mother was so excited they were eating at the newest restaurant in town. Ever since her mother and father had divorced, the two of them rarely ate out. They had to watch carefully the money they spent each week. However, tonight was a celebration. Makenzie's mom had received a promotion at her job and a gift certificate from her colleagues at work to go out and celebrate with her daughter. Both had been overwhelmed by the generosity of those working with her mother.

As the two sat down to eat, the waiter asked if they would like an appetizer. Makenzie's eyes roamed the menu, but nothing caught her eye. Makenzie's mother ordered a sampler platter for them to share, and she wondered what all would come with the appetizer since she hadn't seen the platter on the menu. She didn't have to wonder too long as the waiter brought a large dish to their table.

Makenzie's mother put two fried pieces of meat on her plate. She knew it wasn't chicken, but she did not know exactly what her mother was expecting her to try.

Trusting her mother, Makenzie bit into the tender, fried meat. It was delicious and tasted just like chicken. She quickly ate both pieces, hoping there would be more for her to try. She almost wished she hadn't even ordered a meal. She could make a meal off the appetizer since it was that good.

When the waiter came back to refill their drinks, he looked at Makenzie's plate and then at her as he spoke, "So, I see you really like frog legs; I've never tried them before, but I've been told our restaurant makes the best ones around."

Makenzie stared in horror at the remaining food on her plate and then at the waiter. She managed to nod her head but could not say anything. She looked up at her mother, but her mom looked just as shocked as she did.

Finally, Makenzie managed a smile as she picked up the remainder of the appetizer ready to take another bite. She might have been eating frog legs, but they tasted just like chicken.

Maybe new experiences weren't so bad after all.

Text Questions

1. Which title would be a good alternative for this text?
   a. "What Is It?"
   b. "Tasty New Treat"
   c. "Frogs, Toads, and Other Critters"
   d. "The Special Day"

2. Which paragraph best explains why Makenzie and her mother needed a special night out together?
   a. first paragraph
   b. second paragraph
   c. third paragraph
   d. fourth paragraph

3. Which sentence from the text helps you to explain your answer for question two?
   a. Ever since her mother and father had divorced, the two of them rarely ate out.
   b. Both had been overwhelmed by the generosity of those working with her mother.
   c. As the two sat down to eat, the waiter asked if they would like an appetizer.
   d. Trusting her mother, Makenzie bit into the tender, fried meat.

4. Which is a synonym for the word *celebration* as it is used in the first paragraph?
   a. ceremony
   b. gala
   c. coronation
   d. community

5. In the last line of the story—"maybe new experiences weren't so bad after all"—what might Makenzie be referring to besides eating new foods?
   a. learning to live with a new family situation
   b. learning to go to a new school
   c. learning to eat with chopsticks
   d. learning to speak Spanish

Name_____

Hoping for the Best

The sound from Miranda's alarm clock would not stop. Miranda reached over and hit the snooze button to stop the reverberations of the noise echoing in her room. The action brought her a few moments of peace and quiet.

On a normal day, Miranda jumped out of bed even before the alarm clock could ring. She did not mind getting up early; in fact, she loved morning because she could complete her two-mile run before most of her family was even beginning to stir. She ran every morning so she could be the best she could be. However, this morning was different. This morning, she was going to the doctor. She would find out whether the pain in her leg was something that could be easily healed or would stop her from doing the thing she loved most: running with the track team.

As the alarm rang out again, Miranda knew she could no longer stall. She cut off the offending noise and rose from her bed. She could hear her mother rattling pans down in the kitchen. She knew she was making her favorite breakfast of pancakes and bacon. Her mother always made her favorites whenever Miranda was facing a crisis, but she'd never faced anything like this before.

Sighing into the quiet of the room, she grimaced slightly as she placed her foot on the ground to stand up. The pain, which radiated down her right leg and just underneath her knee, was bad but not unbearable. Surely, Miranda thought, the injury would not be as bad as her overactive imagination had decided it would be.

She shook her head to clear her thoughts and readied herself to join her mother. As she walked into the kitchen, her mother smiled at her. Miranda instantly felt comforted. If nothing else, Miranda at least knew one thing was certain. She was not alone in this and that would make all the difference, no matter what the day brought.

Text Questions

1. Which adjective best describes Miranda?

   a. negative
   b. demure
   c. determined
   d. stubborn

2. Which paragraph from the text helps you to explain your answer for question one?

   a. first paragraph
   b. second paragraph
   c. third paragraph
   d. fourth paragraph

3. What is the title of the text "Hoping for the Best" most likely referring to?

   a. Miranda is hoping to make the track team at her school.
   b. Miranda is hoping to get good news from the doctor.
   c. Miranda is hoping her mother is making her favorite breakfast.
   d. Miranda is hoping she can have time to sleep longer.

4. Which word best describes Miranda's mother?

   a. supportive
   b. annoying
   c. frustrating
   d. manipulative

5. What does the word *radiated* mean as it is used in the fourth paragraph?

   a. glowed
   b. spread
   c. stopped
   d. tingled

Name_____

Not So Easy

Sarah had five dogs that she had to walk each day. She was paid by her neighbors to walk their dogs because most of them did not get home from work until very late. Sarah would go to their homes, one at a time, and then she would walk each dog for a short time before moving on to the next dog.

Normally, Sarah loved her job. In fact, she knew she would need all the money she could get with the plans she had for the future. When she graduated high school, she wanted to go to college and become a veterinarian. She knew it would take a lot of hard work and dedication, but she could not imagine a life in which she couldn't work with animals. She wanted to help any animal she ever saw that was hurt or in need. When she was little, she was always trying to put bandages on the arms and legs of her stuffed pets.

This afternoon, though, Sarah just couldn't enjoy her work. All of her friends were meeting at Charlie's Cheeseburger Palace, and she'd heard from her friend Claire that Tim was going to be there, too. Sarah had a crush on Tim and was jealous that everyone would be there, except her.

As Sarah arrived at the first house, inspiration struck! She would simply go to each house and get each dog and walk all the dogs at one time. That way, she could still complete her job, get paid, and still have time to go and meet her friends.

Thirty minutes later, Sarah knew the brilliant idea she'd had was not so brilliant after all. She was sitting on the curb of the road, desperately trying to untangle three different leashes. Two of the dogs would not stop growling at each other, and her arm was exhausted from trying to keep all the dogs walking and not running.

Sarah had learned an important lesson. There were no shortcuts in doing a good job. She would just have to go and meet her friends on another day.

Text Questions

1. Why does Sarah most likely work a job each day?
   a. She needs the money to eat out with her friends.
   b. She needs the money to save for college.
   c. She needs the money to pay her cell phone bill.
   d. She needs the money to save for a dog of her own.

2. Which line from the story best shows that Sarah always wanted to be a veterinarian?
   a. Sarah had five dogs that she had to walk each day.
   b. Normally, Sarah loved her job.
   c. She wanted to help any animal she ever saw that was hurt or in need.
   d. When she was little, she was always trying to put bandages on the arms and legs of her stuffed pets.

3. Which words best describe Sarah's new plan for walking the dogs?
   a. a big mistake
   b. a brilliant plan
   c. an ingenious idea
   d. a mistaken identity

4. What does the phrase "inspiration struck" mean as it is used in the fourth paragraph?
   a. Sarah was hit by a car.
   b. Sarah was afraid of lightning strikes.
   c. Sarah had a new idea.
   d. Sarah knew she needed to quit her job.

5. Based on the text, what will Sarah probably do next?
   a. She will quit her job.
   b. She will try again to walk all of the dogs at the same time.
   c. She will beg her parents to buy her a dog of her own.
   d. She will continue to walk the dogs the way she used to do the job.

Name_____

The Amazing Win

Mandy couldn't believe she was at the concert with her best friend, Tamara. The past two days had seemed like a dream. She had wanted so much to be able to go and see her favorite band who were coming to Nashville for one show only, but tickets had been much too expensive. She did not have the money to buy even one ticket, much less two so her best friend could go with her. Her mother had suggested she and Tamara try and win the tickets from the local radio station. The station was set to give away ten tickets.

Each afternoon, Mandy and Tamara would rush home from the high school and begin to listen to the radio, waiting for their chance to call in to win. They listened intently and tried calling but were never the winners. Eight tickets were quickly gone and eventually only two remained to be given away. They knew their chances were not good, but the two girls continued to try.

When the signal was given to call in for the last two tickets, both Mandy and Tamara quickly dialed the number. Mandy could not believe it when her phone began to dial and the radio station answered. She put the call on speaker, and both girls listened intently as the disc jockey asked a trivia question about the band that had to be answered before they could receive the coveted tickets. Both girls were so excited to have the chance to win the tickets, that when the question was asked, they froze. Neither could remember the correct answer to the question. Just then Mandy's mother walked into Mandy's room. She heard the question through the speaker and saw the girls' dilemma. Without missing a beat, she supplied the correct answer for Mandy to repeat. The tickets were theirs!

Mandy and Tamara screamed and ran over and hugged Mandy's mother, wondering out loud how she had known the answer. Mandy's mom laughed and assured the girls that all she had heard for an entire week was the two girls talking about the band. She had learned plenty about the group, but it was all thanks to their obsession.

Text Questions

1. Why is Mandy unable to get tickets to the concert?
   a. She has no way to get anywhere so she can purchase the tickets.
   b. She cannot afford the price of the tickets.
   c. Her mother will not let her go to the concert.
   d. She has no one to go with to the concert.

2. Why is the story titled "The Amazing Win?"
   a. because the mother knew the answer to the trivia question when the girls did not
   b. because Tamara was lucky to get through to the radio station
   c. because Mandy did not even try to win
   d. because none of the characters in the story had phones

3. Which is a synonym for the word *dilemma* as it is used in the third paragraph?
   a. moment   c. idea
   b. problem   d. memory

4. Which paragraph best explains how Mandy's mother was able to answer the trivia question?
   a. first paragraph   c. third paragraph
   b. second paragraph   d. fourth paragraph

5. Which sentence from the text helps you to explain your answer for question four?
   a. Each afternoon, Mandy and Tamara would rush home from the high school and begin to listen to the radio, waiting for their chance to call in to win.
   b. She heard the question through the speaker and saw the girls' dilemma.
   c. The tickets were theirs!
   d. Mandy's mom laughed and assured the girls that all she had heard for an entire week was the two girls talking about the band.

Name_____

The Unexpected Invitation

Sam was definitely nervous. It was his first day at a new school, and lunch was only thirty minutes away. For most people his age, lunch was the best part of the school day. Lunch involved time to talk with your friends, catch up on what everyone one is doing, and, of course, eat. Sam, however, didn't know anyone. When it came time to go to lunch, he knew he would have no idea where to sit or with whom to sit.

Sam knew he should be used to changing schools by now. His mother was in the military, so his family moved a lot. He had really liked his old school and hated leaving his two best friends. They still talked to each other through texting and emails, but it wasn't the same as getting to see them every day. He wondered how long they would stay friends. He didn't want to lose them as friends, but he knew it would be tough to stay close.

"I know this is hard on you," his mother had said as he got ready for school this morning, "and I'm really sorry you have to keep doing this." When Sam looked in her eyes, he saw the regret she felt at making the family move yet again, but he didn't want her to feel that way. She was the one who had things hard, not him. She had been ready to defend not just her family but her country. She never hesitated in her duty to serve others. Sam admired her so much. He hugged her and told her not to worry. He assured her he would be fine. He had wanted to mean it when he said the words, but there was still always this part of him that worried when they moved.

The lunch period came quickly and, as Sam stood up to walk to the cafeteria, a voice behind him said, "Excuse me." Sam turned around and realized the red-headed boy was talking to him. He was surrounded by a group of three boys and two girls. One of the girls spoke up, "Would you like to eat lunch with us?"

Sam looked at the faces of each person in the group and could tell they genuinely wanted him to join them for lunch. He smiled and nodded yes. The unexpected invitation was exactly what he needed.

Text Questions

1. Why does Sam feel guilty that he's worried about his day?
   a. because compared to what his mother does, he doesn't feel like he has that much to be worried about
   b. because he knows he always makes friends easily
   c. because he already has friends from his old school
   d. because he and his mother were arguing before he left the house

2. Which paragraph from the text helps you to explain your answer for question one?
   a. first paragraph
   b. second paragraph
   c. third paragraph
   d. fourth paragraph

3. What will most likely happen to Sam when he goes to lunch?
   a. The group will leave him and sit somewhere else.
   b. He will find a different group of friends and join them.
   c. He will become friends with the group that invited him to lunch.
   d. He will decide to sit by himself.

4. Why does Sam's family move a lot?
   a. Sam's father is in the military.
   b. Sam's family moves to be near other relatives.
   c. Sam's mother is in the military.
   d. Sam has been in some trouble at his old school and needs a fresh start.

5. Which title would be a good alternative for this text?
   a. "The New Beginning"
   b. "What's for Lunch?"
   c. "The Impossible Dream"
   d. "School Mania"

Name_____

Capturing the Moment

The sun was shining, and the water was just right. Mason couldn't believe he was at the beach. His entire life he had wanted to see the ocean. Up until now, he had only seen pictures of it or seen videos of it on television or the movies. Nothing compared to actually standing on the beach—his toes buried in the sand, the wind in his face, and the amazing smell of the ocean air. He was beginning to think he wouldn't mind it if they never went back home to Kentucky.

"Mason, come see what I found," his sister Lauren yelled.

Mason walked over to Lauren and saw the tiny seashell she was holding in the palm of her hands. The shell was white with swirls of purple. There was not a blemish anywhere on the surface. It was the smallest shell he had ever seen.

"That's really cool, Lauren. What are you going to do with it?"

"I wanted to take it home and show my friends, but I'm worried there might be a tiny creature inside. I wouldn't want to hurt it just because I thought it had a pretty house, so I am going to put it back in the water."

Mason knew how much Lauren wanted to save the shell. He could tell by the way she was looking at it so wistfully. Then he had an idea. "Hang on a minute, Lauren. Don't throw it back into the water just yet."

Mason ran over to the area where his mother and father were seated underneath a colorful umbrella. He dug inside one of the bags until he found what he was looking for and then hurried back over to meet his sister.

She grinned from ear to ear when she saw what he had brought. "Of course," she said, "that's a great idea!" Mason pulled out the camera and took a picture of Lauren with her shell. Then he took several close-up pictures so they could remember all the swirls of color on the shell before Lauren placed the perfect shell back into the water. By the smile on Lauren's face, he knew he had solved her problem. He just hoped pictures of the trip would be enough to remind him of how wonderful the beach really was.

Text Questions

1. Using information from the text, what type of relationship does Mason most likely have with his sister?
   a. a terrible relationship
   b. a caring relationship
   c. a tumultuous relationship
   d. a troubled relationship

2. What does the word *wistfully* mean as it is used in the sentence "He could tell by the way she was looking at it so wistfully"?
   a. longingly
   b. mournfully
   c. peacefully
   d. carefully

3. Why did Mason take a picture of the shell?
   a. So Lauren could always remember the moment.
   b. So Lauren could have a picture to look at so she could draw the shell.
   c. So he and Lauren could try out the family's new camera.
   d. So his parents would see him being nice to his sister.

4. Which part of the story lets the reader know that Mason had never seen the ocean before the trip described in the text?
   a. the title
   b. first paragraph
   c. the concluding paragraph
   d. none of the paragraphs

5. Which title would be a good alternative for this text?
   a. "Tiny Seashell"
   b. "Snapshots of the Sea"
   c. "Beach Memories"
   d. "How to Save Sea Creatures"

Name_____

Welcome Home

"Surprise!" Voices shouted at Missy as she walked through the front door of her house. She could not believe they were having a party for her. Her first thought was that it wasn't her birthday, but she knew why everyone was there before anyone even had to explain.

"We are so glad you are home from the hospital," her best friend, Tammy, began to explain. "Everyone just wanted to show you how glad we were that you were finally coming home."

Missy could only nod and smile. She knew if she tried to talk, she would start to cry. She was so happy to be home, and she was equally thrilled by the show of support from her friends and family. It hardly seemed possible that she had been in the hospital for over a month. Ever since the accident, she had trouble keeping up with the passing of time. Finally, after all the hugs and welcome-home greetings, Missy found herself standing beside Tammy. Tammy was the first to speak. "I am still so sorry about what happened."

"You don't have any reason to be sorry," Missy said, squeezing her best friend's hand.

"I just don't understand," Tammy began, "why you got hurt, and I didn't even have a scratch."

Missy thought back to the day they had been riding their bikes and a car had jumped a curb, hitting them both. Tammy had somehow managed to walk away from the accident, while Missy had ended up in the hospital with life-threatening injuries.

Missy smiled at Tammy. "I would never want anything to happen to you just like you never wanted anything to happen to me. The good news is, we are both here now, and we're both okay."

Tammy smiled back and then nodded to the front door. "Actually, we still have one little bit of good news to share." Missy looked through the open door and saw a big red bow wrapped around the handles of a brand-new bicycle. On the handle bars was a new helmet. The doctors credited her old one with saving her life. Missy could hardly wait to try out her welcome-home gift.

Text Questions ··

1. What emotion does Tammy feel about the accident?

   a. sadness

   b. guilt

   c. happiness

   d. frustration

2. Which sentence from the text helps you to explain your answer for question one?

   a. Voices shouted at Missy as she walked through the front door of her house.

   b. "Everyone just wanted to show you how glad we were that you were finally coming home."

   c. It hardly seemed possible that she had been in the hospital for over a month.

   d. "I just don't understand," Tammy began, "why you got hurt, and I didn't even have a scratch."

3. What will Missy most likely do with the new bicycle?

   a. Sell it because she will never want to ride again.

   b. Ride it as soon as she is able.

   c. Give it to Tammy.

   d. Give it to charity.

4. What can the reader determine about the relationship between Tammy and Missy?

   a. Since the accident, they are no longer friends.

   b. They are good friends.

   c. They became friends after the accident.

   d. They will never speak to each other again once the party is over.

5. Why is Missy unable to speak when she first arrives?

   a. Her vocal chords have been damaged in the accident.

   b. She is overcome with emotion.

   c. She does not want to talk to Tammy.

   d. She doesn't know why everyone is at her house.

Name_____

Howling in the Night

The noises from the woods came every evening without fail. Each night, at nine o'clock, Trey and his friends could hear howling from the woods that surrounded their neighborhood. Trey's best friend Donovan was convinced there were werewolves living in the area. Tonight, the boys were determined to find out what was going on.

"I told my parents we were playing video games all night," Marcus said to no one in particular.

"I wish we were playing games," Trey confessed to the group. "I'm a little worried about what we're going to find." Trey's flashlight shook in his hand, giving away just how nervous he was.

No one in the group made fun of him. They were all a bit scared, but they were also determined. "We all agreed we want to know where the noise is coming from," Marcus reminded them. "I'm tired of wondering if something is going to come out of the woods someday and grab my little sister. I know my parents don't think there's anything out there, but I want to know."

"At least we aren't trespassing," Donovan spoke up. "Trey's family owns all this land." The minute Donovan stopped speaking, a terrible howl ripped through the night. All three boys stopped in their tracks for just a minute before racing toward the noise. The sound was getting closer and closer, and the trio knew that at any moment they would finally know what was making the mysterious noises.

Trey was the first to stop in his track, and the other two boys were so close, they bumped into his back. "You've got to be kidding me!" All three boys laughed when they spotted the "werewolf" they had heard each night. A hound dog stood in the woods howling at the moon. The sound echoed through the woods, making it reverberate through the night, sounding louder and more mournful than any howl ever made by a dog.

"Who's up for some video games?" Marcus asked. All three boys raced him back to the house.

Text Questions

1. Which sentence helps show that Marcus is concerned about his family's safety?
   a. "I told my parents we were playing video games all night," Marcus said to no one in particular.
   b. "We all agreed we need to know where the noise is coming from," Marcus reminded them.
   c. "I'm tired of wondering if something is going to come out of the woods someday and grab my little sister."
   d. "Who's up for some video games?" Marcus asked. All three boys raced him back to the house.

2. Why do the boys think werewolves might be living in the woods?
   a. They found large paw prints in the neighborhood.
   b. They have heard unusually loud howling coming from the woods.
   c. They have found tufts of fur in a barbed-wire fence that edges the neighborhood.
   d. They saw a werewolf last week.

3. What is the problem in the story?
   a. The boys are lost in the woods.
   b. The boys believe there are werewolves near their neighborhood.
   c. The boys need to prove to each other how brave they are.
   d. The boys have to save Marcus's sister from a werewolf.

4. What does the word *trespassing* mean as it is used in the sentence, "At least we aren't trespassing"?
   a. taking a shortcut through someone's property
   b. being on someone's property without permission
   c. stealing from someone else's property
   d. vandalizing someone else's property

5. What do the three boys most likely do with the remainder of their night?
   a. play video games
   b. hunt for more werewolves
   c. tell their parents what happened
   d. call all their friends

Name_____

Dangerous Falls

Taye and Summer were enjoying their canoe ride. Summer had never been canoeing before, but she loved being on the water. Taye was experienced since he'd been several times with his family, so Summer knew she had an excellent guide for her first time out. All of their friends had taken one route on the river, but she and Taye had slipped away from the group and tried a different route. They were hoping to beat the group back and surprise them by being first.

Summer began to notice that the smooth and easy waters were starting to become a bit more turbulent. She also noticed that Taye was beginning to look a bit concerned, as the boat began to be moved by the rapidly flowing water. "Is everything all right?" she asked her guide as she sat up a bit straighter, trying to see what was ahead of them.

"I'm not sure," Taye admitted as he too looked ahead at the waters that were moving faster than normal. Summer and Taye heard the noise at the same time. The sound of rushing water was loud to their ears. They didn't have to see it to know what was coming. "There's a waterfall up ahead," Taye said to Summer,

even though she already knew what was coming. "You're going to have to paddle hard, if we're going to avoid this. Can you do it?" Summer nodded her head vigorously, even though she was suddenly terrified.

She and Taye worked hard to move the canoe away from the swiftly running stream, aiming the small boat for the nearby banks. At one point, Summer felt sure the pull of the water was about to take total control of the boat, but somehow she and Taye found the strength to guide the canoe near the edge. Summer looked up and saw a branch hanging over her head. She grabbed the branch and wrapped her feet around the seat in front of her so she would not be pulled from the boat. Then she used all of her strength to pull the boat along with her closer to the bank.

Finally, they were out of the dangerous water. Taye pulled the canoe to the side of the bank, and he and Summer walked along the edge to see the waterfall up ahead. When they both saw the huge drop-off, they knew they'd had a close call. It would be a long walk back, but they were safe, and that was what mattered.

Text Questions

1. What is the main problem in the story?
    a. Taye and Summer want to surprise the others by getting back first.
    b. Taye and Summer have taken a shortcut that is dangerous.
    c. Taye and Summer cannot get along with each other.
    d. Summer does not know how to guide a canoe.

2. How do Summer and Taye know they are in danger?
    a. The water begins moving swiftly.
    b. They hear the noise of the waterfall.
    c. The boat begins to be dragged by the swiftly moving current.
    d. all of the above

3. After reading the text, what can you determine about Summer?
    a. She thinks quickly in a crisis.
    b. She and Taye are best friends.
    c. She will never go canoeing again.
    d. She will blame Taye for everything that happened.

4. Which title would be a good alternative for this text?
    a. "Canoeing Fun"
    b. "Adventure Outdoors"
    c. "Just in Time"
    d. "Summer and Taye"

5. What lesson did Summer and Taye most likely learn from their experience?
    a. to never canoe again
    b. to always stay with the group
    c. to not choose each other as partners
    d. to canoe close to the bank

Name_____

The Walking Dead?

Rick slowed down for his friends to catch up. He didn't want to be by himself. It was starting to get dark, and he'd told his parents he'd be home before it did. The only way to make it in time was to take the shortcut, which was right through the middle of the cemetery.

Matthew and Phil caught up to Rick just as he opened the gate. "What are you doing?" Matthew asked.

"Taking the shortcut back. I can't be late."

"Just call your parents," Phil suggested.

"I can't. I forgot my phone, and I know you two don't have one yet, so it's either take the shortcut or we all get in trouble for being late."

None of the boys wanted that. They were all supposed to get to spend the night at Rick's house. They'd gone up to the park to play basketball for a while but had lost track of time. They knew, just like Rick did, that they'd promised they'd be back before dark. The two boys

reluctantly followed Rick into the cemetery. The creaking of the gate as it closed behind them made the boys walk faster.

Halfway through the cemetery, they heard a noise. It sounded as if someone was following them. They looked over their shoulders but saw nothing. No one wanted to admit he was scared, but it was obvious in the way each of them began to move more quickly.

The sound of footsteps grew louder, and the boys didn't even bother to pretend they weren't afraid. They took off running.

"There's the gate up ahead," Phil screamed as the three boys aimed for the exit, flinging open the gate and then slamming it behind them as they stood safely on the sidewalk and just across the street from Rick's house.

None of the boys saw the gray raccoon that watched them as they ran the rest of the way to Rick's front door.

Text Questions

1. Why do Rick and his friends decide to take the shortcut through the cemetery?
    a. They like doing daring things.
    b. They need a quicker route home.
    c. They want to see if they spot a ghost.
    d. They are lost.

2. List three things in sequential order that happen in the story.

    a. _____

    b. _____

    c. _____

3. Which adjective best describes how the boys feel about taking the shortcut through the cemetery?
    a. excited
    b. apprehensive
    c. sympathetic
    d. apathetic

4. What is most likely the cause of the mysterious noises in the cemetery?
    a. a spirit
    b. the caretaker
    c. an animal
    d. another boy

5. What will most likely happen the next time Rick promises his parents he will be home at a certain time?
    a. He will use the cemetery for a shortcut.
    b. He will remember to be on time.
    c. He will not go anywhere again.
    d. He will be late next time.

Name_____

The Noise Upstairs

It was the first time Bracey's parents had left her home alone for the night. She had assured them she was old enough to stay by herself, so they had finally agreed. Of course, before her parents had left for their date night, they had made sure Bracey had her phone charged and knew the numbers to call if she needed help. They also checked all the locks. Bracey had nodded and smiled through all of their instructions, determined she would not need to call them.

As darkness fell, Bracey admitted she wasn't as confident as she had been when her parents first left. She got up and made sure all the doors and windows were locked. She decided she would turn on the television so the house wasn't too quiet, but as she walked over to pick up the remote, she heard something. A noise upstairs stopped her in her tracks. She had never heard anything like it before. She didn't know what to do. Should she investigate the sound? Should she call for help? Should she go upstairs?

Bracey decided to sit beside the front door and wait. The noise continued. There was a *scratch, scratch,* *scratch, creak* sound that came every few minutes. Bracey stared up the steps, wondering what could be up there and hoping whatever it was didn't come down the stairs.

Finally, she heard the sound of her parents' car pulling into the driveway, their car lights flooding the windows of the house. Bracey jumped up and opened the door, trying to appear calm, even though her heart was racing.

"Did everything go okay?" her father asked. But before she could answer, he continued, "I wondered if that scraping noise would drive you crazy. I meant to warn you there was a branch that was scraping against the window upstairs. It's kept me awake the past two nights. I'm going to have to cut it down tomorrow. Did you notice it at all?"

Bracey couldn't believe the noise she had heard had been a branch brushing against an upstairs window, but she was so relieved that was all it had been.

She smiled as she answered her dad, "Just barely!"

Text Questions

1. Why do Bracey's parents check so many things before they leave?
   a. They have had several robberies in the past years.
   b. They were leaving too early for their reservation and needed to kill some time.
   c. They wanted to make sure everything was safe before they left Bracey.
   d. They wanted to test Bracey to see if she could handle things.

2. Why does Bracey most likely try to appear calm to her parents when she opens the front door, even though the text states that her heart was racing?
   a. She wanted her parents to be worried about her.
   b. She liked to always look her very best.
   c. She didn't want to worry her parents.
   d. She didn't know how else to act.

3. Why does Bracey most likely sit by the front door once she gets scared?
   a. She has nowhere else to sit.
   b. She is close to an exit from the house.
   c. She is closer to the telephone.
   d. She always sits in that spot.

4. What happens to make Bracey feel safer?
   a. She goes to investigate the noise.
   b. She calls the police.
   c. Her neighbor comes over and sits with her.
   d. Her parents arrive home.

5. Why does Bracey most likely tell her parents that she barely noticed the noise?
   a. She doesn't want them to think they can't leave her home alone again.
   b. She usually doesn't tell the truth.
   c. She didn't want them to ask her any questions.
   d. She really didn't notice the noise.

Name_____

Whitewater Rafting

The water rushed up to meet the boat. Michael could feel the raft slam down to meet the waves. He held on tightly to his oar, remembering all the instructions he had been given during the earlier training. He shouted in delight as the group hit the next set of rapids. Whitewater rafting was amazing!

Last week, his father surprised his family by telling them he had the money to take them on a weekend trip to go whitewater rafting. Michael's sister Tia had immediately agreed. Two years older than Michael, she was always ready to try anything. Even his mother had seemed excited about the family trip. Michael had agreed to go, but inside he had been nervous. He was glad he hadn't let his nerves stop him from trying. He was having a great time.

As the group hit a clear section of water, the guide let everyone out to swim. The cool water felt great, but Michael was ready to hit the rapids again. Before long, the group was climbing back into the raft, and they were off. The first set of rough water wasn't bad. Everyone did exactly as the guide instructed, and the

small craft dodged the worst of the tight places. The second set was where trouble started. Michael could feel the raft refusing to budge in the direction he tried to steer. Suddenly, they hit a rock, and Michael felt his body fly out of the raft. He plunged into the water and went under.

At first, he panicked. The icy-cold water that had felt good earlier now took his breath away. The words of his instructor began pouring through his head, and he calmed down. He felt as if he was right beside him, talking him through, telling him everything he needed to do. The next thing he knew, he was breaking the surface of the water, and strong hands were pulling him back in. As he landed in the safety of the raft, everyone was glad he was back in, but then they all started to laugh.

"What?" he asked the group looking at him.

"You never let go of our oar," his father pointed out. "Great job!"

Michael laughed, too. He guessed he had "held on" to everything the instructor had said.

Text Questions

1. Which adjective best describes Michael?

   a. daring   b. cautious   c. happy   d. flamboyant

2. Why is the family able to go on the trip?

   a. They have vacation time from school.
   b. They are taking a week-long trip before school starts.
   c. They take family trips every month.
   d. They have some extra money they can use for a weekend trip.

3. Based on information from the text, the next time Michael is invited to go whitewater rafting, what will he most likely do?

   a. He will likely go again.
   b. He will never go again.
   c. He will think of an excuse so he does not have to go again.
   d. He will go as long as he can bring his own oar.

4. Why is everyone staring at Michael when he is pulled back into the raft?

   a. They were worried he was dead.   c. He had mud all over him.
   b. He had been pulled back into a different raft.   d. He was still holding onto the oar.

5. Why does Michael most likely not tell the rest of his family that he is nervous about the trip?

   a. because everyone else is so excited about the trip
   b. because he is embarrassed that he feels nervous
   c. because he doesn't like to talk to his family
   d. because he is jealous of his sister

Name_____

The Haunted Woods

The campout had been Peter's idea, but he was beginning to regret it. All he had wanted to do was have some of his friends over for a campout in the back of his yard. He had never wanted to pitch the tent so far from the house, but Noah had insisted they were too close to the house. Before he knew what was happening, Noah had somehow convinced everyone to move the campsite to the woods. Peter would never admit it to the others, but he really didn't like the woods at night.

"Isn't this great?" Frank said to the group. "It's the first time our parents have agreed to let us camp in the backyard." All the other boys shouted in agreement except for Peter. Peter didn't want to stay there, but he would never admit that to the others. Everyone seemed to be having a good time, and Peter started to relax. Maybe this wasn't such a bad idea after all. The sound of a twig snapping stopped everyone's laughter. Three of the boys grabbed their flashlights and pointed the beams at the woods, but no one could see anything.

"Is anyone there?" Frank hollered out into the darkness, but no answer came. The boys decided it had been nothing and began to talk again when they heard another twig snap. This time, instead of turning on their flashlights, they all became quiet. They moved closer to each other, and everyone listened for any noises that might help them identify what was out there in the darkness of the woods.

Peter looked around at the group and somehow felt responsible. After all, it was his campout. Even if he hadn't wanted to come out into the woods, everyone was here because he had invited them. Before anyone could say anything to stop him, he grabbed his flashlight, turned the beam on high, and headed towards the sound of noise. The other boys watched, frozen, as he rushed into the woods and disappeared into the darkness. Then they all jumped up, ready to help, but before they could even gather their own flashlights, Peter came back to the camp, leading his dog Jackson by the collar. Jackson barked and bounded at the boys, licking them all in the face. Everyone agreed Jackson wasn't so scary when they could see him and not just hear him!

Text Questions

1. Which title would be a good alternative for this text?
   a. "The Twig in the Woods"
   b. "The Campout in the Forest"
   c. "Dogs in the Night"
   d. "Don't Make a Sound"

2. Why are most of the boys excited about camping out?
   a. It's the first time they've been allowed to camp away in the backyard.
   b. It's the first time they've all camped out together.
   c. It's the first time they've camped out all year.
   d. It's the first time Peter has been invited to camp out with everyone.

3. Which paragraph from the text helps you to explain your answer for question two?
   a. first paragraph
   b. second paragraph
   c. third paragraph
   d. fourth paragraph

4. Why does Peter feel it is his responsibility to find out what is making the noise?
   a. He invited everyone over to stay the night.
   b. He knows he is the bravest one in the group.
   c. He knows the woods better than anyone else.
   d. He knows his dog is making all the noise.

5. What is the main problem in the story?
   a. Peter doesn't want to camp near the woods.
   b. The boys hear an unidentified noise in the woods.
   c. None of the boys want to stay at the campsite.
   d. Jackson is lost, and no one can find him.

Name_____

Missing!

As the students entered the classroom, they could all tell something was wrong. Their teacher was crying. Paige Thomson was the first to ask if there was anything they could do.

"Everything is fine, Paige," Mrs. Williams tried to smile as she spoke. "I've just lost something that was very important to me, and I don't think I will be able to find it."

"What did you lose?" Clint Holloway asked. "Maybe we can help you look for it."

Mrs. Williams looked at their sincere faces and finally answered. "Well, I left an old newspaper on the corner of my desk. The newspaper belonged to my grandmother. The headline was about the assassination of President Kennedy. I had hoped to share the paper with you today in history class. The paper is old, but it is also special because I can remember my grandmother telling me the story of what all happened on that day.

She gave me the newspaper before she died, so it is something I have that belonged to her. When I came back from lunch, the newspaper was gone."

The other students looked at each other, wondering if one of them had taken the paper and hoping that no one would do something like that to the teacher. Everyone liked Mrs. Williams. No one in the room could imagine anyone wanting to upset her.

Trevor Simpkins spoke up for the entire class. "We'll help you look, Mrs. Williams. If we all work together, we're bound to find it."

Mrs. Williams smiled at the group of students. She knew they might not find the missing paper, but even if they didn't, she knew she should still feel very lucky. She had a group of students who genuinely cared about her and each other, and that was probably the best thing she could ever hope to find!

Text Questions

1. Why is the old newspaper so important to Mrs. Williams?
   a. She likes vintage things.
   b. Her grandmother gave her the newspaper.
   c. She collects old newspapers.
   d. She had not yet read the newspaper.

2. Which sentence best explains your answer for question one?
   a. As the students entered the classroom, they could all tell something was wrong.
   b. "I've just lost something that was very important to me, and I don't think I will be able to find it."
   c. "The newspaper belonged to my grandmother."
   d. "The paper is old, but it is also special because I can remember my grandmother telling me the story of what all happened on that day."

3. List three things in sequential order that happen in the story.

   a. _____

   b. _____

   c. _____

4. Why do the students most likely want to help Mrs. Williams?
   a. They won't have to start class if they are helping the teacher.
   b. They like the teacher and want to help her find the missing newspaper.
   c. They want to read the paper for themselves.
   d. They want to straighten up the classroom as they look for the paper.

5. What does Mrs. Williams realize is even more important than the missing newspaper?
   a. that she still has a job
   b. that no one took her purse
   c. that her students care about her and each other
   d. that her grandmother loved her

Name_____

Surprise Visitors

Mack and Marshall were twins. They did nearly everything together. Mack, however, would be the first to admit that Marshall was the more daring of the two. He liked to take risks, and he would try nearly anything; whereas, Mack was more reserved and careful with his decisions.

Each afternoon, when weather would permit, the two brothers would go hiking. After being in school all day, being able to go outside and do something was especially great. Their parents had warned them though about the dangers of wild animals. They were vigilant as they hiked and tried to do all the right things to keep each other safe. Unfortunately, one day, that wasn't enough as Mack and Marshall stumbled upon a black bear's cub. Immediately, the boys knew they were in trouble. If the mother bear were near, she would assume anything or anyone near her cub was a threat. She would not hesitate to attack.

Before the boys could retreat from the area, they heard the sounds of the mother bear approaching fast. Both boys froze, knowing they shouldn't run but desperately looking for somewhere to hide. At the last possible second, Mack pointed over the small cliff. It was risky, and he was afraid, but he knew he and Marshall couldn't stay there. Both boys scrambled down the side of the cliff and stood precariously on a small ledge that jutted out about five feet below them. They could hear the mother bear as she entered the area. Her paws moved restlessly at the ground, and she let out sounds of distress. It seemed to take forever before they finally heard the sounds of her retreating from the area, along with her small cub.

The two boys crawled back up from the ledge and both sat down for a minute to catch their breath. Mack used his cell phone to call his parents and ask them to bring the car and meet them at the road at the base of the trail. He didn't explain what had happened but simply said the two boys were too tired to hike the rest of the way home. With the way his heart was still racing, he knew that much was definitely true.

As the boys headed for the trail that would take them to the car, they made sure the bears' prints were going in an entirely different direction.

Text Questions

1. Which paragraph best describes the personalities of the two brothers?
   a. first paragraph
   b. second paragraph
   c. third paragraph
   d. none of the paragraphs

2. When Mack calls their parents, why does he most likely not tell them about the bears?
   a. He doesn't want them to come searching for the bears.
   b. He wants his parents to see they are safe before telling them about the bears.
   c. He doesn't like to tell his parents anything.
   d. He wants Marshall to tell the story to their parents.

3. What does the word *vigilant* mean as it is used in the second paragraph?
   a. watchful
   b. careless
   c. reckless
   d. afraid

4. What is the main problem in the story?
   a. The boys are forbidden by their parents to go hiking.
   b. The boys run into a black bear's cub while they are hiking.
   c. The boys are afraid to tell their parents what happened.
   d. The boys had a bad day at school and go hiking to forget what happened.

5. Why is it unusual that Mack made the decision for the twins to go down the cliff?
   a. Mack is the more reserved of the twins.
   b. Mack is afraid of heights.
   c. Mack is not good at making decisions.
   d. Mack loves bears and would not want to hide from them.

Name_____

Safe and Sound

Patricia's mom was just turning off the highway when they saw the man in front of them drop a small bag out of his car window. A small tail poked out of the opening. They watched as the bag tumbled down the slope and landed near the river. Something felt wrong about the situation, so the two decided to pull the car over and check things out.

As they got out of the car, they realized the hike down the bank was rocky. Patricia's mom was still wearing her heels from work, and there was no way she would be able to make the climb down the side of the hill. "Let me go, Mom," Patricia begged her mother as she pointed to her tennis shoes. "I can make the climb easily."

Her mother looked torn. She had a feeling she knew what was in the bag, and if they waited too long to retrieve it, it would be too late, but she didn't feel good about letting her daughter go down the hill alone. Her daughter's foot was much too small though for them to trade shoes, and the house was still too far away for her to go home and get a different pair of shoes. Reluctantly, she agreed to let Patricia make the climb

down but on one condition: "Don't open the bag until you bring it all the way up, and if you can't make the climb back up with the bag in your hand, then you'll just have to leave it behind for now until we can get your father and come back." Patricia agreed and made the climb down. It was easier than she thought because many of the rocks made steps where she could climb down. She grabbed the bag and thought she heard a sound from inside, but she had promised her mother she wouldn't look, so she began the climb back up. Again, the climb was made easier rather than harder by the placement of the rocks. She used them to guide herself quickly up the top of the hill.

When she reached the top, she handed the bag to her mother. Her mother untied the string, and just as she had suspected, inside was a small, gray kitten. The kitten looked none the worse for wear but extremely happy to be released from the bag.

Patricia looked at her mother with tears in her eyes. Her mother squeezed her tight and said, "Let's get our newest family member home."

Text Questions ....

1. Why is Patricia's mother torn about letting her daughter make the climb?
   a. She doesn't think Patricia is a good climber.
   b. She is worried about Patricia climbing down the hill by herself.
   c. She is worried Patricia will ruin her clothes.
   d. She wants to go straight home.

2. Why does Patricia's mother most likely let her go down the hill?
   a. She knows there is most likely an animal inside, and it will die if they don't release it soon.
   b. She thinks there is money in the bag, and it will make them all rich.
   c. She is nosy and wants to know what is in the bag.
   d. She knows Patricia likes to climb.

3. Which paragraph best explains the conditions Patricia's mother has set up before she will allow her daughter to climb down the embankment?
   a. first paragraph   c. third paragraph
   b. second paragraph   d. fourth paragraph

4. What type of relationship do Patricia and her mother most likely have?
   a. a difficult relationship   c. a sensitive relationship
   b. a trusting relationship   d. a fragile relationship

5. Which of the following statements from the text is a fact?
   a. "I can make the climb easily."   c. Something felt wrong about the situation.
   b. Inside was a small, gray kitten.   d. She had a feeling she knew what was in the bag.

Name_____

The Missing Party

Cade's class, for once, was in a hurry to get back inside from recess. The teacher had planned a party for everyone because they had been so good the last few weeks. Before they left, she had set out all the treats on a long table. He couldn't wait to get back and have a delicious snack and some extra free time with his classmates.

As the teacher gave the signal to go inside, everyone lined up. The others were just as excited as Cade. This would be the first party they had been given this school year. As they entered the classroom, everyone froze in their tracks. The table where all the party food had been before they had left for recess was empty! All that remained were a few crumbs.

"What happened?" Kaitlynn Jeffreys shouted to no one in particular.

All of the students began to mumble at once. Then they noticed the cutout paw prints on the floor. There was a trail of tiny gray prints leading away from the table and down the hall.

"It looks like a mouse has taken all of our food," their teacher declared. "We'd better follow those prints and go rescue our party before it's too late."

Excited now, the students lined up and began to follow the construction paper cutout paw prints out the door and down the hall. The prints took them all over the school and finally outside the library doors.

"Surprise!" shouted the librarian and her assistants as the class entered the room. There on two tables were all the treats for the party. Stuffed mice were sitting all around the food, and there were tons of books about mice placed all around the edges of the table. Cade couldn't wait to eat, but he also couldn't wait to check out one of the great-looking books the librarian had placed around the tables.

Text Questions

1. What is the main problem in the story?
   a. The treats have vanished from the classroom.
   b. The librarian has stolen all the food from the class.
   c. The teacher has decided the students no longer deserve a party.
   d. No one brought any food for the party.

2. Which of the following statements about the text is a fact?
   a. The food for the party is no longer in the classroom.
   b. The food looked delicious.
   c. The party day was the best day ever.
   d. The mice books were the best books in the library.

3. What will most likely happen next?
   a. The children will go looking for more food.
   b. The children will be upset because the librarian took their party.
   c. The children will enjoy the party and check out some books from the library.
   d. The children will take library books and hide them around the school.

4. Which adjective best describes how Cade feels by the end of the story?
   a. frustrated
   b. angry
   c. excited
   d. annoyed

5. Why has the teacher most likely moved the party to the library?
   a. The children will want to check out books as well as eat.
   b. The children have to get extra exercise looking for the party.
   c. The children won't eat in the classroom.
   d. She didn't mean to set up the party in the classroom originally.

Name_____

Flying High

The pilot's voice announced to the passengers that the plane would be landing soon and for everyone to fasten their seat belts. Rhonda could not believe the plane was already landing. She had been so nervous about her first time on an airplane. She was sure the trip would drag by, but she had loved flying, and the trip had gone so much quicker than she had expected. Her parents had been nervous, too. They had wanted Rhonda to have a chance to spend part of her summer with her grandparents, but they had been worried about putting her on a plane by herself. It had taken a lot of discussions to convince them to let her go, but eventually they had agreed. In just a few minutes, she would be with her grandparents, and she could tell them all about her first plane trip. She couldn't wait.

Rhonda looked out the window, and all of a sudden, she saw smoke coming from the side of the plane. Emergency signs began to flash, and the pilot's voice came across again, this time explaining to the passengers that they were having problems with one of the engines but that he would get them all safely on the ground. Rhonda looked around the plane and noticed several people looked worried. They were so close to landing, but she wondered if any of the other passengers had looked out their windows and seen the smoke.

Feeling more alone than she ever had, Rhonda closed her eyes tightly and began picturing her family and thinking about how much she loved them. The wheels making contact with the pavement startled her, and she opened her eyes to find they were safely on the ground. The plane eased to a stop, and the sign came on that everyone could safely remove their seat belts and stand up. All the passengers erupted in cheers for the crew that had brought them all safely to the ground.

Now that it was over, Rhonda was no longer afraid. Instead, she was thinking about how she would tell the story to her grandparents and how exciting her first plane flight had been. She also decided that when she called her parents, she wouldn't mention any of what had just happened. After all, she still had a return ticket that she wanted to use!

Text Questions

1. Why is the plane flight exciting to Rhonda?
   a. She has always loved planes.
   b. It is her first time flying.
   c. She loves to travel.
   d. She wants to be a pilot when she is older.

2. What is the main problem in the story?
   a. Rhonda's parents don't want her to go on the trip.
   b. Rhonda's grandparents want her to spend the summer with them.
   c. Rhonda does not want to leave all her friends for the summer.
   d. The plane has problems just as it is about to land.

3. Which paragraph best explains how Rhonda reacts to the pilot's announcement that there is a problem with the plane?
   a. first paragraph
   b. second paragraph
   c. third paragraph
   d. fourth paragraph

4. What will Rhonda most likely do when it is time to return home?
   a. have her parents drive her home
   b. refuse to go home
   c. use her return ticket and fly home
   d. ride a bus home

5. When does Rhonda first realize there is a problem with the plane?
   a. when the pilot makes the announcement
   b. when she sees some of the other passengers are upset
   c. when she sees smoke outside of her window
   d. She never realizes there is a problem.

Name_____

The Pilfered Pies

Deidre couldn't wait to get home. Her mother was preparing food for the town's bake sale, and she always let Deidre sample some of the food before she took the rest to the sale. Deidre's favorite thing to eat was her mother's apple pie. Her mother would cut up the pies and sell them by the slice, and she always saved at least one slice for Deidre and her father. No one made better pies than her mother. In fact, at the county fair, she always won the blue ribbon for her baking skills.

The smell of cinnamon greeted Deidre as she walked into the house. Already, her mouth was beginning to water. She hollered to let her mother know she was home from school, but she didn't hear any answer. She headed straight for the kitchen, assuming her mother would be in there finishing up her baking, but there was no sign of her mother there, either. Deidre looked around the kitchen and also realized there was no sign of her mother's apple pies. Her heart sank. What if her mother had forgotten to save her a piece? She had been thinking about that pie all day. Normally, she could simply go to the bake sale, but she couldn't this weekend because her father would be arriving any moment to pick her up. It was her weekend to spend time with her father.

Deidre went to her bedroom and finished packing her bag. She was just finishing when she heard the backdoor open and knew her mother was finally home. She went to the kitchen to say hello and, of course, to find out where her pie went. Deidre's mother smiled when she saw her. Before Deidre could ask about the pie, her mother opened the microwave and pulled out an entire pie. Deidre wondered why the pie had been in the microwave when they were always baked in the oven. Before she could ask, her mother explained. "The microwave seemed the best place to keep it fresh while I ran the other pies to the sale. I didn't want the cat to find your treat while I was gone."

"But, Mom," Deidre said, "there's an entire pie here, not just a slice like there usually is."

"I baked one for you to take with you and share."

Deidre really liked the way the mystery of the missing pie had been solved!

Text Questions

1. What does the phrase "her heart sank" mean as it is used in the second paragraph?
   a. Deidre was extremely happy.
   b. Deidre was very disappointed.
   c. Deidre was having problems with her heart.
   d. Deidre was nervous.

2. Why is Deidre anxious to get home?
   a. She wants to help with the bake sale.
   b. She needs to get ready for her weekend with her father.
   c. She can't wait to have some of her mother's apple pie.
   d. She has a lot of homework she needs to complete.

3. Which sentence helps prove that the pies Deidre's mother makes are very good?
   a. Deidre couldn't wait to get home.
   b. In fact, at the county fair, her mother always won the blue ribbon for her baking skills.
   c. The smell of cinnamon greeted Deidre as she walked in the house.
   d. What if her mother had forgotten to save her a piece?

4. What does the phrase "her mouth was beginning to water" mean in the second paragraph?
   a. She couldn't wait to taste the pie.
   b. She needed something to drink.
   c. She was extremely hungry.
   d. She was chewing a piece of gum.

5. Which adjective best describes Deidre's mother?
   a. selfish
   b. loving
   c. stubborn
   d. unforgiving

Name_____

The Guest

The students at Sycamore High School were gathered in the gym. During the middle of their first-period class, the principal had made an announcement for the teachers—they needed to assemble all the students in the gymnasium. Clint had not failed to notice his teacher looked as surprised as everyone else in the class. He also was sure she had not been expecting the announcement because she had been about to hand out a quiz for the class to take.

As they walked down the hall toward the gym, Clint looked around and noticed all the students seemed just as puzzled about what was going on as he did. He heard several teachers behind him whispering and realized with certainty that even the faculty didn't know why they were being asked to gather in the gym.

The students, despite their excitement of being out of class, were unusually quiet as they made their way to the gym. It was as if everyone realized there was about to be some major announcement. As the principal made her way to the microphone, an eerie silence descended on the room. The principal's voice reverberated across the room as she picked up the microphone and began to speak.

"Students, faculty, and staff, I know you are wondering why I have asked you all to join together in the gymnasium on a day when we did not have any planned activity." She paused for just a moment before continuing. "We have an unexpected guest at our school today, and I know that every student here will join with me in giving a round of applause to our surprise visitor. This person once attended Sycamore and is one of our school's most well-known graduates. Please give a round of applause for our governor."

Cheers erupted through the crowd before the principal could even finish giving his name, even though all the students knew who he was. Only last year, he had helped schools across the state receive special funding so every room had been supplied with much needed technology. All the parents might not agree on politics and opinions, but the students could all agree that they were proud that the man standing before them was a graduate of their school.

Text Questions

1. What unexpected event happened during the story?

   a. The students were called away from their classes to gather in the gymnasium.
   b. The students were called out of class to participate in a fire drill.
   c. The students were told they would have an early dismissal day.
   d. The students were excused from taking a test.

2. Why is the visitor special to the high school?

   a. He graduated from their high school.
   b. He lives near their high school.
   c. He has no affiliation with their high school.
   d. He was once a teacher at their high school.

3. Which statement is <u>not</u> a fact about the story?

   a. The students did not know why they were being called out of class.
   b. The teachers did not know why they were assembling in the gym.
   c. The principal did not know why they were having the unexpected assembly.
   d. The guest was a former student of the high school.

4. Why does Clint feel certain his teacher knew nothing about the assembly?

   a. She doesn't look surprised at the announcement.
   b. She was about to pass out a test to her class.
   c. She did not tell everyone about the assembly.
   d. She told the class she knew nothing about the assembly.

5. What might be one reason the principal did not tell the school about the unannounced guest?

   a. She might not have been certain he would be able to come if she announced it, due to his busy schedule.
   b. She wanted to keep the news all to herself.
   c. She was not certain how everyone in the school would react.
   d. She wanted to see how everyone would react.

Name_____

Ready, Set, Race!

"On your mark, get set, go!" The cry of the official set the race in motion. Six small cars built by six boys raced down the track to see which car would come in first place. David watched anxiously, hoping his creation would be first. He had worked for hours making sure the weight of the car would meet the specifications set forth in the rules. He had tires that rotated quickly, and as he raced his car in practice drills, the time was always better than last year's winner.

Trying not to be disappointed when his car took second place, he shook the hand of the winner, Thomas Mallory, and congratulated him on his car. His own father assuring him he had done a great job, offered up the hope that next year he would win the coveted first-place spot. David knew his father was right. There were many boys his age who had not made it to the final round. He knew he should be proud of what he had accomplished, but he had honestly expected to win first place, so he couldn't help but be disappointed.

After talking to his father, David went to the back room to retrieve all of his belongings from a storage locker.

They had at least a two-hour drive back home, and they needed to leave soon if they were to get home before it grew too late. As David opened his locker, he could hear voices talking on the other side of the room. He immediately recognized one as the voice of Thomas Mallory.

"I can't take this prize from David. He was a good sport about losing, but he deserves first place. The modifications I made to the car weren't legal. I am going to go and tell the judges right now. I just hope it's not too late and that David and his family are still here." David couldn't believe what he was hearing. He had won after all! His car had been the faster of the two if all of the rules had been followed. He felt bad for Thomas because he obviously felt guilty about what he had done, but he was glad he was going to tell the truth. David couldn't wait to see the look on his father's face when he told him what had happened.

He was still looking forward to trying again next year, but this year had just become a whole lot sweeter.

Text Questions

1. What is the main problem in the story?
   a. One of the contestants cheats at the race.
   b. One of the contestants ruins David's car.
   c. One of the contestants challenges David to a race.
   d. One of the contestants is unable to participate.

2. Which adjective best describes David's feelings about participating in the race before it began?
   a. confident
   b. nervous
   c. frustrated
   d. angry

3. Which adjective best describes David's feelings about the race after he lost to Thomas?
   a. confident
   b. nervous
   c. frustrated
   d. angry

4. Which paragraph best explains why David believed his car was the best of all the cars that were racing?
   a. first paragraph
   b. second paragraph
   c. third paragraph
   d. none of the paragraphs

5. Why does Thomas decide to confess to the judges?
   a. He knows David knows what he has done.
   b. He feels guilty about what he has done.
   c. He thinks someone saw him changing his car.
   d. His father makes him confess to the judges.

Name_____

The Fire

Janie had been having the strangest dream every night. Over and over, she dreamed there was a fire at her apartment complex. Each night when she had the dream, she would wake up and try to convince everyone to get out of their apartments, but no matter how hard she tried in the dream, she could never wake anyone up. She told her mother about the dream, but her mother told her that it was simply a dream and not to worry.

Exhaustion began to catch up with Janie. Because of the recurring nightmare, she had not been sleeping well. One afternoon, as she arrived home from school, she decided to take a nap on the couch rather than start her homework, which was her normal routine. She felt like she had only just closed her eyes when she smelled smoke. Even half asleep she knew it was just the dream seeming so real again and that she shouldn't worry, but she couldn't help it. She sat up from the couch and began screaming, "Fire!"

As she sat up, she realized there really was smoke just outside her window. She wasn't sleepy any longer. She jumped up and ran out to the balcony. Flames were coming from the apartment below her. Janie grabbed the telephone and dialed for help as she ran outside and began knocking on everyone's doors, urging them to get outside quickly. Unlike in her dream, this time people listened as Janie ran up and down the apartment complex warning people to get out.

The sound of alarms coming down the street was like music to Janie's ears. The fire trucks arrived and began to immediately work on putting out the flames.

Janie's mother pulled into the parking lot at that exact minute. She spied Janie standing outside and rushed to her.

"It wasn't exactly like my dreams," she told her mother, "but it was close enough that I knew what needed to be done."

"You are a true hero," her mother said. "I'm so proud of you." Then her mother added with a smile, "But from now on, I only want you dreaming about happy things."

Text Questions

1. Which event is different in Janie's dream and what actually happened?

   a. In her dream, the entire apartment complex burned to the ground.
   b. In her dream, no one will wake up when she warns them about the fire.
   c. In her dream, the fire department will not answer her emergency call.
   d. In her dream, her mother is trapped in the apartment.

2. Why does Janie fall asleep in the middle of the afternoon?

   a. She is tired because she hasn't been sleeping well at night.
   b. She is hoping to have the dream again.
   c. She likes sleeping on the couch better than sleeping in her bed.
   d. She falls asleep while she is doing her homework.

3. Which title would be a good alternative for this text?

   a. "The Premonition"
   b. "Out of Time"
   c. "Listen"
   d. "Something to Remember"

4. Which paragraph best describes Janie's recurring dream?

   a. first paragraph
   b. second paragraph
   c. third paragraph
   d. none of the paragraphs

5. In the second paragraph, what does it mean when the text states that Janie plans to do something other than her "normal routine"?

   a. She plans to do exactly what she does every day.
   b. She plans to do something different than what she does every day.
   c. She plans to begin a regular routine each day.
   d. She plans to invite friends over to help her.

Name_____

The Best Wish

The candle blew out on her birthday cake with one quick breath. Olivia watched as sparks whirled from the candle and went up in the air. It was almost as if the wish itself were being carried up and away. Olivia wished it really were something special happening. Her wish had not been a selfish one. She had wished her grandmother would be well enough to come home from the hospital and be with their family again. She had lived with them for the past three years, and Olivia missed her so much.

Olivia's mother cut the cake into several slices and began placing each piece on a small dessert plate. Her father put ice cream beside each piece and then helped to pass out plates to all the guests. Olivia took the first bite of cake. The chocolate cake was delicious. She was just about to take a second bite when the phone rang.

Olivia watched her mother answer the phone. She couldn't hear the conversation, but she could tell by the smile on her mother's face that something good had happened. When her mother hung up the phone, she told everyone she had some good news. The hospital had just called, and Olivia's grandmother had made a sudden and remarkable improvement. She was so good, in fact, that she could be dismissed from the hospital the minute they could get there to sign the papers.

Everyone burst into instant chatter at the good news. Olivia hugged her mother, and the guests all agreed that they should go immediately to bring her back home.

Olivia's mother looked at her right before she was ready to leave and then said, "Olivia, you don't look as surprised as everyone else about the news. Did you know something the rest of us didn't know?"

"Mom, I know this sounds crazy, but when I made my birthday wish, it felt like something magical happened. I wished for grandmother to get better and for her to come home. I think the wish really worked."

"You know what, Olivia," her mother said as she gave her one last hug, "I think you're right, and I think you just got the very best present of all!"

Text Questions

1. Which adjective best describes Olivia's birthday wish?
   a. hopeful
   b. pessimistic
   c. ridiculous
   d. surprising

2. Which paragraph best describes the relationship Olivia has with her grandmother?
   a. first paragraph
   b. second paragraph
   c. third paragraph
   d. fourth paragraph

3. What special event happens during the middle of the birthday party?
   a. The family receives a call from the hospital.
   b. Olivia receives a special gift from her parents.
   c. The lights go out in the middle of the party.
   d. Olivia tells her parents she thinks her grandmother will get to come home soon.

4. What will Olivia most likely do on her next birthday?
   a. She will think very carefully before she makes her wish.
   b. She will not make a wish at all.
   c. She will wish for something she didn't get on her last birthday.
   d. She will do nothing special.

5. Which title would be a good alternative for this text?
   a. "The Magical Wish"
   b. "Selfish Wishes"
   c. "Watch What You Wish For"
   d. "Happy Birthday"

Name_____

Catch Us If You Can

Chloe and Kayla Beth were waiting patiently for night to fall. They wanted to catch the fairies making the ring on their lawn. Their parents refused to believe in fairies, but Chloe and Kayla Beth knew they were there.

One night, Chloe had an idea. "Let's go out before it gets dark. We will hide so the fairies don't know we are there. Then we will take pictures of them so we can prove to Mom and Dad that they really exist."

Kayla Beth agreed it was a good plan. The hardest part, she told Chloe, would be finding a night when they could sneak out without worrying their parents. Luck was with them just a week later, when their parents decided to go out to eat. They invited the girls to go, too, but they both told their parents they should go and have a date night without them.

The minute their parents were out of sight, the two girls dressed all in black. They headed out in the direction where they knew the ring would appear. They hid behind a large tree, which had fallen onto the ground, and they waited.

When darkness fell, the fairies came out to play. At first, Chloe and Kayla Beth were so captivated by the sight that they forgot about taking pictures. At the last minute, Kayla Beth remembered her camera and began taking picture after picture. When the fairies finally disappeared, the two sisters ran from their hiding place and through the front door. They wanted to look at the pictures but knew they had precious little time to change and get ready for bed before their parents arrived home.

The minute they were both in their pajamas, Kayla Beth brought the camera over to Chloe's room. They anxiously waited to see the first picture.

"There's nothing there!" Chloe cried in dismay when she saw the pictures showed nothing except the backyard. In each photograph they took, there were no fairies to be found. Kayla Beth and Chloe were so disappointed, they went straight to bed. If they had only looked outside the window, they would have seen two little fairies laughing.

Text Questions

1. What is the problem in the story?
   a. The sisters claim to see fairies, but their parents won't believe them.
   b. The sisters want their parents to have a night out without them.
   c. The sisters forget to take their camera when they see the fairies.
   d. The sisters see strange things each night in their backyard.

2. Why do Chloe and Kayla Beth want to go out at night?
   a. Night is when the fairies come out to play.
   b. They have school during the day.
   c. They think hunting fairies will be more fun at night.
   d. Their parents suggested night would be a better time to go.

3. Why do the girls want to be in bed before their parents get home?
   a. They want to be asleep before they arrive.
   b. They don't want their parents to know what they were doing while they were gone.
   c. Their parents told them a certain time to be in bed.
   d. They are very tired.

4. At the end of the story, why are the fairies laughing?
   a. They know the pictures won't show any fairies.
   b. They think the girls' pajamas have funny designs.
   c. They know the girls are about to get in trouble with their parents.
   d. They laugh all the time.

5. Which title would be a good alternative for this text?
   a. "Now You See Us; Now You Don't"
   b. "Lights Out"
   c. "In the Dark"
   d. "Fairy Tricks"

Name_____

The Stranger's Gift

When Rose was born, she was a very lucky baby. Her father had once saved a little, old lady from drowning. When she was safe on land, she told the stranger that she had magical powers. She assured him that he would someday have a daughter, and when he did, she would come and grant the baby one special wish. Until that time, he was to think very carefully on what he would want to wish for his child.

On the day of his child's birth, he knew she would show up. Sure enough, just before sunset, there was a knock at the door. When he opened the door, the old woman who he had saved stood on his doorstep. "You have a daughter?" she questioned, and he nodded yes.

"Then it is time." The old lady went into the room and stood over the crib of the sleeping newborn. She smiled when she looked at the innocent child. Then she turned to the man and said, "What have you decided on as your wish?"

The man had spent more time worrying about the wish than enjoying the idea of the wish. He knew that wishes could go horribly wrong. One only had to remember the story of King Midas to know that even riches couldn't bring a person happiness.

So with the love of a father, he told the woman he wished she would take her wish and go away. He told her that he had a loving wife and a beautiful new daughter and that he was happy and needed nothing her wishes could bring. All of his wishes had already come true.

The old woman's face broke into a huge grin. She congratulated the man on his wisdom and left the house. As she walked away, she touched a small plant growing at the edge of the yard. Her touch turned it into a beautiful rose bush that was meant to remind the man of his wise decision. Seeing the magical bush blooming in his yard, he knew at least one other problem had been solved this night.

They would name their daughter Rose.

Text Questions

1. Which is a synonym for the word *magical* as it is used in the first paragraph?

   a. horrible
   b. mysterious
   c. unusual
   d. harmful

2. Why does the man not make a wish for his daughter?

   a. He is worried the wish may do more harm than good.
   b. He cannot decide what to wish for.
   c. He had forgotten all about the wish.
   d. He can no longer receive the wish.

3. Which adjective best describes the man's feelings for his new daughter?

   a. protective
   b. insecure
   c. vengeful
   d. resentful

4. Which paragraph best describes how the man has felt about the wish since he was told he'd receive one?

   a. second paragraph
   b. third paragraph
   c. fourth paragraph
   d. none of the paragraphs

5. Why does the woman leave a rose bush blooming in the family's yard?

   a. so he will never forget the wisdom of his decision
   b. so he can always have a fresh bouquet of roses
   c. so he will name his daughter Rose
   d. so he will remember her name was Rose

Name_____

Good Witch, Bad Witch

Sahara was a good witch. She had been raised by two parents who taught her that magic should only be used to help others, so she had spent her life trying to do just that. Unfortunately, not all witches were raised the same as Sahara. In fact, her stepsister Merrell was a witch, and she wasn't very nice at all. Merrell often used her special abilities to play mean jokes on people or to get her way. Sahara tried to go behind Merrell and fix the bad things she had done, but sometimes she was too late, and sometimes she didn't know what all Merrell had done.

Most weekends Merrell was at her mother's, and she and Sahara rarely had to see each other at home, but both girls attended the same school during the day. It was impossible for Sahara to avoid her stepsister all of the time.

Today was one of the days Merrell seemed intent on making everyone's life miserable. She had already made two students drop their lunch trays, and she had

made one student fall. Sahara had sat still long enough. She was ready to challenge Merrell if that was what was needed to get her to stop being so mean.

Just when it looked as if Merrell was about to pull another mean trick on an unsuspecting student, Principal Saunders walked into the room. He took one look at Merrell and seemed to know exactly what she was up to. He smiled at the young witch and motioned for her to follow him. Merrell's smile was wicked, like she was about to play a trick on him, but Sahara saw him shake his head back and forth, and then she watched Merrell frown. Whatever trick she was trying, the trick was not working on the principal. He turned and winked at Sahara and then walked over and removed Merrell from the room.

Sahara wasn't sure what powers Principal Saunders had that could stop Merrell in her tracks, but it really didn't matter. What did matter was that, in her book, he was totally awesome.

Text Questions

1. Which adjective best describes Sahara?
   a. kind
   b. cruel
   c. mysterious
   d. flashy

2. Why is Merrell most likely so different from Sahara?
   a. They were raised by different parents.
   b. They try to be different, so people won't get them confused.
   c. Merrell is trying to become more like Sahara.
   d. Sahara is trying to become more like Merrell

3. What is most likely true about Principal Saunders?
   a. He heard from someone that Merrell was causing problems.
   b. He has some type of magical powers.
   c. He is a friend of Sahara's father.
   d. He is going to be fired as principal.

4. Which paragraph best describes Merrell's personality?
   a. first paragraph
   b. second paragraph
   c. third paragraph
   d. none of the paragraphs

5. What does the word *unsuspecting* mean as it is used in the fourth paragraph?
   a. wary
   b. careful
   c. naive
   d. watchful

Name_____

Mermaids?

Irene often swam in the ocean just as the sun would begin to set. Her parents did not like her to swim alone, so she would invite her friend Ann to join her. The two girls loved how the sun looked as if it touched the ocean right as it set for the evening. There seemed to be something magical about the world at that time of day.

One evening, as the girls were swimming and watching the sun begin to set, they heard a large splash. They both turned and thought they saw the tail of a huge fish dip below the water. Ann told Irene the scales looked as if they had all the colors of the rainbow. Irene assured Ann it was probably just the setting sun playing tricks on her eyes, but she too had seen something in the water.

The next night, the girls were especially watchful as the sun began to set, but this time they were both watching the water rather than the quickly setting sun.

Splash! They both heard the noise at the same time. Imagine their surprise when they turned and there in the water was a girl who was half fish and half girl. She was, in fact, a mermaid. Ann and Irene were so stunned, they couldn't even think of what to say. The mermaid flipped her tail and made water splash on both the girls. She smiled and then swam away.

Night after night, the two girls returned to the ocean, always at sunset, always hoping to catch a glimpse of the mermaid they both knew they had seen. They told their parents, but no one believed them. No matter how many times they went back to the ocean, the mermaid never returned, and after awhile both girls began to believe they had dreamed the entire thing.

As the girls grew older, they had two daughters of their own. The daughters became best friends and loved to swim in the ocean right as the sun was setting. The two girls ran home one night to tell their mothers a most unusual story. They claimed they had seen a mermaid swimming in the ocean. Imagine the girls' surprise when their mothers believed them!

Text Questions

1. Why is this text considered a fantasy?
   a. because the girls go swimming in the ocean
   b. because the girls think swimming at night is magical
   c. because the girls see a mermaid
   d. because the girls think the sun looks as if it touches the ocean each night

2. List three things in sequential order that happen in the story.
   a. _____
   b. _____
   c. _____

3. Why is there most likely a question mark at the end of the title?
   a. because there are no such things as mermaids
   b. because after awhile the girls were not sure if they saw a mermaid or not
   c. because the author could not decide if the title was a good title or not
   d. because titles need end punctuation

4. What special connection do the mothers and daughters share?
   a. They all like to swim.
   b. They all live near the ocean.
   c. They all believe they saw a mermaid.
   d. They all like to watch the sun setting at night.

5. The word *splash* is an example of what type of figurative language?
   a. onomatopoeia
   b. metaphor
   c. personification
   d. simile

Name_____

A Night for a Knight

Mack loved stories about knights and dragons and castles and kings. He wished he could be a brave knight like the ones in his book. He searched the pages of the storybook, rubbing his hands across the pages. Suddenly, he felt something pulling at his hands. All of a sudden, he was falling into the book.

When he opened his eyes, he was no longer sitting in the safety of his room. He was in the middle of a field wearing shiny silver armor. He held a sword in one hand and a shield in the other. He could not believe it; he was a knight! He had little time to adjust to the idea because he felt something breathing near his neck. He looked around and saw a huge, brown horse nudging him with its nose. Mack felt as if the horse was trying to get his attention. Then the horse let out a loud noise and stomped its hoof. Mack looked up just in time to see a dragon in the sky swooping to attack. Fire was aimed straight at Mack, and he was able to hold up his shield just in time to protect himself. He knew he would owe the horse at least five good apples later for saving his life, but right now he still wasn't safe.

Mack knew he had always wanted to be a knight, but now that he was one, he didn't know how good he was with his sword. Would he be able to beat the dragon? The dragon landed on the ground and circled Mack. Mack kept turning to keep his shield between himself and the fire-breathing beast. Suddenly, the dragon attacked. Mack threw up his shield and stabbed with his sword. Mack fought the dragon until his arm felt heavy and tired. He didn't know how much longer he could go on, when suddenly he felt his sword pierce the scaled flesh of the beast. Then he felt himself falling and falling. When he landed, he was back in his room. His knight's clothes were gone, and he was back in his bed with his book.

He looked at the pages of the book and saw the horse that had saved him. He could have sworn it winked at him. When he turned the page, he saw the dragon was no more and the castle was safe.

Text Questions

1. What type of words are *knight* and *night*?

   a. synonyms
   b. homonyms
   c. antonyms
   d. affixes

2. How does the horse save Mack?

   a. He gives him time to use his shield as protection.
   b. He pushes Mack out of the way.
   c. He rides Mack away and off to a safer place.
   d. He shields Mack from the dragon.

3. At first, how does Mack feel about being a knight?

   a. surprised
   b. terrified
   c. afraid
   d. nervous

4. Which paragraph from the text helps you to explain your answer for question three?

   a. first paragraph
   b. second paragraph
   c. third paragraph
   d. none of the paragraphs

5. Which adjective best describes a knight?

   a. handsome
   b. brave
   c. cowardly
   d. friendly

Name_____

The Last of the Unicorns

The small animal hid, frightened and alone. The unicorn was the last of his kind. Hunters were fast on his trail, and he had no idea where to go for help. All he knew was he could not run much longer. He was growing weaker by the moment, but if he gave up now, he knew he would die.

Hiding for the moment behind a large tree, the unicorn looked up, startled to see a small gnome sitting on the branch of the tree. He didn't know if he could communicate with the gnome, but he knew he had to try.

The gnome's eyes lit up with excitement when he realized he could understand the unicorn. He could feel all of his sorrow and all of his fear. He knew, without a doubt, that he could not let the hunters find the unicorn. Even if it cost him his own life, he vowed to the unicorn he would do everything he could to protect the majestic and magical beast.

Quickly and quietly, the gnome led the unicorn deeper into the woods. They covered their trail using magic dust so the hunters would be confused and unable to follow. They ran for days, resting only very little until they came to a huge waterfall. The gnome had heard stories that the place inside the forest existed, but he had never been brave enough to travel the great distance to find out if the stories were true. When he saw the waterfall, he hugged the neck of the unicorn and whispered in his ear that they had finally arrived.

The unicorn bent down on one knee, and motioned for the gnome to climb onto his back. He held on tight as they raced through the waterfall and came out on the other side.

The land that greeted them was magical indeed. The gnome knew he would never want to leave, and he was especially sure the unicorn would not want to go either, for there in a field just off to their left was a herd of unicorns.

Text Questions

1. Which statement is a fact about the story?
   a. Unicorns are the most beautiful of all magical creatures.
   b. The gnome agreed to protect the unicorn.
   c. The magical land behind the waterfall was the prettiest place in the world.
   d. Everyone loves stories that have a gnome as a main character.

2. List three things in sequential order that happen in the story.

   a. _____

   b. _____

   c. _____

3. What does the unicorn learn once he enters the land behind the waterfall?
   a. He is not the last unicorn.   c. He and the gnome will be friends forever.
   b. He can swim.   d. He does not have to hide anymore.

4. Which paragraph best explains the gnome's commitment to the unicorn?
   a. first paragraph   c. third paragraph
   b. second paragraph   d. none of the paragraphs

5. Who knew about the magical land hidden behind the waterfall?
   a. the hunters
   b. the unicorn
   c. the gnome
   d. No one knew about it; they simply stumbled across the magical place.

Name_____

The Book of Spells

Cameron's job was to find the book of spells and to destroy it. He had been scouring the countryside for days, following different leads. Some had led him closer to the book, while others had simply been false clues given by those hoping to keep him away from the book. Little did they know, Cameron had some help of his own that would offer him much needed assistance in finding the book. He had a magical compass given to him by none other than Merlin.

Merlin needed the book of spells destroyed. He had warned Cameron over and over again that the spells inside the book were to be used only to help the side of evil. The book could not be altered or changed for good. Merlin had convinced Cameron that the only way to save innocent people from the wicked spells inside the book was to destroy it.

Cameron used his compass to help guide him, but even the compass was not always perfect. Finally, though, Cameron was convinced he was in the right place at the right time. The compass was going crazy, pointing north and then twirling in circles faster and faster. He was certain the book was inside the building he was about to enter. He withdrew his sword from its sheath and prepared to enter the building.

The minute he walked in, he could feel the power of the book calling him. He could almost believe the book was saying his name, begging him to read its text and to save it. Cameron, however, had one more trick up his sleeve. Having been forewarned by Merlin, he knew exactly what to do. He placed two small wads of fabric in his ears to block out the pleas of the magical book. He raised his wand over the cover and repeated the words Merlin had told him to say.

Within seconds, the noises in his head cleared, and the book was gone. Cameron left the room, exhausted but relieved, and began the long journey home to tell Merlin the good news.

Text Questions

1. Why is this text considered a fantasy?
   a. The text is set back in time.
   b. The text talks about the power and use of magic.
   c. The text was written by Cameron.
   d. The text is written in first-person point of view.

2. Why is Cameron on a quest to find the book?
   a. He must destroy the book because it can only be used for evil.
   b. He must find the book and bring it back to Merlin.
   c. He must find the book and save it for himself.
   d. He must destroy the book so Merlin cannot use it.

3. Which paragraph best explains how Cameron is able to locate the book?
   a. first paragraph
   b. second paragraph
   c. third paragraph
   d. fourth paragraph

4. Which adjective best describes Cameron?
   a. determined
   b. annoying
   c. magical
   d. angry

5. Why does Merlin not want the spells for himself?
   a. The spells can never be used for good.
   b. He already has all the spells he needs.
   c. He fears Cameron would steal the spells before getting the book to him.
   d. He cannot read the spells written in the book.

Name_____

Super Powers

Misty had always wanted to be a superhero. Every Halloween, she designed costumes so she could look like a hero. She often had a mask or a cape or some other design to her costumes so everyone could tell she was someone who could save the world. As many times as she had pretended to be a hero, no one was more surprised than she when she actually developed her own special powers.

One day, as she looked into the mirror, Misty realized she could no longer see herself. She had become invisible! She had no idea what had caused the transformation or how long her powers would last, but she wasn't about to waste a second. She hit the streets running, looking for criminals, and surprising them when they didn't realize anyone was there. By the end of the day, she had stopped three bank robbers and two shoplifters. It had been a wonderful day even if she hadn't been able to wear a cool superhero costume.

The next day, she woke-up and discovered she was still invisible. She went back out and did much of what she had done the day before. Whispers of some unknown hero were starting to spread through the streets. Newspaper journalists scrambled to write stories, but no one knew who the new hero was or where to find the helpful citizen. Misty smiled to herself. If they only knew, she thought, they wouldn't believe it. She could barely believe it herself. After an entire week of being a superhero, Misty was starting to become a bit tired. Being a hero was a good thing, but it took a lot of work to run from place to place, catching criminals and tying up bad guys. She was tired and cranky, and since she couldn't see her reflection, she had no idea if she looked as bad as she was starting to feel.

The next morning, Misty woke up and caught sight of her reflection in the mirror. She grinned when she saw that she could see herself again. She knew it was the end to her days as a superhero, but it didn't mean she had to stop helping people. That day, as she went into work, she held the door open for three people and helped two elderly people carry their groceries. Granted, she wasn't saving the world anymore, but it still felt good to help in any way she could!

Text Questions

1. How does the reader know Misty has a fascination with superheroes?
   a. She reads about them all the time.
   b. She only watches movies with superheroes.
   c. She makes all her Halloween costumes be superhero costumes.
   d. She has posters of superheroes all over her bedroom.

2. What superhero power does Misty develop?
   a. flight
   b. invisibility
   c. super strength
   d. mind control

3. Which paragraph shows that Misty is starting to become tired of being a superhero?
   a. first paragraph
   b. second paragraph
   c. third paragraph
   d. fourth paragraph

4. How is Misty changed by what has happened to her?
   a. She realizes she can help people even if she isn't a superhero.
   b. She no longer makes her own Halloween costumes.
   c. She gets rid of all the mirrors in her house.
   d. She no longer keeps her money in the bank.

5. Why is Misty so happy to see her reflection?
   a. She realizes she still looks really pretty.
   b. She realizes she is no longer invisible.
   c. She realizes she has other special powers.
   d. She realizes she can be both a superhero and a regular girl.

Name_____

Bright Lights

The twinkling lights in the sky captured Carole's attention. She had seen the lights before but thought they were fireflies. Now she realized the lights were too far away and too bright to be the common flying insect she had mistaken them for the other night.

Going outside, she grabbed a pair of binoculars and tried to see them more clearly. Even with the magnified lenses, she could not discern what the lights really were.

"Mother!" Carole yelled so she would join her outside.

Her mother came running outside when she heard Carole's urgent call. "What's wrong?" she asked her daughter. "You sounded like something was upsetting you."

"I wanted you to see these lights before they disappeared. This is the second time I've seen them, but I can't decide what they are."

Carole's mother gazed at the twinkling lights, but she too was perplexed by what they could be. "I don't know what they are, but whatever it is, the lights are beautiful."

The next morning, Carole's mother brought her the newspaper while she was still in bed. "Wake-up, sleepyhead. I want you to see the newspaper. Apparently, a lot of people saw your lights last night. Some people are saying they are lights from UFOs. Other people are claiming they are fairy lights."

Carole scanned the paper, surprised to see the lights captured in the grainy black-and-white photo that made up part of the front page of the paper. She didn't know what she thought the lights were, but she did agree with one comment she read as she scanned the newspaper article.

The lights were magical. That was all she knew for sure.

Text Questions

1. Why does Carole most likely want her mother to see the lights?
   a. to see if she knows what they are
   b. to see if she will come when she calls for her
   c. to see if she can see the lights
   d. to see if her mother thinks the lights are caused by spaceships

2. What does the word *perplexed* mean as it is used in the sentence "She too was perplexed by what they could be"?
   a. puzzled
   b. amazed
   c. infatuated
   d. upset

3. What is the main problem in the story?
   a. Carole and her mother never agree about anything.
   b. Carole's mother thinks she is trying to hide something from her.
   c. Carole keeps seeing mysterious lights that she cannot identify.
   d. Carole's mother tries to protect her by not letting her see the strange lights.

4. Which statement is a fact about the story?
   a. The lights are the most unusual things anyone has ever seen.
   b. Carole is the best daughter a mother could have.
   c. Other people besides Carole have seen the lights.
   d. People are always terrified by lights that look like UFOs.

5. Why does Carole's mother want her to see the newspaper the next morning?
   a. so she will know other people have seen the lights, too
   b. so she can protect Carole from all the hurtful things people are saying about her
   c. so she can see if Carole ever reads the newspaper
   d. so she can throw it away as soon as Carole is finished reading it

Name_____

The Talking Animals

Selena had always wanted to go to the zoo. When her parents had finally agreed to take her, she didn't want to leave, even when her parents had gotten tired of seeing all of the amazing animals. She had finally convinced them to sit down at the small café and let her finish exploring. She hoped they could stay until closing time, especially since she didn't know when they would have a chance to come back.

As Selena wandered in and out of different areas, she kept feeling herself pulled back to study the monkeys. She didn't know why she was so fascinated by the creatures, but whenever she looked at them, she felt some type of instant connection.

"Excuse me," a voice said very near to her ear. Selena jumped because she had thought she was all alone. She turned, but there was no one there.

"Excuse me," the voice said again.

This time, Selena turned in a complete circle. There was no one there except her and the monkeys.

"Over here," the voiced echoed one last time. This time, Selena really looked and was shocked to find the voice was coming from one of the monkeys. At first, she couldn't believe it, but when the monkey spoke again, she knew she had heard correctly. "I was just wondering if you could take my picture and put it in the newspaper. It's been quite a while since anyone has."

"Certainly," Selena stammered. She was shaking as she grabbed her camera from around her neck. She found herself asking the monkey to say "bananas" right before she snapped the picture, and then she wondered if perhaps she was the one "going bananas."

She hurried to get her mother and father and dragged them both back to the monkey cage. From that point on, none of the monkeys would talk.

Selena felt a little foolish and knew her parents didn't believe her, but it didn't really matter. She had talked with the animals today even if she was the only one who knew it.

Text Questions

1. Which title would be a good alternative for this text?
   a. "Fun at the Zoo"
   b. "Monkeying Around"
   c. "Watch Out!"
   d. "Conversation with the Animals"

2. What happens in the story to make this text fall under the genre of fantasy?
   a. Selena has extraordinary strength.
   b. Selena sees a mermaid at the zoo.
   c. Selena hears a monkey talk to her.
   d. Selena uses a snake as a lasso to save her parents.

3. List three things in sequential order that happen in the story.

   a. _____

   b. _____

   c. _____

4. Why is Selena so excited about her trip to the zoo?
   a. She heard there will be talking animals at the zoo.
   b. She has never before been to the zoo.
   c. She is helping with one of the exhibits.
   d. She is friends with one of the workers at the zoo.

5. What does it mean when Selena thinks she might be "going bananas?"
   a. going crazy
   b. going places
   c. going with someone
   d. going everywhere

Name_____

Ancient Times

Jason and his family were on vacation visiting Greece for the first time. Jason was especially excited because he had been reading every book he could about the Greek gods and goddesses. He was fascinated by all of the mythology and could not wait to see the ancient ruins that were once the temples of the various deities.

At one of the ancient temples, Jason had walked away only a few feet from his parents when he felt the strangest presence near him. He looked down and found that a circle of light had appeared at his feet. He bent down in the ruse of tying his shoe, but all the while, he was staring at the light.

Before he knew it, the light became similar to a television screen. Jason could suddenly see the world hundreds of years earlier! It was as if he was viewing the past through a time portal. More than anything, Jason wanted to touch the portal and see if he could go through, but he was scared if he did, he would never find his way back. Too enthralled to even think about yelling for his parents, Jason watched the ancient view until he began to see the portal shrink, and he knew it was time for them to go.

On the ride back, his parents asked him several times if anything was wrong. Jason simply shook his head. He knew there was no way his parents would believe him without proof, and he didn't have any to give them. He knew he had been given a special opportunity, though, and it was one he would never forget.

Text Questions

1. Which statement is a fact about the story?
   a. The Greek gods and goddess were the most interesting deities in mythology.
   b. Jason and his family were visiting Greece.
   c. Greece is the most amazing place to take a vacation.
   d. Everyone should visit Greece at least once.

2. What does the word *deities* mean as it is used in the first paragraph?
   a. rulers
   b. gods and goddesses
   c. pharaohs
   d. citizens

3. Which paragraph best describes the portal Jason is viewing?
   a. first paragraph
   b. second paragraph
   c. third paragraph
   d. fourth paragraph

4. Why are Jason and his family in Greece?
   a. His father is on a business trip.
   b. They are there on a family vacation.
   c. His mother insisted they go.
   d. Jason won a trip in a contest.

5. What can one infer about Jason after reading the story?
   a. He will continue to be fascinated with Greek mythology.
   b. He will try to run away from his family and enter the portal.
   c. He will start learning all about ancient Roman mythology, too.
   d. He will never want to visit Greece again.

Name_____

Searching for Big Foot

Sightings of Big Foot had been seen in the woods near Leroy's house for years. Leroy was not a fan of the supernatural stories. He did not believe in things like Big Foot, the Loch Ness monster, or the Abominable Snowman. However, he knew the town relied on the tourist dollars that the supposed sightings brought to the town. People were anxious to catch even just a slight glimpse of the creature, even if Leroy wasn't.

One evening, Leroy could not find his cat, Stymie. Stymie was now fifteen years old and hard of hearing, so hollering for him did no good. He knew he would have to go looking for him and that meant a trek into the woods. Leroy went inside and changed into his best hiking boots and then grabbed a flashlight in case it got dark before he could find his cat.

Leroy might not believe in Big Foot, but it didn't mean he still wasn't a little nervous whenever he entered the woods. After all, if people weren't seeing Big Foot, they were seeing something. It was possible, Leroy believed, that there was some other extra-large creature in the woods. Maybe it was a bear or a huge deer that confused the tourists.

As Leroy walked, the noises of the woods started to make him extremely nervous. Even though he knew his cat probably couldn't hear him, he still hollered his name just to break the silence of the night. After looking for over an hour, Leroy was tired and dejected. He decided to head back to his house, hoping Stymie had returned while he was gone. As he turned around, Leroy caught sight of something huge and furry. It was a flash of something running. He only saw it for a moment, but it was enough to make him realize that whatever it was, it was huge. Instead of running away, he ran toward where he had seen the giant creature.

There in the mud were several large footprints.

Leroy ran the rest of the way home. Spotting Stymie on the porch, he snatched the cat, went inside, and locked the front door.

Text Questions

1. Which adjective best describes Leroy?
   a. skeptical
   b. gullible
   c. popular
   d. friendly

2. Which is a synonym for the word *trek* as it is used in the second paragraph?
   a. run
   b. journey
   c. vacation
   d. adventure

3. Why does Leroy become nervous when he is in the woods?
   a. He begins thinking about the Big Foot sightings.
   b. He hears a lot of noises.
   c. He fears he has become lost.
   d. He forgot to bring his cell phone with him.

4. What can one infer Leroy will now think about anyone who claims to have seen Big Foot?
   a. He will not believe them.
   b. He might think they are telling the truth.
   c. He will not want to listen to them.
   d. He will have no different opinion than before his trip into the woods.

5. Which title would be a good alternative for this text?
   a. "Seeing Is Believing"
   b. "The Ancient Curse"
   c. "Lions and Tigers and Bears"
   d. "Creepy Crawlies"

Name_____

A Dream Come True

Wanda had always loved watching birds. She was amazed that almost all birds could fly. She felt sorry for the ones that couldn't. What was the point of wings if not for flying?

One night, at a carnival, Wanda and some of her friends went into a booth to have their fortunes told. As Wanda placed her palm into the hands of the exotic fortune-teller, the woman tilted her head and looked at Wanda with a mysterious glint in her eye.

"Tonight, I will tell your fortune for free," she informed Wanda, "because yours is quite fascinating." Wanda listened intently as the fortune-teller continued. "For one night only, your life will change dramatically. You will finally be given what you have wished for your entire life, but the gift is fleeting. Enjoy it while it lasts." The fortune-teller dropped Wanda's hand and then looked exhausted. She told the others to come back later. She claimed she was too exhausted to read any more fortunes that night.

Wanda and her friends all laughed at the dramatic way the fortune teller had acted around her, and they teased Wanda the rest of the night, asking her over and over what she most wanted. Wanda laughed along with them, but she couldn't help but wonder if something might happen.

That night, when Wanda finally began to fall asleep, she started to feel a tingling in her toes. She thought perhaps they were falling asleep, but then the tingling moved up her entire body. She suddenly had the strongest feeling that she could fly. She rose from the bed and began to move her arms. Sure enough, she could fly just like one of the birds she had so often admired. She did not hesitate, remembering the fortune-teller's words that the gift would not last for long. She went outside and began to fly. She spent hours traveling through the air. She never thought to call anyone else for fear it would end her gift. Finally, exhausted, she collapsed on her bed and fell into a deep sleep.

When she woke the next morning, the magical feeling was gone, and she could no longer fly. She wouldn't have even believed it had happened at all if it weren't for the open window she saw in her bedroom.

Text Questions

1. Why does Wanda like birds?
   a. She is fascinated by flight.
   b. She is amazed by their feathers.
   c. She wants to be an ornithologist when she is older.
   d. She likes all animals.

2. What does the word *fleeting* mean as it is used in the third paragraph?
   a. permanent
   b. brief
   c. unusual
   d. special

3. What convinces Wanda the events of the night before actually happened?
   a. She is extremely tired.
   b. She finds a feather on her bed.
   c. She sees the window is still open.
   d. She is not convinced that any of it was real.

4. What will most likely happen the next time Wanda goes to a carnival?
   a. She will not visit the fortune-teller's booth.
   b. She will visit the fortune-teller's booth.
   c. She will ride all of the rides.
   d. She will eat lots of cotton candy.

5. Why does Wanda not let anyone else know she can fly?
   a. She is having too much fun to call anyone.
   b. She doesn't know anyone she can call.
   c. She is scared if she tells anyone, the gift will end.
   d. She does not have a way to call anyone.

Name_____

The Birthday Surprise

To the average person, Ollie Mei was just a dog. She had two floppy ears, one wagging tail, and one perpetually wet nose. But what the average person didn't realize was that Ollie Mei could play the piano. You heard me. She was a musician—secretly, of course. While her owners—Tabitha and Travis—knew of her talent, Ollie Mei had made it clear that she wanted to keep it under wraps. She had no desire to become famous. She was a shy dog, you see.

On the eve of Travis's fortieth birthday, Tabitha received the terrible news that the hired band couldn't make it. Apparently, the lead singer had the flu and had passed it on to his bandmates. Tabitha was distraught. It was too late to hire another band, and

there wasn't enough time to find a DJ. Ollie Mei could see how upset Tabitha was, so she decided to help her out, making this one exception for her favorite treat-giver.

As everyone gathered to take pictures and eat cake, Ollie Mei realized it was time to make her entrance. She trotted over to the piano, gracefully tapping on several keys before finding the beginning notes. When the crowd started singing "Happy Birthday to You," Ollie Mei played along, hitting every note effortlessly. The guests all cheered, and Tabitha and Travis were thrilled. It really was the happiest of birthdays, thanks to Ollie Mei and her exceptional talent.

Text Questions

1. What does the phrase "keep it under wraps" mean as it is used in the sentence, "While her owners—Tabitha and Travis—knew of her talent, Ollie Mei had made it clear that she wanted to keep it under wraps"?
   a. tell everyone
   b. wrap a present
   c. rap a song
   d. keep it a secret

2. Which adjective best describes Ollie Mei?
   a. selfish
   b. selfless
   c. energetic
   d. irritated

3. Why was Tabitha upset?
   a. She had to cancel the party.
   b. The DJ canceled.
   c. The band canceled.
   d. Travis was turning forty.

4. Which sentence helps prove that Tabitha and Travis were pleased with Ollie Mei's performance?
   a. When the crowd started singing "Happy Birthday to You," Ollie Mei played along, hitting every note effortlessly.
   b. The guests all cheered, and Tabitha and Travis were thrilled.
   c. To the average person, Ollie Mei was just a dog.
   d. Tabitha was distraught.

5. What do you think will most likely happen after Ollie Mei plays "Happy Birthday to You"?
   a. She will dance on the piano.
   b. She will bark at the crowd.
   c. She will play another song.
   d. She will sing another song.

Name_____

Lucky Pair of Shoes

Football practice had just ended, and Jeremy took a seat on the cold, metal bench next to three of his teammates.

"Another good practice, guys," Jeremy said, wiping the drops of sweat and rain from his face. "We're sure to beat Lincoln High next week if we keep playing like that!"

All four boys were covered from head to toe in mud, but the smiles on their faces made it obvious that they didn't seem to mind. Football practice was usually fun, but when you get to practice in the mud, it's a whole different game. There was talk about canceling the practice due to the weather, but the upcoming game against Lincoln High School was just too important. Lincoln High had taken home the championship trophy the past two years, but Jeremy was sure this was the year North High was going to take it back.

"I gotta get home before it gets dark," said Victor, as he started to pack up his backpack. "Last week I was ten minutes late, and I had to hear about it the entire night. I'll see you guys tomorrow at school."

Victor headed off down the street, as the other three boys started unlacing their dirty cleats and replacing them with clean sneakers from their bags.

"Have you guys seen my shoes?" asked Jeremy, with a confused look on his face. "I know I put them in here this morning."

"Isn't that them over there?" said Tommy, pointing to a pair of shoes resting under a nearby tree. "It looks just like them."

Tommy was right—the shoes did look exactly like his shoes, but who took them out of his bag? Probably just one of his teammates trying to be funny.

"Very funny, guys, but now they're going to be all wet!" Jeremy walked over to grab the shoes, but to his surprise, they were completely dry. "That's weird," he muttered, but he walked back to the bench without giving it much more thought. As he slipped the first shoe on over his muddy sock, an unusual tingling sensation overcame his body.

"Um, guys," he said, "I'm not sure if these are my shoes."

Text Questions

1. What did Jeremy think was unusual when he found his shoes?

   a. The shoes were a different color.
   b. The shoes were completely clean.
   c. The shoes were completely dry.
   d. The shoes were the wrong size.

2. What happened when Jeremy put one of the shoes on his foot?

   a. He saw a flash of light.
   b. He could see into the future.
   c. His voice changed.
   d. He felt a tingling sensation.

3. Which adjective best describes Jeremy's thoughts about the game against Lincoln High?

   a. optimistic
   b. furious
   c. anxious
   d. ambivalent

4. Why is this text considered a fantasy?

   a. because the boys are playing football in the rain
   b. because Jeremy's friends play a trick on him
   c. because the shoes seem to have magic powers
   d. because Jeremy can't seem to find his shoes

5. Based on the title, what is most likely to happen next?

   a. Jeremy leaves the shoes where he found them and walks home barefoot.
   b. Jeremy wears the shoes during the football game, and his team loses again.
   c. Jeremy wears the shoes home and starts to discover their magical powers.
   d. Jeremy loses the shoes on his way home from football practice.

Tracking Sheet

NONFICTION

Disasters		Biographies		American History		Animals	
Page 9		Page 24		Page 40		Page 55	
Page 10		Page 25		Page 41		Page 56	
Page 11		Page 26		Page 42		Page 57	
Page 12		Page 27		Page 43		Page 58	
Page 13		Page 28		Page 44		Page 59	
Page 14		Page 29		Page 45		Page 60	
Page 15		Page 30		Page 46		Page 61	
Page 16		Page 31		Page 47		Page 62	
Page 17		Page 32		Page 48		Page 63	
Page 18		Page 33		Page 49		Page 64	
Page 19		Page 34		Page 50		Page 65	
Page 20		Page 35		Page 51		Page 66	
Page 21		Page 36		Page 52		Page 67	
Page 22		Page 37		Page 53		Page 68	
Page 23		Page 38		Page 54			
		Page 39					

FICTION

Mythology		Fairy Tales/ Folklore		Historical		Contemporary Realism		Mystery/ Suspense/ Adventure		Fantasy	
Page 71		Page 87		Page 103		Page 117		Page 133		Page 148	
Page 72		Page 88		Page 104		Page 118		Page 134		Page 149	
Page 73		Page 89		Page 105		Page 119		Page 135		Page 150	
Page 74		Page 90		Page 106		Page 120		Page 136		Page 151	
Page 75		Page 91		Page 107		Page 121		Page 137		Page 152	
Page 76		Page 92		Page 108		Page 122		Page 138		Page 153	
Page 77		Page 93		Page 109		Page 123		Page 139		Page 154	
Page 78		Page 94		Page 110		Page 124		Page 140		Page 155	
Page 79		Page 95		Page 111		Page 125		Page 141		Page 156	
Page 80		Page 96		Page 112		Page 126		Page 142		Page 157	
Page 81		Page 97		Page 113		Page 127		Page 143		Page 158	
Page 82		Page 98		Page 114		Page 128		Page 144		Page 159	
Page 83		Page 99		Page 115		Page 129		Page 145		Page 160	
Page 84		Page 100		Page 116		Page 130		Page 146		Page 161	
Page 85		Page 101				Page 131		Page 147		Page 162	
Page 86		Page 102				Page 132				Page 163	

Answer Key

166

Answer Key

Nonfiction

Disasters

Page 9 The Great Quake
1. d
2. a
3. b
4. d
5. Answers will vary but could include the following: The enormous loss from the disaster caused the San Francisco earthquake to become known as the "Great Quake." The earthquake caused the loss of over five hundred people and destroyed thousands of acres of the city of San Francisco.

Page 10 The Chicago Fire
1. b
2. a
3. a
4. d
5. c

Page 11 The Dust Bowl
1. a
2. b
3. a
4. b
5. a

Page 12 The Galveston Hurricane
1. b
2. c
3. c
4. c
5. d

Page 13 The Black Death
1. b
2. a
3. b
4. d
5. b

Page 14 Pompeii
1. a
2. Answers will vary but could include the following: The disaster in Pompeii happened so quickly that many of the citizens were unable to escape. Like the disaster of the sinking of the *Titanic*, there were many who were simply trapped. The remains of those in Pompeii were preserved under layers of volcanic ash. These remains were found later by archeologists. This is similar to the discovery of the *Titanic* by Robert Ballard. His expedition found that many of the artifacts were preserved as they rested at the bottom of the ocean.
3. c
4. d
5. d

Page 15 The Sticky Explosion
1. a
2. a
3. b
4. a
5. Answers will vary but could include the following: Equipment should have been checked carefully and all safety measures should have been maintained. The tanks holding the molasses should have been large enough to hold the amount of molasses.

Page 16 The *Hindenburg*
1. c
2. d
3. b
4. d
5. Answers will vary but could include the following: Many of the passengers survived the explosion of the Hindenburg because they were able to get to safety by reaching the ground after the explosion occurred. It is possible that some were able to jump to safety while others may have been helped out of the exploding aircraft.

Page 17 The *Titanic*
1. a
2. c
3. c
4. d
5. a

Page 18 The Twin Towers
1. c
2. a
3. a
4. c
5. Answers will vary but could include the following:
   a. In 2001, two planes flew into the Twin Towers.
   b. The south tower fell in less than one hour after being attacked.
   c. The north tower fell next.

Page 19 The New Madrid Fault
1. c
2. a
3. d
4. a
5. Answers will vary but could include the following:
   a. Reelfoot Lake in Tennessee was created.
   b. Landscape in the area was permanently changed.

Answer Key (cont.)

Page 20 Mount St. Helens: A Deadly Volcano
1. Answers will vary but could include the following: The people who refused to evacuate from the area surrounding Mount St. Helens most likely did so because they did not realize the situation was as dangerous as it was about to become.
2. d
3. b
4. a
5. c

Page 21 Cherynobyl: A Nuclear Disaster
| 1. d | 3. d | 5. a |
| 2. c | 4. d | |

Page 22 The Space Shuttle Catastrophe
| 1. d | 3. b | 5. c |
| 2. a | 4. c | |

Page 23 Hurricane Katrina
1. Answers will vary but could include the following:
   a. People did not have the money to evacuate.
   b. People did not have transportation to be able to leave the city.
2. b
3. d
4. b
5. d

Biographies

Page 24 William Driver
1. Answers will vary but could include the following: William Driver is best known as the owner of the United States flag known affectionately as "Old Glory." He saved the flag from destruction during the Civil War.
2. d
3. a
4. d
5. b

Page 25 Thomas Jefferson
| 1. b | 3. b | 5. c |
| 2. d | 4. d | |

Page 26 King Tut
1. Answers will vary but could include the following: Tutankhamun's burial tomb was amazingly well-preserved, and people around the world have been able to see the items that were in his tomb as they have been on tour and shown in museums all over the world.
2. c
3. d
4. Answers will vary but could include the following:
   a. King Tut was born around 1341 B.C.
   b. King Tut died and was buried in the area known as the Valley of the Kings.
   c. In 1922, Howard Carter discovered the tomb.
5. d

Page 27 Butch Cassidy
1. b
2. d
3. c
4. Answers will vary but could include the following: Robert Leroy Parker would grow up to become the infamous bank robber, Butch Cassidy. Cassidy's main target would be the Union Pacific Railroad, and the railroad company would eventually drive the bank robber out of the United States and into South America.
5. d

Page 28 Milton Hershey
1. b
2. Answers will vary but could include the following: Milton Hershey was determined to succeed as a candy maker. He spent years studying the making of candy and built his Hershey factory in Pennsylvania. He was also determined to help his hometown, which he did, by providing funds, jobs, and unique opportunities for those who reside there.
3. b
4. d
5. a

Page 29 Helen Keller
1. a
2. d
3. b
4. Answers will vary but could include the following: Helen Keller became deaf, blind, and mute as a young child after an unexpected illness. Her teacher Anne Sullivan was eventually able to communicate with and help teach Helen Keller. Keller would go on to college, and she would remain friends with her teacher until Anne Sullivan's death.
5. c

Answer Key *(cont.)*

Page 30 Harry Houdini

1. a   3. d   5. b
2. c   4. c

Page 31 Benjamin Franklin

1. d   3. b   5. b
2. a   4. c

Page 32 Anne Frank

1. d   3. b   5. d
2. c   4. b

Page 33 Amelia Earhart

1. Answers will vary but could include the following: Amelia Earhart was the first female to fly across the Atlantic Ocean. She would later die as she flew her plane across the Pacific.
2. c
3. d
4. Answers will vary but could include the following:
   a. She was born in 1897 in Atchison, Kansas.
   b. During World War I, she volunteered for the Red Cross.
   c. In 1937, her plane would become lost at sea.
5. b

Page 34 Elvis Presley

1. a   3. b   5. b
2. a   4. c

Page 35 Laura Ingalls Wilder

1. c   3. a   5. a
2. c   4. a

Page 36 Rosa Parks

1. b   3. c   5. b
2. a   4. d

Page 37 Princess Diana

1. d
2. b
3. Answers will vary but could include the following:
   a. She was born July 1, 1961.
   b. She began dating Prince Charles.
   c. She married the prince in 1981.
4. a
5. a

Page 38 Levi Strauss

1. c
2. a
3. b
4. c
5. Answers may vary slightly but should include some of the following information: Strauss decided to move to California to expand his opportunities. He decided the miners needed a good pair of work pants, so he began constructing his first pair of jeans.

Page 39 Jesse James

1. d   3. a   5. a
2. b   4. d

American History

Page 40 History

1. b
2. b
3. c
4. Answers will vary but could include the following: The decisions you make will affect generations that come after you. This is how the world is connected through history.
5. d

Page 41 Slavery

1. c   3. a   5. d
2. a   4. c

Page 42 Independence

1. b   3. d   5. a
2. c   4. c

Page 43 The Louisiana Purchase

1. b   3. a   5. b
2. a   4. d

Page 44 The Wild West

1. a
2. b
3. Many former slaves moved away from the South and to the West hoping to find a better way of life.
4. b
5. d

Answer Key (cont.)

Page 45 Early Inventions
1. d
2. a
3. Answers will vary but could include the following: Electricity was important in the past and is still important today. With the invention of skyscrapers, electricity allowed elevators to reach the highest floors of buildings. Light bulbs powered by electricity also helped work to continue even after dark. Today, electricity is still used for these purposes as well as new inventions such as electric cars.
4. d
5. b

Page 46 Women's Suffrage
1. b   3. d   5. b
2. c   4. a

Page 47 The Roaring Twenties
1. c
2. b
3. Answers will vary but could include the following: Inventions for completing housework made the tasks that were generally handled by women easier to complete. This freed up time for women to do things besides housework.
4. b
5. d

Page 48 The Great Depression
1. b   3. d   5. c
2. a   4. c

Page 49 World War II
1. a
2. c
3. c
4. Answers will vary but could include the following:
    a. Roosevelt insists in his speech that the United States must be willing to fight for "Four Freedoms."
    b. Pearl Harbor is attacked.
    c. America enters World War II.
5. a

Page 50 The Iron Curtain
1. d   3. c   5. b
2. a   4. b

Page 51 Civil Rights
1. a   3. c   5. a
2. d   4. a

Page 52 The Race into Space
1. b   3. a   5. a
2. b   4. c

Page 53 The American-Indian Movement
1. a
2. b
3. c
4. Answers will vary but could include the following: Living conditions were not good in the reservations. Tribes began to sue for what had been promised to them under the original treaties.
5. c

Page 54 Vietnam
1. b   3. a   5. c
2. b   4. a

Animals

Page 55 Animal Rights
1. c   3. c   5. c
2. a   4. a

Page 56 Bats
1. d   3. a   5. c
2. c   4. a

Page 57 Monkeypox
1. c
2. b
3. First, it is important to note that, unlike some other diseases, this particular disease is hard to spread from person to person. To become infected, a person must eat or be bitten by an infected animal.
4. b
5. c

Page 58 Migration
1. d   3. a   5. a
2. c   4. a

Page 59 Pythons
1. b   3. b   5. d
2. c   4. d

Page 60 Bedbugs
1. a   3. c   5. b
2. a   4. a

Answer Key (cont.)

Page 61 Sleeping Sickness
1. c
2. d
3. c
4. Answers will vary but could include the following: Ticks can carry a disease known as Lyme disease. Symptoms include a rash and fever. This is similar to some of the symptoms experienced with sleeping sickness. Also, the disease is carried by ticks that are found only in certain areas.
5. b

Page 62 Elephants
1. b   3. a   5. b
2. d   4. b

Page 63 Sheep
1. a   3. a   5. c
2. a   4. a

Page 64 Jellyfish
1. Answers will vary but could include the following:
   a. Their bodies are made of material that is soft and jellylike.
   b. They can range in size.
   c. They have extensions that hang from their bodies that are called tentacles.
2. d
3. d
4. b
5. a

Page 65 Ticks
1. d   3. a   5. a
2. a   4. b

Page 66 Chinchillas
1. b   3. d   5. a
2. c   4. a

Page 67 Animal Experiments
1. d
2. a
3. d
4. Answers will vary but could include the following: Animal testing should be allowed for medical research. Animal research should not occur if cosmetics or perfumes are being tested.
5. c

Page 68 Service Animals
1. b
2. a
3. a
4. a
5. Answers will vary but could include the following: Animals should not be used for service. It is cruel to have an animal become attached to a person and for the person to become equally attached to the animal, only to remove the animal when it is needed elsewhere. The animal should be treated as a pet and allowed to bond with the person it is helping.

Fiction

Mythology

Page 71 Mythology
1. b   3. d   5. d
2. a   4. b

Page 72 Echo
1. c   3. b   5. d
2. a   4. c

Page 73 Greek Mythology
1. b   3. b   5. a
2. a   4. b

Page 74 Hephaestus
1. d   3. a   5. c
2. b   4. a

Page 75 Creation
1. b
2. a
3. c
4. Answers will vary but could include the following: Creation myths are still used in today's movies and literature. This shows how important their influence is even today.
5. b

Page 76 Poseidon
1. a
2. Answers will vary but could include the following: According to the text, Poseidon sometimes used his powers to cause terrible storms. However, he also used his powers to help the Greek people.
3. c
4. d
5. b

Answer Key (cont.)

Page 77 The Titans
1. d
2. a
3. d
4. d
5. Answers will vary but could include the following: The Titans were the original rulers of the Greek world according to mythology. The Titans' children eventually banished them and became the twelve rulers who resided on Mount Olympus. The Titans are still important in today's modern culture.

Page 78 Cyclops
1. d
2. a
3. a
4. b
5. Answers will vary but could include the following: The Cyclops were giant in size and could help build walls for entire cities. They helped create thunderbolts for Zeus, and they captured Odysseus and devoured several members of his crew.

Page 79 Horus
1. c   3. d   5. d
2. b   4. b

Page 80 Dragons
1. d
2. a
3. Answers will vary but could include the following: A skull and crossbones is a symbol that often represents danger.
4. b
5. d

Page 81 Set
1. d   3. d   5. c
2. b   4. d

Page 82 Persephone
1. d
2. Answers will vary but could include the following: Demeter was so upset, she spent all of her time looking for her daughter and stopped worrying about other things. As the goddess of agriculture, she caused the crops to die and widespread famine to occur.
3. c
4. b
5. d

Page 83 The Underworld
1. a   3. a   5. b
2. b   4. a

Page 84 Medusa
1. d
2. c
3. d
4. a
5. Answers will vary but could include the following:
   a. The king ordered Perseus to bring him back Medusa's head.
   b. Perseus was given help to defeat Medusa by Athena.
   c. Perseus cut off Medusa's head.

Page 85 Athena
1. d
2. Answers will vary but could include the following: The goddess of war would need to be wise to keep the people from going to war when they did not need to fight and to be able to keep peace.
3. b
4. c
5. b

Page 86 Zeus
1. b
2. His most famous weapon was the thunderbolt, which he used as needed to maintain control.
3. a
4. b
5. a

Fairy Tales/Folklore

Page 87 A Messed-Up Fairy Tale
1. a
2. Answers will vary but could include the following: Tiffany thought she was the princess of her family and that everyone should do whatever she asked them to do. She was always bossing her family around, screaming things like, "Get me some chocolate milk!" She never asked nicely.
3. c
4. c
5. b

Answer Key (cont.)

Page 88 Dragon Achoo

1. b	3. a	5. a
2. d	4. b	

Page 89 The Tortoise and the Snail

1. c
2. c
3. a
4. Answers will vary but could include the following:
   a. The tortoise and the snail decide to race.
   b. The tortoise takes off and leaves the snail.
   c. The snail is picked up by a bird.
5. c

Page 90 Let Down Your Hare

1. b	3. c	5. b
2. d	4. d	

Page 91 Beauty and the Bear

1. a	3. b	5. b
2. b	4. d	

Page 92 Let Me In!

1. d
2. a
3. c
4. b
5. Answers will vary but could include the following: The moral of the story is that you cannot change the true nature of a beast and neither could the apologetic pig. Wolves eat pigs, and the pig was like takeout dinner delivered to their door.

Page 93 The Curse

1. a	3. b	5. a
2. d	4. a	

Page 94 The Cat's Meow

1. a	3. c	5. a
2. c	4. c	

Page 95 All That Glitters

1. b
2. b
3. a
4. c
5. Answers will vary but could include the following:
   a. There was a princess who wanted to get married.
   b. She held a party to find a husband.
   c. She was married one week later.

Page 96 Little Miss

1. a	3. c	5. b
2. a	4. c	

Page 97 Little Blue Riding Hood

1. d
2. c
3. d
4. a
5. Answers will vary but could include the following:
   a. Blue is walking through the woods.
   b. She discovers an elf caught in a trap.
   c. She releases the elf, and she gives him her wish.

Page 98 The Old Woman and the Doctor

1. c	3. c	5. Answers will vary.
2. d	4. a	

Page 99 The Unusual Mice

1. a	3. a	5. a
2. b	4. a	

Page 100 The Sweet Touch

1. b	3. a	5. a
2. d	4. a	

Page 101 What Is True?

1. a	3. c	5. d
2. b	4. a	

Page 102 An Unusual Friendship

1. a	3. c	5. c
2. c	4. a	

Historical

Page 103 The Great Inventor

1. Answers will vary but could include the following:
   a. Mattie's father tells her they will visit Mr. Edison.
   b. Mattie and her father visit Mr. Edison's home.
   c. Mattie sees the phonograph.
2. d
3. a
4. b
5. a

Page 104 Saying Goodbye

1. a	3. d	5. c
2. c	4. a	

Page 105 The Land of the Free

1. d	3. b	5. b
2. a	4. c	

Answer Key *(cont.)*

Page 106 Everyone's Dream
1. c   3. c   5. d
2. a   4. a

Page 107 Making a Difference
1. c   3. d   5. a
2. c   4. a

Page 108 Disaster in the Sky
1. d   3. d   5. c
2. c   4. c

Page 109 A Twist of Fate
1. b   3. c   5. a
2. b   4. a

Page 110 The Man on the Moon
1. a   3. b   5. d
2. c   4. a

Page 111 The British Are Coming
1. a
2. b
3. b
4. a
5. Answers will vary but could include the following:
   a. Cal hears the news the British are coming.
   b. Cal rushes home.
   c. Cal's father arrives later that evening.

Page 112 The Unending Dust
1. c   3. c   5. b
2. b   4. a

Page 113 A Time for Hope
1. b   3. b   5. a
2. c   4. d

Page 114 The Teddy Bear
1. a   3. a   5. a
2. b   4. b

Page 115 Gone Too Soon
1. a   3. d   5. a
2. c   4. b

Page 116 Troubling Thoughts
1. a   3. a   5. d
2. b   4. c

Contemporary Realism

Page 117 Forgiving
1. c
2. d
3. a
4. a

5. Answers will vary but could include the following:
   a. Juanita does not want to face the class at lunch.
   b. She tries to hide from the class by sneaking into the library.
   c. The teacher and her classmates find her and tell her they are like family and everything is fine.

Page 118 The Lucky Break
1. a   3. d   5. a
2. b   4. a

Page 119 Lost and Found
1. c   3. d   5. a
2. a   4. c

Page 120 Don't Stop the Music
1. d   3. b   5. b
2. c   4. a

Page 121 The Unexpected Gift
1. d   3. a   5. a
2. c   4. b

Page 122 Winter Blues
1. a   3. b   5. d
2. a   4. a

Page 123 High in the Sky
1. c
2. Answers will vary but could include the following:
   a. Sandra is enjoying the hot-air balloon ride.
   b. Sandra starts to feel bad.
   c. Sandra passes out.
3. a
4. c
5. c

Page 124 Unexpected Help
1. d   3. a   5. b
2. a   4. a

Page 125 The Day Off
1. a   3. b   5. c
2. c   4. c

Page 126 Tastes Like Chicken
1. b   3. a   5. a
2. a   4. b

Page 127 Hoping for the Best
1. c   3. b   5. b
2. b   4. a

Answer Key *(cont.)*

Page 128 Not So Easy
1. b   3. a   5. d
2. d   4. c

Page 129 The Amazing Win
1. b   3. b   5. d
2. a   4. d

Page 130 The Unexpected Invitation
1. a   3. c   5. a
2. c   4. c

Page 131 Capturing the Moment
1. b   3. a   5. c
2. a   4. b

Page 132 Welcome Home
1. b   3. b   5. b
2. d   4. b

Mystery/Suspense/Adventure

Page 133 Howling in the Night
1. c   3. b   5. a
2. b   4. b

Page 134 Dangerous Falls
1. b   3. a   5. b
2. d   4. c

Page 135 The Walking Dead?
1. b
2. Answers will vary but could include the
   following:
   a. Rick and his friends realize they are going to
      be late getting back home.
   b. They decide to take a shortcut through
      the cemetery.
   c. They hear something following them.
3. b
4. c
5. b

Page 136 The Noise Upstairs
1. c   3. b   5. a
2. c   4. d

Page 137 Whitewater Rafting
1. b   3. a   5. a
2. d   4. d

Page 138 The Haunted Woods
1. a   3. b   5. b
2. a   4. a

Page 139 Missing!
1. b
2. d

3. Answers will vary but could include the
   following:
   a. The students find their teacher crying.
   b. She says she is missing an important
      newspaper.
   c. Everyone agrees to do everything they can
      to help her find the missing paper.
4. b
5. c

Page 140 Surprise Visitors
1. a   3. a   5. a
2. b   4. b

Page 141 Safe and Sound
1. b   3. c   5. b
2. a   4. b

Page 142 The Missing Party
1. a   3. c   5. a
2. a   4. c

Page 143 Flying High
1. b   3. b   5. c
2. d   4. c

Page 144 The Pilfered Pies
1. b   3. b   5. b
2. c   4. a

Page 145 The Guest
1. a   3. c   5. a
2. a   4. b

Page 146 Ready, Set, Race!
1. a   3. c   5. b
2. b   4. a

Page 147 The Fire
1. b   3. a   5. b
2. a   4. a

Fantasy

Page 148 The Best Wish
1. a   3. a   5. a
2. a   4. a

Page 149 Catch Us If You Can
1. a   3. b   5. d
2. a   4. a

Page 150 The Stranger's Gift
1. b   3. a   5. a
2. a   4. c

Page 151 Good Witch, Bad Witch
1. a   3. b   5. c
2. a   4. a

Answer Key *(cont.)*

Page 152 Mermaids?
1. c
2. Answers will vary but could include the following:
   a. The girls go swimming at night.
   b. They see a mermaid.
   c. Their daughters go swimming in the same place and spy a mermaid.
3. b
4. c
5. a

Page 153 A Night for a Knight
1. b   3. a   5. b
2. a   4. b

Page 154 The Last of the Unicorns
1. b
2. Answers will vary but could include the following:
   a. The unicorn realizes he is in danger.
   b. The gnome offers to protect the unicorn.
   c. The two escape to safety.
3. a
4. c
5. c

Page 155 The Book of Spells
1. b   3. c   5. a
2. a   4. a

Page 156 Super Powers
1. c   3. c   5. b
2. b   4. a

Page 157 Bright Lights
1. a   3. c   5. a
2. a   4. c

Page 158 The Talking Animals
1. b
2. c
3. Answers will vary but could include the following:
   a. Selena and her parents go to the zoo.
   b. Selena separates from her parents.
   c. A monkey talks to Selena.
4. b
5. a

Page 159 Ancient Times
1. b   3. c   5. a
2. b   4. b

Page 160 Searching for Big Foot
1. a   3. a   5. a
2. b   4. b

Page 161 A Dream Come True
1. a   3. c   5. c
2. b   4. b

Page 162 The Birthday Surprise
1. d   3. c   5. c
2. b   4. b

Page 163 Lucky Pair of Shoes
1. c   3. a   5. c
2. d   4. c